BEHAVIOR MODIFICATION

a practical approach for educators

JAMES E. WALKER

Professor and Chairman,
Department of Specialized Educational Development,
Illinois State University,
Normal, Illinois

THOMAS M. SHEA

Professor, Department of Special Education,
Southern Illinois University,
Edwardsville, Illinois

SECOND EDITION

with 23 illustrations

The C. V. Mosby Company

ST. LOUIS • TORONTO • LONDON   1980

Cover photograph by Gerald S. Upham

SECOND EDITION

Copyright © 1980 by The C. V. Mosby Company

All rights reserved. No part of this book may be reproduced in any manner without written permission of the publisher.

Previous edition copyrighted 1976

Printed in the United States of America

The C. V. Mosby Company
11830 Westline Industrial Drive, St. Louis, Missouri 63141

Library of Congress Cataloging in Publication Data

Walker, James Edwin, 1941-
    Behavior modification.

    Bibliography: p.
    Includes index.
    1. Teaching. 2. Behavior modification.
3. Individualized instruction. 4. Handicapped
children—Education—United States. I. Shea, Thomas M.,
1934-   joint author. II. Title.
LB1027.W29 1980   371.1′02   79-21107
ISBN 0-8016-5338-X

GW/M/M 9 8 7 6 5 4 3 2 1   02/B/266

To
Gwenn, Jamell, and Jabrina
and
Dolores, Kevin, and Keith

Preface

This second edition of *Behavior Modification: A Practical Approach for Educators* has been extensively revised to improve its readability and usability. Revisions are based on developments in the field of behavior management reported in the literature since the original manuscript was prepared and on feedback from professionals and students.

During the last decade there has been a proliferation of behavior management philosophies, techniques, and instructional methodologies that has increased the complexity of the educator's responsibilities and functions. New information is being published almost daily on the various perspectives of human behavior, including the psychoanalytic-psychodynamic, biophysical, environmental, and behavioral points of view. Of these perspectives the behavioral, or more specifically the behavior modification point of view, appears to have had the most significant impact on classroom and school management procedures and practices. However, because of their overall importance in the broad field of behavior management and their impact on the development of the discipline of behavior modification, the theories and techniques associated with the psychoanalytic-psychodynamic, biophysical, and environmental perspectives are reviewed in this new edition.

Revisions in the text are, in large part, a result of direct and indirect feedback from students and faculty who have studied the original edition. We have been informed of the text's strengths and weaknesses by many undergraduate and graduate students of education, by teachers participating in in-service programs, and by our professional colleagues. We have attempted in this revision to retain the text's strengths and eliminate its weaknesses.

The text is written to provide experienced teachers, teachers-in-training, parents, and paraprofessionals with a practical guide for the application of behavior modification techniques in general and special educational settings. It is designed to aid teachers working in self-contained classes and resource centers, teachers engaged in itinerant and consultative service, and elementary and secondary regular classroom teachers having responsibility for normal and handicapped children. It may be used as a basic text for preservice and in-service courses and as a self-study guide.

The discipline of behavior modification is introduced in Chapter One through examples of classroom and school research studies. This chapter includes a presentation on the application of behavior modification techniques to individualized education programs (IEPs), mandated for all handicapped children by Public Law 94-142. Chapter One concludes with an overview of the psycho-analytic-psychodynamic, biophysical, environmental, and behavior modification perspectives of human behavior and educational practice.

The basic principles of behavior modification are presented in Chapter Two. The exposition of each principle is supplemented by practical examples from classroom teaching experiences.

In Chapter Three the reader is given step-by-step instructions for modifying behavior in the classroom. Each step is discussed and exemplified. Chapter Three includes an extensive list of reinforcers for use in the classroom and school setting.

Several specific methods of increasing acceptable behavior and decreasing unacceptable behavior are reviewed in Chapters Four and Five.

Chapter Six is an overview of behavior modification procedures and practices for implementation by educators willing to involve parents in coordinated home-school management programs. The chapter includes a parent-teacher interview technique for assessment purposes. The material in this chapter is also applicable to the training of paraprofessionals.

Chapter Seven is an overview of several behavior management techniques associated with the psychoanalytic-psychodynamic, biophysical, and environmental theoretical perspectives presented in Chapter One.

In the final chapter the ethics of behavior management are discussed in detail. The chapter concludes with guidelines for the ethical application of interventions suggested in the text.

Quizzes and skill-building projects are presented at the end of Chapters Two through Seven. Answers to the quiz questions are presented in Appendix A. Several journals, textbooks, and films available for supplemental study are listed in Appendix B. Multiple copies of work sheets and forms presented earlier are provided at the end of the text. These can be removed for use by the reader.

The text is written in nontechnical language for maximum readability by a broad audience of professionals, paraprofessionals, college students, and parents. This style was chosen because, in our opinion, the professional literature loses much of its significance and impact when it relies on unnecessary technical jargon.

The primary goal of this work is the *ethical*, *effective*, and *efficient* management of the behavior and learning problems of children as they learn to explore, manipulate, and ultimately control their world for their personal satisfaction and benefit and for the benefit of society.

We would like to acknowledge the assistance and support of our many colleagues, friends, and long-suffering students who have been exposed to and have responded to the materials in this text. We have profited greatly by their comments.

Jean Wilhaber has served as our right arm throughout the writing process by typing, correcting, and retyping the not-always-organized manuscript.

James E. Walker
Thomas M. Shea

Contents

Behavior modification

a practical approach for educators

CHAPTER ONE

An introduction to behavior modification

Ms. Justine watches as Tami, wiping her eyes with a tissue from the decorative dispenser on the corner of the teacher's desk, slowly leaves the fourth-grade classroom. It has been a long, trying day for both of them.

As the little Swiss clock on the desk chimes 4 o'clock, Ms. Justine leans back in her chair to ponder her dilemma. Right now, she hates teaching. She hates reprimanding and scolding children, especially Tami, who tries so very, very hard to sit still and pay attention during her lessons. It seems as if this little drama has happened with Tami and some of the other children a dozen or more times since the school year began last month.

The children are too active to settle down to their lessons. Ms. Justine yells and hollers, scolds and reprimands; but it doesn't appear to help. They never change. Perhaps they never will.

Something must be done. The children have to learn their lessons. Tami is 2 years behind in reading and a full year behind in spelling; she has practically no measurable skills in subtraction and division. Tami must be helped. She must learn these skills before the end of the school year or confront another failure in the fifth grade.

Ms. Justine knows her present methods of behavior management are not only ineffective but are taking too much out of her personally. She is exhausted when she gets home after school. Her stomach is always upset. She is grouchy and short-tempered with her husband and children.

Perhaps there are more effective methods Ms. Justine could apply in an effort to help Tami and the others attend to their lessons.

Larry sits in the gym bleachers, anxiously waiting for Mr. Veritas to finish organizing the volleyball game. The whole class, except Larry, is choosing sides and preparing to begin the game.

Larry wishes he could be part of the activity, but he can't. He's afraid to let the others know that he's a poor player. He doesn't know exactly why he's a poor player, but every time a group game is organized, he must refuse to participate. He says, "No, I won't," "I can't," "I don't feel good," or "That's a dumb game."

Larry knows Mr. Veritas is unhappy with him but also very concerned about him. But Larry just can't play those games. He thinks it's really too bad that Mr. Veritas doesn't like him, because Mr. Veritas is a nice guy and would be an interesting friend.

Mr. Veritas quickly organizes the teams, and the volleyball game begins. He feels that he must hurry and talk to Larry.

"Poor kid," Mr. Veritas thinks, "he's really OK, but he just won't play team games. Perhaps he refuses because of his weight problem. No, others in the class are as rotund as Larry, and they play team sports. Perhaps

Larry is afraid he's not a good-enough player. I'll talk to him again and see what I can do to help."

Perhaps there are effective methods for helping Larry increase his participation in team activities.

Ms. Komfort hums a little tune to herself as she cruises along Interstate 55 out of Memphis. What a marvelous day! What a great year it has been at John F. Kennedy Elementary School with her 25 first graders!

For the first time in her teaching career, Ms. Komfort has interested, responsive, and enthusiastic children in her class. If the last 4 months of the school year are as good as the first 5 months, she will remain in teaching forever.

"Sure hope it continues," she thinks.

Perhaps there are techniques to help Ms. Komfort maintain her children's enthusiasm for learning throughout the year.

Teachers wish to teach; it is what they are trained to do, their function, and the purpose for which they are employed and assigned to a school, a classroom, and a group of children for approximately 180 days each school year. Frequently teachers are frustrated in efforts to attain their goals because of the behavioral and remedial problems of the individual children in their classrooms.

As a result of the theoretical, experimental, and pragmatic efforts of many scholars and practitioners during the twentieth century, teachers have been made increasingly aware of a number of variables that must be considered if effective and efficient classroom transactions are to be established between teachers and children. Teachers have become keenly aware that:

1. Every child is a unique individual, *similar* to all other children in many respects yet *different* from all other children.
2. No single set of therapeutic or remedial procedures is effective under *all condi-*

tions with *all children*. We must remain open-minded and give thoughtful consideration to many theoretical and methodological points of view if we are to effectively aid children.

3. No matter how well designed and executed classroom-centered intervention processes may be, their effectiveness will be limited unless they relate to the individual child's needs and desires (Caplan, 1963; Morse, 1964).

Educators have also become aware that in reality the child's cognitive, affective, and psychomotor learning domains are inextricably interwoven. We understand that the child acts and reacts as a whole being. We recognize that a remedial intervention in the cognitive domain may influence the child's affective behavior, that intervention in the psychomotor domain will in all probability affect the child's cognitive and affective learning, and so on.

EXAMPLE

Todd, a 6-year-old first grader, was diagnosed by a neurologist as "a hyperactive child with suspected minimal brain damage." According to his teacher, Todd was disruptive in the classroom, constantly running about, hitting children, tearing paper, and so on.

Todd's neurologist prescribed medication to slow the boy down in school. The medication has been effective in modifying Todd's behavior. He has begun to learn his ABCs and numbers; he has learned to use scissors for cutting-and-pasting activities; his behavior has improved in the classroom, especially during group activities. Todd has been heard to say, "See how good I am," and "I'm a big boy, now."

It is evident that changes in Todd's hyperactive psychomotor behavior have influenced his cognitive skills (learning his ABCs and numbers) and his affective behavior (in group activities). His self-concept has improved.

EXAMPLE

Scott, an 11-year-old fifth grader with a visual-perceptual handicap, had experienced difficulty in throwing and catching a ball and in running bases.

Scott is now enrolled in a program that includes physical therapy, visual-perceptual training, and adaptive physical education. As a result of these interventions he has developed skills in throwing, catching, and running.

Scott's teacher has noted that as Scott is increasing his competency in the psychomotor area, he is also improving cognitively (in such activities as reading and writing) and socially (his group behavior and peer relationships have improved).

Again, it is evident that changes in one learning domain influence the individual's competency in the other areas of learning.

• • •

This text is written from the point of view of learning theory and behavior modification. Behavior modification, however, is but one of the conceptual frameworks available to the practitioner for use in efforts to change behavior. *Behavior modification is not a panacea that can effectively solve all problems of all children.*

Other models (biophysical, psychoanalytic-psychodynamic, and environmental) have made and continue to make significant contributions to our knowledge of the behavior of children (Rhodes and Tracy, 1972a, 1972b). The reader is encouraged *not* to cast aside these other points of view—not to become an exclusivist.

In the remainder of this chapter the reader is introduced to the field of behavior modification and provided several examples of classroom, school, and home behavior modification research selected from the contemporary behavior therapy literature. The chapter concludes with an overview of the following models of behavior: psychoanalytic-psychodynamic, biophysical, environmental, and behavior modification.

BEHAVIOR MODIFICATION IN THE CLASSROOM, SCHOOL, AND HOME: EXAMPLES FROM THE RESEARCH

Behavior modification interventions have been applied effectively in various settings (home, school, office, factory, camp, and playground) with many types of individuals (old, young, rich, poor, male, female, normal, and maladjusted) having a diverse range of problems (psychoses, autism, neuroses, marital conflicts, learning problems, lack of motivation, and speech problems). The examples presented here were selected for their diversity rather than their representativeness of the total field of behavior modification. They have been confined to studies on children's behavior and learning in the classroom, school, and home.

After reviewing the examples, the reader is encouraged to continue to study the research literature for a broader understanding of this discipline. To facilitate exploration of the literature, lists of the appropriate journals, texts, and films are provided in Appendix B. These references have been selected as the most meaningful for the teacher-practitioner of a regular class, a resource room, or a special class.

Case 1—*Extinguishing tantrums*

Williams (1959) reported the case of a 21-month-old boy who had tantrums at bedtime. When his parents put the child to bed in the evening and left the room, he would cry and scream until they returned. Initially, they attempted to modify his going-to-bed behavior by reading him a bedtime story, but this approach was not successful; he would cry and scream until the book was removed from sight.

The researchers designed an intervention that removed the child's reinforcer for crying and screaming (a parent in the room) and consequently extinguished the inappropriate behavior (tantrums). The parents were instructed (1) to put the child in his bed after they had attended to his needs, (2) to bid the child "goodnight," (3) to leave the room, and (4) to close the door behind them. They were not to return to the child's room that evening.

After 10 nights of this new routine, the behavior was extinguished. A 2-year follow-up study revealed that the behavior recurred only once. This recurrence was the result of an error made by a visiting aunt with good intentions.

Case 2—*Increasing peer interaction*

Allen and associates (1964) conducted a study of a nursery school girl who was 4 years, 3 months of age. It was observed that the girl would not interact with other children in the school. In addition, she did not respond to their attempts to interact with her; she preferred the company of adults.

The girl did not appear withdrawn or fearful of the other children. She had a varied repertoire of unusually well developed physical skills. "She was superior to the other children in climbing, jumping, and riding; the use of creative paints and clay; songs; nature collections; mature verbalizations; and willingness to keep the nursery clean."

A social reinforcer (adult attention) was successfully utilized to increase her interactions with the other children in the nursery school.

Case 3—*Decreasing stuttering*

Richard and Mundy (1965) reported the case of a 9-year-old boy who was a chronic stutterer.

Social reinforcement and tangible rewards contingent on points were used to decrease the stuttering behavior. The boy was reinforced for not stuttering; he was ignored when stuttering occurred.

The investigators reported a dramatic decrease in the inappropriate behavior.

Case 4—*Modifying academic performance*

Lovitt and Smith (1974) studied an 11-year-old girl who performed erratically on subtraction problems. The study was designed to explore the effects of withdrawal of positive reinforcement, contingent on incorrect answers. The contingency specified that for each incorrect answer 1 minute of recess time would be lost.

This six-phase, multiple-baseline intervention effectively eliminated her erratic performance in subtraction.

Case 5—*Increasing classroom verbalizations*

Rosenbaum and Kellman (1973) implemented a shaping intervention to change the behavior of a third-grade girl who did not respond in class. Speech was first reinforced in a one-to-one setting with an adult. The elements of the regular school situation were gradually introduced into the one-to-one setting. Finally, the treatment procedures were transferred to the classroom setting.

Two and a half months after the treatment was terminated, the child was still speaking freely in her regular classroom.

Case 6—*Decreasing off-task behavior*

Simmons and Wasik (1973) used small-group contingencies and special activities to modify the behavior of a group of first graders. The instructional model used in the classroom was based on small-group work in designated learning centers or areas.

Before initiation of the study, the children frequently engaged in out-of-center behaviors that reduced the overall efficiency of the instructional model and increased the time the teacher and her aide devoted to behavior management.

When small-group contingencies were applied, the children had to behave (in their small groups) in a specific manner to obtain the rewards (special activities). The children's out-of-center behavior was reduced.

Case 7—*Eliminating abusive behavior*

Whitehurst and Miller (1973) reported the use of punishment to reduce the abusive behavior of two preschool boys on a nursery school bus. Their abusive behavior decreased when the punishment (retention on the bus until the second time it passed their house on the trip home after school) was imposed.

Case 8—*Modifying social and academic behaviors*

Sacks (1974) developed a study to (1) investigate how to modify the social and academic performance of preschool children who were under the supervision of teacher-trainees, (2) ascertain whether social or tangible rewards were more reinforcing to the children, and (3) determine if the teacher-trainees presented the rewards to the children with consistency and accuracy. For this research study the investigator instructed eight teacher-trainees in behavior modification techniques, including the appropriate presentation of reinforcers.

The results of the study demonstrated that the preschoolers' performance did improve in the following areas: (1) staying with their group, (2) complying with teacher requests, (3) identifying the letters of the alphabet, and (4) counting objects from one to twenty.

It was not possible for the investigator to determine if social or tangible reinforcers had more effect on the social and academic performance of the children. However, it was demonstrated that the teacher-trainees were successful in presenting both social and tangible reinforcers with accuracy and consistency.

Case 9—*Using the school administrator as a reinforcer*

Darch and Thorpe (1977) developed "the principal game" for their research study. The subjects in this study were ten disruptive fourth-grade boys, ranging in age from 9 years, 3 months to 11 years, 1 month. The principal game involved using the school principal as a social reinforcer for the boys. The game was in effect during social studies class. During this class the prize for winning the game was a chance to engage in conversation with the principal.

The results of the study demonstrated that the school principal was an effective reinforcer of on-task behavior during social studies class.

Case 10—*Improving reading*

Cook and White (1977) investigated the reinforcement potency of children's reading materials with a group of third graders. They conducted their study in two parts.

In the first part of the study, 96 children stated their personal listening preferences for three types of reading materials: (1) heritage, (2) contemporary, and (3) McGuffey—in that order.

The second part of the study included 193 third-grade children who listened to audiotapes of the preferred materials as a reward for correct responses during reading class and for completion of individual reading exercises. Thus, listening to audiotapes of preferred reading materials served as a reinforcer.

The results of the study demonstrated that the use of audiotapes of selected reading materials as a reinforcer was an excellent reward for participation during reading class and for completion of individual reading assignments.

Case 11—*Assessing parent-teacher training*

Koegal and associates (1978) assessed the generalization effects of materials present in parent-teacher training programs. They conducted a brief demonstration for parents on how to teach an autistic child a specific behavior. This demonstration was sufficient to teach the parents how to work with that particular behavior. However, generalization of the learned technique to other behaviors did not occur as a result of training.

However, the teaching of behavior modification procedures to the parents was effective in helping them modify a variety of child behaviors.

Case 12—*Reinforcing emotionally disturbed children*

Clements and Tracy (1977) conducted a study with ten emotionally disturbed boys, aged 9 to 11 years. The purpose of the investigation was to ascertain if touching (patting and hugging) and verbal reinforcement were effective means of modifying the boys' inappropriate social behavior in the classroom. Tactile and verbal reinforcers were applied by the same teacher with all of the boys. Each received the following reinforcers, in random order: tactile, verbal, tactile and verbal, and control (no cues or reinforcers).

The results of the study demonstrated that touching is an effective reinforcer, especially when paired with a verbal reinforcer.

Case 13—*Training profoundly retarded children*

Casebeer (1977) designed a training program for the education of profoundly mentally retarded children. The ten children studied ranged in age from 4 years, 10 months to 11 years, 1 month. They were nonverbal and were not toilet trained.

The training program was designed to develop the children's skills in the following areas: gross and fine motor coordination, sensorimotor skills, form perception, visual training, imitation, grooming, self-help skills, toileting, self-concept, socialization, and language development. The reinforcers presented during the training program were food, verbal praise, and tactile stimulation.

The results of the training and reinforcement demonstrated improvement in all areas.

Case 14—*Using peer tutoring to improve performance*

Coyne (1978) conducted a behavior modification study in which college students were the subjects. The purpose of the study was to investigate the effectiveness of peer tutoring as a method of improving academic performance in contrast to more traditional study methods. The study was conducted with students in an introductory educational psychology course.

The results demonstrated that the performance of the students in peer tutoring improved for each student who was paired with a study peer who was performing more proficiently in the course examinations during the baseline phase. These results were not found for the students who studied by traditional methods.

Case 15—*Teaching lipreading*

Johnson and Kayes (1976) applied behavior modification techniques to teach lipreading (or speech reading) to a 9-year-old deaf, multihandicapped boy. The child was diagnosed as emotionally disturbed and mentally handicapped, and because of his inappropriate behaviors he was unable to remain in a classroom group long enough to acquire an adequate level of proficiency in lipreading. In this study both token and social reinforcers were applied to enhance the probability that the subject would acquire lip reading skills.

The results demonstrated that token and social rewards were effective in shaping lipreading behavior. The subject learned to read both voiced and nonvoiced names of objects.

Case 16—*Effects of teacher approval*

Thomas and associates (1978) investigated the effects of teacher approval and disapproval of the behaviors of students in ten seventh-grade classes. They found that the majority of the teachers in the study displayed rates of student disapproval that were higher than their approval rates. They also found approval and disapproval of student behavior to be associated with student on-task and off-task behaviors.

Among the on-task behaviors approved of by the teachers were (1) hand raising before speaking, (2) listening to the teacher and not interrupting, (3) working quietly at the assigned place, (4) requesting permission to leave the work location, (5) being quiet, and (6) doing extra work when the assignment was completed. Off-task behaviors disapproved of by the teachers included (1) making unnecessary noise, (2) moving about the room when unnecessary, and (3) giving the appearance of daydreaming or showing disinterest in the lesson.

In general, the results of the study demonstrated that the teachers tend to take appropriate behavior for granted: they make few efforts to reward it. They expend more time reinforcing the inappropriate behaviors of students.

Case 17—*Correcting arithmetic assignments*

Hundert and Bucher (1978) conducted a research project to determine if students could self-score their arithmetic assignments with accuracy. Two studies were conducted.

In the first study the subjects were boys of an average age of 10 years, 4 months. They corrected their arithmetic assignments and turned them in to the teacher. Reinforcers for correcting the work accurately consisted of tokens that could be exchanged for various backup rewards. Throughout this study accuracy in the students' rating of their assignments was maintained. However, little change in the students' arithmetic performance was found.

In the second study the subjects were 17 male students of an average age of 15 years,

3 months. The teacher conducted continuous, then intermittent checks on the accuracy with which the students rated their arithmetic assignments. During the first phase of this study the students' accuracy in grading their work was reinforced as in the first study. In the second phase of the study the self-rating accuracy of the students was checked publicly. A penalty was applied for inaccuracies, and a bonus was given for accuracy.

The results of the second study demonstrated that students tend to exaggerate their reporting of accuracy when they are reinforced for rating their assignments. However, these exaggerations can be reduced and maintained at low levels by intermittent public checks of student accuracy.

• • •

The reader's attention is directed to the variety of target behaviors, ages, handicapping conditions, group compositions, experimental settings, and specific interventions applied in the research cases. Once again, the reader is encouraged to refer to the journals, textbooks, and films presented in the appendixes and to continue the study of the broad field of behavior modification.

PUBLIC LAW 94-142

On November 29, 1975, President Gerald R. Ford signed Public Law (P.L.) 94-142, which in a bipartisan effort was passed by both the House of Representatives and the Senate by overwhelming margins (404 to 7, and 87 to 7, respectively). This landmark legislation, known as the *Education of All Handicapped Children Act of 1975,* mandates that throughout the United States *a free, appropriate public education be provided for all handicapped children.*

Congress emphasized the key elements of the act in its use of the words *free, appropriate, public,* and *all.* It is the intention of

Congress that *all* handicapped children receive an education regardless of their race, religion, sex, or the characteristics of their particular handicaps. They are to receive an education that is *appropriate* to their individual needs. This education is to be *free* (without cost) to the child and the parents or guardian. Finally, the handicappped child's *free, appropriate* education is to be provided by the *public* school system rather than in private school or institutional settings (Shea, 1978).

The Education for All Handicapped Children Act of 1975 is having and will continue to have a significant impact on the structure and operation of the total educational establishment in the nation for many years to come. Its provisions will affect education from the preschool to the university level, in general and special education programs. It will effect regular elementary and secondary education teachers as well as special education teachers. It will have a significant impact on both handicapped and nonhandicapped individuals.

Among the provisions of P.L. 94-142 of greatest significance to the topics presented in this text are (Abeson and Weintraub, 1977):

1. Each handicapped individual needing special education and related services is to have an individualized education program (IEP) written in response to his or her individual educaional needs.
2. Parents are to be involved in the child's IEP. As partners with professionals in the child's education, parents will have several important functions. They will participate in the child's assessment, the IEP development process, the approval of the IEP and special placement, and the evaluation of the IEP. Parents may participate directly in the child's educational program.
3. The regular and special classroom

teachers are to be fully participating members of the IEP decision-making team under the provisions of P.L. 94-142. As the professionals primarily responsible for the delivery of services to the handicapped individual, the teacher —general or special—will have full and active involvement in the IEP development, implementation, and evaluation.

4. Handicapped children are to be placed in the least restrictive environment necessary to meet their unique educational needs. This provision requires that the handicapped child be placed in an educational environment that is as close to a normal or regular school program as feasible, yet one that is responsive to the child's individual educational needs. A child's special educational needs *only* will be met in a special education service program. The child's normal childhood needs will be met in the regular classroom and school setting. This concept is frequently referred to as mainstreaming, an often misunderstood term. Mainstreaming can be defined as

. . . a belief which involves an educational procedure and process for exceptional children, based on the conviction that each such child should be educated in the least restrictive environment in which his educational and related needs can be satisfactorily provided. This concept recognizes that exceptional children have a wide range of special educational needs, varying greatly in intensity and duration; that there is a recognized continuum of educational settings which may, at a given time, be appropriate for an individual child's needs; that to the maximum extent appropriate, exceptional children should be educated with non-exceptional children; and that special classes, separate schooling, or other removal of an exceptional child from education with non-exceptional children should occur only when the intensity of the child's special education and related need is such that they cannot be satisfied in an environment including non-exceptional children, even with provisions of supplementary aides and services. (Council for Exceptional Children, Delegate Assembly, 1976, p. 3)

Individualized education programs

A key provision of P.L. 94-142 is the individualized education program (IEP) to be written for each child who is declared eligible for special education services. The IEP must be developed in response to each child's individual educational needs.

In P.L. 94-142 the IEP is described as

. . . a written statement for each handicapped child developed in any meeting by a representative of the local educational agency or an intermediate educational unit who shall be qualified to provide, or supervise the provision of, specially designed instruction to meet the unique needs of handicapped children, the teacher, the parents or guardian of such child, and, whenever appropriate, such child, which statement shall include (A) a statement of the present levels of educational performance of such child, (B) a statement of annual goals, including short-term instructional objectives, (C) a statement of the specific educational services to be provided to such child, and the extent to which such child will be able to participate in regular educational programs, (D) the projected date for initiation and anticipated duration of such services, and appropriate objective criteria and evaluation procedures and schedules for determining, on at least an annual basis, whether instructional objectives are being achieved. (Public Law 94-142, Section 4)

As noted previously, the law specifically requires the direct participation of parents, teachers, and when appropriate the handicapped child in the IEP development process. In addition, P.L. 94-142 mandates that the child be integrated into the regular school programs for educational activities unless such integration is detrimental to the child's overall educational progress.

Analysis of the description of the IEP in P.L. 94-142 suggests the following minimum requirements under the law:

1. The child's educational performance must be assessed and the resultant data included in the written IEP.
2. The results of the assessment must be translated into annual goals and short-term instructional objectives. These annual goals and short-term instructional objectives form the base on which the child's educational program is designed.
3. The educational program must be written in response to the child's individual needs as stated in the goals and instructional objectives.
4. An objective evaluation procedure must be designed and implemented to ascertain the effectiveness of the instructional program.

A correlation can be made between the IEP process and the steps in the behavior modification process, described in detail in Chapter Three. The behavior modification process requires the following steps:

Collection of baseline data (IEP assessment phase)

Selection of objectives for the behavior change program (IEP short-term instructional objectives phase)

Design and implementation of a specific behavior change intervention or strategy (IEP instructional or educational program phase)

Collection of intervention data to evaluate the effectiveness of the behavior change intervention (IEP evaluation phase)

It appears that both regular and special education teachers trained in behavior modification procedures will find this training a valuable asset in their efforts to develop meaningful IEPs for handicapped children.

MODELS OF HUMAN BEHAVIOR

What makes us behave as we do toward ourselves, others, and our environment? How can we change our behavior and the behavior of others from inappropriate to appropriate? From unacceptable to acceptable? From destructive to constructive? From "bad" to "good"?

These questions embody our purpose— our goal. They are the age-old queries that have gnawed at our intellect and emotions since the beginning of time.

What makes us behave as we do? How can our behavior be changed?

Four of the responses theoreticians have made and continue to make to these questions are the psychoanalytic-psychodynamic, biophysical, environmental, and behavior modification explanations of human behavior. In this section these theoretical constructs are related to the behavior of children.

Historical perspective*

According to Hewett and Forness (1974), there are four historical determiners of our behavior toward ourselves and others:

1. The need and desire to *survive* in a harsh and hostile environment
2. *Superstition,* or the need to respond in some manner to the unknown
3. *Science,* or the need to investigate, analyze, and explain the unknown
4. *Service,* or the need to assist, guide, protect, and make whole, fellow human beings of lesser fortune

Humans have moved back and forth among these determiners of behavior throughout recorded history, first emphasizing one explanation then another as our knowledge and environment have demanded. We have striven for a scientific explanation of behavior but have frequently regressed to less rational explanations during trying times. However, during each historical period we have developed some explanation of our behavior, which is frequently a combination of two or more of the historical determiners.

As we progressed toward the world of the nineteenth and twentieth centuries, our explanations of human behavior focused more and more on science and service, and less and less on survival and superstition. However, with all of our contemporary knowledge of human beings and our environment, the elements of survival and superstition still exist in our explanations of human behavior.

Each of the models of human behavior presented here is an explanation of behavior; each has led to the development of an educational strategy or methodology for application with children having behavior problems.*

Psychoanalytic-psychodynamic model

As used in this text, the psychoanalytic-psychodynamic model refers to a group of theoretical constructs that have evolved during the past several decades from the original theoretical formulations of Freud (1933, 1949). These formulations have in common a belief in the existence of a dynamic intrapsychic life. Proponents of this model vary in their views on the following: the impact of the environment on the individual's intrapsychic life, the basic instinctual forces energizing psychic life, and the functions of the components of the personality (Munroe, 1955; Roberts, 1975).

---

*The reader is especially referred to Hewett and Forness (1974), Kanner (1964), and Rhodes and Tracy (1972a, 1972b) for excellent overviews and discussions of our attitude toward and treatment of the handicapped during the various historical periods.

*The material on the psychodynamic-psychoanalytic, biophysical, environmental, and behavior modification models of behavior is adapted from Shea, T. M. *Teaching children and youth with behavior disorders,* St. Louis: The C. V. Mosby Co., 1978, Chapter 1.

Fig. 1. Etiology of behavior from the psychoanalytic-psychodynamic perspective. (From Shea, T. M. *Teaching children and youth with behavior disorders.* St. Louis: The C. V. Mosby Co., 1978.)

The effects of nonintrapsychic variables, such as the environment and heredity, have been discussed by Adler and Jung (Munroe, 1955), Berne (1964a, 1964b), Erikson (1950, 1974), Harris (1969), Sullivan (1953), and many others.

Psychoanalytic-psychodynamic theorists see the causes of human behavior as being within the individual. Behavior is determined by a dynamic intrapsychic life. The relationship between the individual and behavior problems from the psychoanalytic-psychodynamic perspective is depicted in Fig. 1.

Freud perceived the personality as being composed of three interrelating components: the id, the superego, and the ego.

The id is the lusty infant who wants immediate gratification. Physical pleasure is what the id is after, and it will use the libido (sexual energy) to get what it wants. The id's typical remark in the personality dialog is "Gimmie. I want it. Now!" Because of its animalistic anti-social nature, the rest of the personality and society have kept the id mostly unconscious. It still influences us, but unconsciously. . . .

The super-ego is the conscience. Should and shame are the staples of its vocabulary, and its favorite line is, "You should be ashamed of yourself!" While the id is predominantly unconscious, the super-ego is partly conscious and partly unconscious. The unconscious part contains the "remonstrations and rules we were taught, "Don't do that. Don't play with . . . Nasty! Nice people don't. . . ." The super-ego is judgmental.

Between the id and the super-ego lives the hero and executive of the Freudian personality structure, the ego. Not only is he caught between the id and the super-ego and forced to moderate their conflicting pressures, he also is the one who is mostly aware of outside, social reality. Thus, his line to the others is, "Now, let's be realistic about this. . . ." The ego generally straddles the conscious and the unconscious. In a healthy personality he is the manager and can call the shots without being overpowered by the id or the super-ego. Each of the three parts has a genius all of its own. The ego's armamentarium includes his "ego defenses." Sublimation, for example, is the redirection of socially unacceptable impulses into acceptable channels: Don't play in the toilet, dear. Why don't you go out and play in the sandbox? A large part of our work as teachers is to provide socially acceptable outlets for otherwise destructive desires. (Roberts, 1975, pp. 6-7)

Efforts to apply psychoanalytic-psychodynamic theories to educational processes have led teachers to develop the psychoeducational, or the psychodynamic-interpersonal educational, strategy, which is

. . . concerned with the psychic orgin and meaning of maladaptive behavior, as well as the child's interpersonal relationships with others, particularly the teacher. This orientation, shared by most psychotherapists, is consistent with the high priority given by them to understanding psychological causal factors and the develoment of a positive, trusting relationship between adult and child in formal education training. (Hewett, 1968, p. 9)

Significant contributions to this educational strategy have been made by Berkowitz and Rothman (1960), Bettelheim (1950), Bower (1961), Glasser (1965), Morse (1965), Redl and Wineman (1951, 1952), and others. Although diversification exists among these theorists and practitioners, the primary objectives and methodologies to be applied in the educational setting remain relatively constant.

A primary goal is to understand why the child is behaving as he is in school. This goal may be achieved by some through interpretation of behavior in a psychodynamic context, using psychoanalytic concepts. Others may view the child more in relationship to his total environment and be concerned with understanding why he lacks adaptive capacities for dealing with the stresses and demands associated with learning and adjustment in school. For the teacher, a major goal is the communication of acceptance to the child and the establishment of a secure and meaningful relationship. Formal educational goals are of secondary importance. (Hewett, 1968, pp. 17-18)

In the classroom emphasis is placed one (1) developing a mentally healthy atmosphere; (2) accepting the child and the pathological conditions without reservation; and (3) encouraging and assisting the child in learning, beginning at a level and under circumstances in which the child can perform successfully. Assuming the role of educational therapist, the teacher accepts the child, tolerating and interpreting the child's behavior.

Psychoanalytic-psychodynamic theories no longer dominate programs for the education of behavior-disordered chldren, as was the situation in the 1950s and 1960s. However, this theoretical perspective remains a dominant force in contemporary American society in such forms as popular literature, child care books, movies, novels, television shows, and casual conversations.

In Chapter Seven several of the intervention strategies associated with the psychoanalytic-psychodynamic model are reviewed in some detail.

Biophysical model

The biophysical theory of the etiology of learning and behavior problems of children places emphasis on organic origins of human

Fig. 2. Etiology of behavior from the biophysical perspective. (From Shea, T. M. *Teaching children and youth with behavior disorders*. St. Louis: The C. V. Mosby Co., 1978.)

behavior. The proponents of this conceptual model postulate a relationship between physical defects, malfunctions, and illnesses, and the behavior exhibited by the individual. This relationship is depicted in Fig. 2.

Although not the dominant theory of causation in the education of children, the biophysical model does have proponents among professionals and parents concerned with severely emotionally disturbed, learning-disabled, perceptually handicapped, and developmentally disabled children.

The practitioner who is influenced by the biophysical model is concerned primarily with changing or compensating for the individual's malfunctioning organic mechanisms or processes that are causing the unacceptable behavior.

Some proponents of this theoretical perspective believe that the individual's external environment is an unimportant factor in the behavior problem (Rimland, 1969). Others accept the importance of the external environment and believe that this is the factor that triggers an inherent organic predisposition within the individual organism (Rosenthal, 1963).

As a result of extensive biophysical research with children having severe behavior disorders (autistic, schizophrenic children), Rimland concluded:

Why do psychiatrists and psychologists believe there are people whose mental disorder is functional rather than organic? Why do they reject the plausible premise that the "functional" cases differ from the organic cases only in that our knowledge is at present too limited to identify the "organic" defect in the "functional" cases? (p. 703)

Rimland's prediction is that as our knowledge and understanding of human behavior and the physical organism develop, we will find that psychosocial factors have a minor influence in the etiology of severe behavior disorders.

Biophysical handicaps can be divided into four groups (National Foundation–March of Dimes, 1975):

1. *Structural defects:* One or more parts of the body are defective in size or shape (spina bifida, clubfoot, cleft lip).
2. *Functional defects:* One or more parts of the body are malfunctioning (blindness, deafness).
3. *Inborn errors of metabolism:* The body is unable to convert certain chemicals to other chemicals needed for normal body functioning (phenylketonuria [PKU], Tay-Sachs disease).
4. *Blood diseases:* The blood is unable to conduct its normal functions (sickle cell anemia, hemophilia).

These organic defects may be a consequence of either heredity or environment (trauma). Environmental effects may occur before, during, or after birth.

Several curative and preventive medical interventions have been developed to mitigate or modify the effects of biophysical defects. Among these interventions are prenatal and postnatal health care, proper nutrition and diet, megavitamin and similar therapies, general and specific physical examinations, symptom control medications, and genetic counseling. These interventions are presented in detail in Chapter Seven.

Among the proponents of biophysical theories as they apply to the education of children and youth are Cruickshank and others (1961), Fernald (1943), Frostig and others (1961), Getman (1962), Itard (1962), Kephart (1960), Seguin (Kanner, 1964), and Strauss and Lehtinen (1947).

An excellent summary of this theoretical perspective as it applies in the educational setting is provided by Hewett (1968):

The primary goal of the sensory-neurological strategy is to discover the child's sensory and neurologically based deficit, often through extensive observation and diagnostic testing. Once these deficits are uncovered, the child is viewed as a learner who must be trained to accurately perceive and comprehend stimuli and to demonstrate motor efficiency before he is given complex learning tasks. (p. 24)

In the special classroom setting the teacher who is influenced by the biophysical model will emphasize order and routine in the classroom and daily schedule, frequent repetition of learning tasks, the sequential presentation and learning of tasks, and a reduction or elimination of extraneous environmental stimuli.

Environmental model

The impact, actual and potential, of the environment on human behavior is a dominant theme in contemporary society. Many decisions made by governments, corporate groups, and individuals are made with a conscious awareness of the relationship between people and the environment. Environmental impact studies are standard, accepted components of all proposals to construct highways, airports, dams, lakes, industrial complexes, high-rise buildings, and so on. Both professionals and lay persons are increasingly concerned with any environmental change that may affect human behavior, such as those concerning recreation areas, water pollution, waste disposal, strip mining, or nuclear power. Many are concerned with the effects of environmental changes on employment, human services, neighborhood composition, and so on.

Sociology traditionally is the study of the development, structure, interaction, and behavior of organized groups of human beings. Sociology is composed of a number of subgroups focusing on specific areas of this social science, such as social psychology, small-group study, or educational sociology.

In an educational setting sociology focuses on the formal and informal composition of and interactions among groups. It is concerned with groups both within an organization and outside of it that affect the organization. As it applies to the education of children, sociology is the study of social forces that in some manner affect these individuals.

Ecology is the study of the interrelationships between an organism and its environment. As it applies to the education of children, ecology is the study of the reciprocal relationship between the child or group and others (individuals, groups, and objects) in the environment.

Sociology and ecology as etiological models of human behavior are depicted in Fig. 3.

The sociological theory of greatest importance to educators of children with learning and behavior problems is the deviance perspective.

The deviance perspective focuses on mental illness as the breaking of social rules. In particular, mental illness is related to implicit rules governing ordinary social interaction. From a deviance perspective, two important questions arise. (1) What are the social forces promoting conformity or rule-breaking? (2) What relationships exist between those enforcing the rules and those breaking the rules? (Des Jarlais, 1972, p. 263)

In an effort to respond to these two central questions, sociologists have generated several theoretical models to account for deviant behavior. Reviewed by Des Jarlais (1972), these frameworks include:

Anomie: The theory of anomie as a cause of mental illness was proposed by Durkheim (1951). Anomie is defined as a lack of social rules or inhibitors within the structure of a society that effectively limit or regulate individual and group behaviors. This phenomenon occurs in

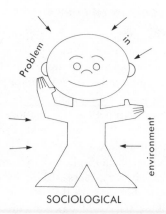

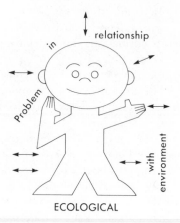

Fig. 3. Etiology of behavior from the sociological and ecological perspectives. (From Shea, T. M. *Teaching children and youth with behavior disorders.* St. Louis: The C. V. Mosby Co., 1978.)

rapidly developing or changing societies, such as contemporary society, in which socially sanctioned norms have not evolved or been institutionalized rapidly enough to monitor the efforts of individuals and groups to attain their needs and desires.

Social disorganization: The theory of social disorganization was developed from the findings of a series of urban studies. Among the researchers associated with this school of thought were Hawley (1950) and Park and Burgess (1925). This perspective attempts to measure and characterize the differences between communities considered organized or "natural" and communities considered disorganized. Characteristics of the organized community, in opposition to those of the disorganized community, include low crime and delinquency rates, stable family units, and a low rate of mental illness. The sources of such characteristics of the community (both organized and disorganized) are assumed to be related to such variables as the availability of employment, education, religious services, recreational facilities, and the like. The disorganized community lacks appropriate services.

Cultural transmission: Sutherland and Cressey (1960) proposed the theory of cultural transmission. Cultural transmission theorists maintain that deviant behavior is learned behavior. Mental illness, a form of deviance, is learned through differential association: it is a result of the individual's associations with persons and groups who are in some manner teaching deviance. Of course, the reverse is true in the learning of nondeviant behavior.

Labeling theory: The labeling of children who deviate from the norms and rules of the school and community as emo-

tionally disturbed, behavior disordered, delinquent, learning disabled, retarded, and so on, has long been a concern of educators. Many fear the effects of the label and its implications for the child's behavior and educators' expectations of the child.

The sociological theory of labeling emphasizes that one does not become a deviant by breaking rules. One must be labeled a deviant before the social expectations defining the particular form of deviancy are activated. Once an individual is officially labeled a deviant, this person assumes the role expectations of that particular form of deviance in order to conform to the expectations of society. This theoretical perspective is closely related to Parson's (1951) concept of the sick role. He proposed four societal expectations that encourage individuals labeled "sick" to assume this role:

1. Sick persons are relieved of their normal role obligations.
2. Because they are sick, they are not morally responsible for their condition.
3. Sick persons must express their desire to return to normal functioning.
4. Sick persons must seek technically competent help from appropriate caretakers (psychiatrists, psychologists, social workers, teachers).

Reviewed by Wagner (1972), a variety of interventions have evolved out of sociological and ecological theories. Many of these interventions are reviewed in some detail in Chapter Seven.

The application of the environmental model in educational programs for children is characterized by (1) an awareness of the impact of the environment on the group and/or individual and the monitoring and manipulation of the environment for the therapeutic benefit of the individual and/or group, and (2) an awareness of the dynamic reciprocal interrelationship that exists between the group and/or individual and the environment and the monitoring and manipulation of this relationship for the therapeutic benefit of the individual and/or group.

Behavior modification model

Behavioral psychology is the predominant educational psychology taught in American colleges and universities today (Roberts, 1975).

The statement "What you do is influenced by what follows what you do" (Sarason and others, 1972, p. 10) is an excellent summary of the essence of the behavioral theory, specifically in reference to behavior modification. Although behavior modification is the primary focus of this text, a brief overview of this model is presented here to facilitate the reader's efforts to compare and contrast it with the three previously presented models of human behavior.

The behavior modifier is concerned primarily with what behavior an individual exhibits that is inappropriate or unacceptable and what intervention can be designed and imposed to change this observable behavior.

For the behavior modification practitioner behavior is defined as all human acts that are observable and measurable, excluding biochemical and physiological processes (Roberts, 1975).

The practitioner sees the causes of human behavior as existing outside of the individual, in the environment. Thus, the individual's behavior is primarily determined by external forces. The relationship between the individual and his or her behavior as perceived by the behaviorist is depicted in Fig. 4.

Those adhering to the behavior modification model assume that all human behavior (adaptive and maladaptive) is the conse-

Fig. 4. Etiology of behavior from the behavior modification perspective. (From Shea, T. M. *Teaching children and youth with behavior disorders.* St. Louis: The C. V. Mosby Co., 1978.)

quence of the lawful application of the principles of reinforcement.

According to Roberts, the principles of reinforcement are:
1. The reinforcement must be appropriate. If one reinforcer does not work, another may be tried.
2. Reinforcement follows the behavior. According to "Grandma's law," you eat your vegetables first, then you may have dessert. (This important law is further exemplified in the section on contingency contracting in Chapter Four.)
3. The behavior should be reinforced as soon as possible after it occurs. Teachers who do not return papers or who delay their return a long time are guilty of professional misconduct in the perception of the behaviorist.
4. Many small rewards will be more effective than a few big ones.

These rules are an indication of the behavior modifier's belief that human behavior is controlled by the individual's impinging environmental stimuli (Kameya, 1972). The individual's behavior is changed by manipulation of the environment.

Behavioral theory, including behavior modification techniques and their applications to individual and group behavior problems, has its roots in the writings and research of Bandura (1969), Eysenck (1960), Hull (1943), Pavlov (1941), Skinner (1953, 1971), Thorndike (1932), Watson (1930), and Wolpe (1961), among others. Although there has been and continues to be heated debates among theorists relative to various theoretical constructs and interventions within this theoretical model, practitioners have successfully applied its principles to a variety of human problems. Among the problem behaviors that have been changed as a consequence of the application of behavior modification interventions are psychoses, autism, neuroses, marital conflicts, specific learning problems, motivational handicaps, and speech problems. Researchers and practitioners have successfully modified tantrums, verbal and physical aggression, interpersonal interaction patterns, eating habits, mutism, and so on.

Various behavior modification interventions in the school have been successfully implemented with exceptional children by Haring and Phillips (1962), Hewett (1968), Orme and Purnell (1970), Walker and Shea (1974), Zimmerman and Zimmerman (1962), and others.

The goal of behavior modification interventions in the classroom with behavior-disordered children (and, indeed, with all individuals) is best summarized by Hewett (1968).

The basic goal for the behavior modifier is the identification of maladaptive behaviors which interfere with learning and assisting the child in developing more adaptive behavior. Every child is considered a candidate for learning something regardless of his degree of psychopathology and other problems. This "something" may only represent a starting point (e.g., chair sitting) and be but a small part of the eventual "something" the teacher hopes to accomplish (e.g., reading), but care will be taken to insure its mastery before more complex goals are introduced. The child's behavior is viewed in the broadest possible context without rigid adherence to a priority ranking of behavioral goals on the basis of inferences regarding emotional conflicts or brain dysfunctions (p. 34).

There are a variety of specific behavior modification interventions that may be applied in the effort to change inappropriate behavior. These interventions are presented in detail with practical examples in this text.

The procedures for applying behavior modification in the educational setting require the teacher to (1) observe and clarify the behavior to be changed; (2) select potent reinforcers at the appropriate time; (3) design and impose, with consistency, an intervention technique based on the principles of reinforcement; and (4) monitor and evaluate the effectiveness of the intervention.

SUMMARY

In this introductory chapter several classroom and school research studies exemplifying various applications of behavior modification procedures are presented to familiarize the reader with the versatility of this discipline.

The research studies are followed by a brief overview of several relevant parts of P.L. 94-142, the Education for All Handicapped Children Act of 1975. The components of the individualized education programs (IEPs) mandated for each handicapped child under this federal legislation are presented.

Four models of human behavior—psychoanalytic-psychodynamic, biophysical, environmental, and behavior modification—are briefly reviewed. The models are not compared or contrasted with each other; each one contributes to our understanding of human behavior, and the reader is encouraged to thoroughly investigate all of them.

In the remainder of this text our primary purpose is to present and explore with the reader the behavior modification model and its application to children in the educational setting. Interventions associated with the other three models are reviewed in Chapter Seven.

REFERENCES

Abeson, A., and Weintraub, F. Understanding the individualized education program. In S. Torres (Ed.), *A primer on individualized education programs for handicapped children.* Reston, Va.: The Foundation for Exceptional Children, 1977.

Allen, K., Hart, B., Buell, J., Harris, F., and Wolf, M. Effects of social reinforcement on isolated behavior of a nursery school child. *Child Development,* 1964, *35,* 511-518.

Bandura, A. *Principles of behavior modification.* New York: Holt, Rinehart & Winston, 1969.

Berkowitz, P., and Rothman, E. *The disturbed child.* New York: New York University Press, 1960.

Berne, E. *Games people play.* New York: Grove Press, Inc., 1964. (a)

Berne, E. *Principles of group treatment.* New York: Oxford University Press, Inc., 1964. (b)

Bettelheim, B. *Love is not enough.* New York: The Free Press, 1950.

Bower, E. M. *The education of emotionally handicapped children: A report to the California Legislature.* Sacramento: California State Department of Education, 1961.

Caplan, G. Opportunities for school psychologists in the primary prevention of mental disorders in children. *Mental Hygiene,* 1963, *47,* 525-540.

Casebeer, C. A. A teacher planned program for the profoundly mentally retarded. *Education and Training of the Mentally Retarded,* February 1977, *12,* 66-68.

Clements, J. E., and Tracy, D. B. Effects of touch and verbal reinforcement on classroom behavior of emotionally disturbed boys. *Exceptional Children,* April 1977, *43,* 453-454.

Cook, V. J., and White, M. A. Reinforcement potency of children's reading materials. *Journal of Educational Psychology,* June 1977, *41,* 226-232.

Council for Exceptional Children, Delegate Assembly. Mainstreaming. *CEC Update,* 1976, 7(4), 3.

Coyne, P. D. The effects of peer tutoring with group contingencies on the academic performance of college students. *Journal of Applied Behavior Analysis,* Summer 1978, *11,* 305-307.

Cruickshank, W., Bentzen, F., Ratzenburg, F., and Tannhauser, M. *A teaching methodology for brain-injured and hyperactive children.* New York: Syracuse University Press, 1961.

Darch, C. B., and Thorpe, H. W. The principal game: A group consequence procedure to increase classroom on-task behavior. *Psychology in the Schools,* July 1977, *14,* 341-347.

Des Jarlais, D. C. Mental illness of social deviance. In W. C. Rhodes and M. L. Tracy (Eds.), *A study of child variance.* Vol. 1. *Conceptual project in emotional disturbance.* Ann Arbor: The University of Michigan Press, 1972.

Durkheim, E. *Suicide.* New York: The Free Press, 1951.

Erikson, E. H. *Childhood and society.* New York: W. W. Norton & Co., Inc., 1950.

Erikson, E. H. *Dimensions of a new identity: The 1973 Jefferson lectures in the humanities.* New York: W. W. Norton & Co., Inc., 1974.

Eysenck, H. J. *Behavior therapy and the neuroses.* New York: Pergamon Press, Inc., 1960.

Fernald, G. *Remedial techniques in basic school subjects.* New York: McGraw-Hill Book Co., 1943.

Freud, S. *New introductory lectures on psychoanalysis.* New York: W. W. Norton & Co., Inc., 1933.

Freud, S. *An outline of psychoanalysis.* New York: W. W. Norton & Co., Inc., 1949.

Frostig, M., LeFever, W., and Whittlesey, J. R. B. *Developmental Test of Visual Perception.* Palo Alto, Calif.: Consulting Psychologists Press, 1961.

Getman, G. N. *How to develop your child's intelligence.* Luverne, Minn: Author, 1962.

Glasser, W. *Reality therapy.* New York: Harper & Row, Publishers, Inc., 1965.

Haring, N. G., and Phillips, E. L. *Educating emotionally disturbed children.* New York: McGraw-Hill Book Co., 1962.

Harris, T. A. *I'm OK–You're OK: A practical guide to transactional analysis.* New York: Harper & Row, Publishers, Inc., 1969.

Hawley, A. *Human ecology: A theory of community structure.* New York: Ronald Press Co., 1950.

Hewett, F. M. *The emotionally disturbed child in the classroom: A developmental strategy for educating children with maladaptive behavior.* Boston: Allyn & Bacon, Inc., 1968.

Hewett, F. M., and Forness, S. R. *Education of exceptional learners.* Boston: Allyn & Bacon, Inc., 1974.

Hull, C. L. *Principles of behavior.* New York: Appleton-Century-Crofts, 1943.

Hundert, J., and Bucher, B. Pupil self-scored arithmetic performance: A practical procedure for maintaining accuracy. *Journal of Applied Behavior Analysis*, Summer 1978, *11*, 304.

Itard, J. M. G. *The wild boy of Aveyron*. New York: Appleton-Century-Crofts, 1962.

Johnson, C. M., and Kayes, J. H. Acquisition of lipreading in a deaf multihandicapped child. *Journal of Speech and Hearing Disorders*, May 1976, *41*, 226-232.

Kameya, L. I. Behavioral interventions in emotional disturbance. In W. C. Rhodes and M. L. Tracy (Eds.), *A study of child variance*. Vol. 2. *Interventions*. Ann Arbor: The University of Michigan Press, 1972.

Kanner, L. *A history of the care and study of the mentally retarded*. Springfield, Ill.: Charles C Thomas, Publisher, 1964.

Kephart, N. *The slow learner in the classroom*. Columbus, Ohio: Charles E. Merrill Publishing Co., 1960.

Koegal, R. L., Glahn, T. J., and Nieminen, G. S. Generalization of parent training results. *Journal of Applied Behavior Analysis*, Spring 1978, *11*, 95-109.

Lovitt, T. C., and Smith, D. D. Using withdrawal of positive reinforcement to alter subtraction performance. *Exceptional Children*, February 1974, *40*, 357-358.

Morse, W. C. Intervention techniques for the classroom teacher of the emotionally disturbed. In P. Knoblock (Ed.), *Educational programming for emotionally disturbed children: The decade ahead*. Syracuse, N.Y.: Division of Special Education and Rehabilitation, Syracuse University, 1964.

Morse, W. C. The crisis teacher. In N. Long, W. C. Morse, and R. Newman (Eds.), *Conflict in the classroom* (1st ed.). Belmont, Calif.: Wadsworth Publishing Co., Inc., 1965.

Munroe, R. L. *Schools of psychoanalytic thought: An exposition, critique, and attempt at integration*. New York: Holt, Rinehart & Winston, 1955.

National Foundation–March of Dimes. *Birth defects: The tragedy and the hope*. White Plains, N.Y.: The Foundation, 1975.

Orme, M. E. J., and Purnell, R. F. Behavior modification and transfer in an out-of-control classroom. In G. Fargo, C. Behrns, and P. Nolen (Eds.), *Behavior modification in the classroom*. Belmont, Calif.: Wadsworth Publishing Co., Inc., 1970.

Park, R. E., and Burgess, E. W. *The city*. Chicago: University of Chicago Press, 1925.

Parsons, T. *The social system*. New York: The Free Press, 1951.

Pavlov, J. P. *Lectures on conditioned reflexes* (2 vols.). New York: International Universities Press, 1941.

Redl, F., and Wineman, D. *Children who hate*. New York: The Free Press, 1951.

Redl, F., and Wineman, D. *Controls from within*. New York: The Free Press, 1952.

Rhodes, W. C., and Tracy, M. L. (Eds.). *A study of child variance*. Vol. 1. *Conceptual project in emotional disturbance*. Ann Arbor: The University of Michigan Press, 1972. (a)

Rhodes, W. C., and Tracy, M. L. (Eds.). *A study of child variance*. Vol. 2. *Interventions*. Ann Arbor: The University of Michigan Press, 1972. (b)

Richard, H., and Mundy, M. Direct manipulation of stuttering behavior: An experimental-clinical approach. In L. P. Ullmann and L. Krasner (Eds.), *Case studies in behavior modification*. New York: Holt, Rinehart & Winston, Inc., 1965.

Rimland, B. Psychogenesis versus biogenesis: The issues and evidence. In S. C. Plog and R. B. Edgerton (Eds.), *Changing perspectives in mental illness*. New York: Holt, Rinehart & Winston, 1969.

Roberts, T. B. *Four psychologies applied to education: Freudian-behavioral-humanistic-transpersonal*. Cambridge, Mass.: Schenkman Publishing Co., Inc., 1975.

Rosenbaum, E., and Kellman, M. Treatment of a selectively mute third-grade child. *Journal of School Psychology* 1973, *11*(1), 26-29.

Rosenthal, D. (Ed.). *The Genain quadruplets: A case study and theoretical analysis of heredity and environment in schizophrenia*. New York: Basic Books, Inc., Publishers, 1963.

Sacks, A. S. Introducing teacher-trainees to behavior modification techniques and their application of those techniques in increasing social and academic behavior of preschool children. *Dissertation Abstracts*, April 1974, *35*, 6562.

Sarason, I. G., Glaser, E. M., and Fargo, G. A. *Reinforcing productive classroom behavior*. New York: Behavioral Publications, Inc., 1972.

Shea, T. M. *Teaching children and youth with behavior disorders*. St. Louis: The C. V. Mosby Co., 1978.

Simmons, J. T., and Wasik, B. H. Use of small group contingencies and special activity times to manage behavior in a first-grade classroom. *Journal of School Psychology*, 1973, *11*(3), 228-238.

Skinner, B. F. *Science and human behavior*. New York: Macmillan Publishing Co., Inc., 1953.

Skinner, B. F. *Beyond freedom and dignity*. New York: Alfred A. Knopf, Inc., 1971.

Strauss, A. A., and Lehtinen, L. E. *Psychopathology and education of the brain-injured child*. New York: Grune & Stratton, Inc., 1947.

Sullivan, H. S. *The interpersonal theory of psychiatry*. New York: W. W. Norton & Co., Inc., 1953.

Sutherland, E., and Cressey, D. *Principles of criminology* (6th ed.). Philadelphia: J. B. Lippincott Co., 1960.

Thomas, J. D., Pusland, I. E., Grant, M. D., and Glynn, T. L. Natural rates of teacher approval and disapproval in grade-7 classrooms. *Journal of Applied Behavior Analysis*, Spring 1978, *11*, 91-94.

Thorndike, E. L. *The fundamentals of learning.* New York: Teacher's College Press, 1932.

Wagner, M. Environmental interventions in emotional disturbance. In W. C. Rhodes and M. L. Tracy (Eds.), *A study of child variance.* Vol. 2. *Interventions.* Ann Arbor: The University of Michigan Press, 1972.

Walker, J. E., and Shea, T. M. Individualizing behavior modifications in a day care center for the severely retarded. *The Journal for Special Educators of the Mentally Retarded,* 1974, *11*(1), 14-22.

Watson, J. B. *Behaviorism.* Chicago: University of Chicago Press, 1930.

Whitehurst, C., and Miller, E. Behavior modification of aggressive behavior on a nursery school bus: A case study. *Journal of School Psychology,* 1973, *2*(3), 123-128.

Williams, C. D. The elimination of tantrum behavior by extinction procedures. *Journal of Abnormal Social Psychology,* 1959, *59*, 269.

Wolpe, J. The systematic desensitization treatment of neuroses. *Journal of Nervous and Mental Disease,* 1961, *132*, 189-203.

Zimmerman, E. H., and Zimmerman, J. The alteration of behavior in a special classroom situation. *Journal of the Experimental Analysis of Behavior,* 1962, 5, 59-60.

CHAPTER TWO

Basic principles of behavior modification

"What you do is influenced by what follows what you do" (Sarason and others, 1972). The consequences and probable consequences of behavior, more than any other factor, determine the behavior that the individual exhibits. In the discipline of behavior modification the consequences of behavior are called reinforcers. Reinforcers may increase, decrease, or maintain behavior.

Reinforcers can be classified in a number of ways. Basically, they are classified as tangible reinforcers (food, drinks, and tokens) and social reinforcers (praise, smiles, and other signs of approval).

For example, why does a child attend school? What reinforces school-attending behavior? A child may go to school because:

1. It is warmer in school than in the home.
2. The people at school give the child more attention than the people at home or in the neighborhood.
3. The child plans after-school activities with friends during the morning recess.
4. The child eats the hot meal provided each noon by the school.

It can be understood, then, that a child attends school for both tangible (heat and food) and social (attention and friends) rewards.

Reinforcers may be positive (rewarding, pleasure giving) or negative (aversive, punishing). Tangible and social reinforcers are positive reinforcers, desirable consequences for which appropriate behavior is exhibited.

A child who considers school an aversive stimulus might exhibit inappropriate behavior in an attempt to avoid school. If the child were successful in this attempt, the inappropriate behavior would increase; thus school-attending behavior would decrease. For example, two situations that would result in an increase in school-avoiding behavior are:

1. The child is allowed to remain at home during the school day because he or she complains of being ill.
2. The child is allowed to remain at home because a homework assignment is not completed.

If the child were not allowed to avoid school by exhibiting these behaviors, they would probably decrease.

Punishment would also be effective in getting a child to attend school. Among the punishments that could be employed are (1) a spanking from the child's father; (2) a reprimand from the child's mother; (3) loss of allowance or the use of a bike; (4) loss of privileges, such as watching television or attending the movies; and (5) the threat of being sent to juvenile court or a detention center.

The consequences of behavior, then, are the determiners of behavior. Human beings tend to repeat behaviors that are, in their perception, rewarded or praised. They tend not to repeat behaviors that are, in their perception, punished.

In the remainder of this chapter some of the basic principles of behavior modification are presented and exemplified. These principles can be systematically applied by the teacher in the classroom and by the parents in the home.

The effective and efficient application of behavior modification techniques involves more than the simple memorization of principles of reinforcement and their application. For effective implementation it is necessary that the practitioner be intuitive, creative, and empathetic.

PRINCIPLES OF REINFORCEMENT

The principles of reinforcement are a set of rules and techniques to be applied in the behavior change process. The successful behavior modifier relies heavily on these principles when planning and implementing a behavior change program.

Principle 1. Reinforcement must be dependent on the manifestation of the appropriate behavior

If we are attempting, via a planned intervention, to increase a specific behavior in an individual, we must reinforce *only* the behavior we are planning to increase. In planning and implementing an intervention, we must *take caution to ensure that undesirable behaviors are not reinforced unwittingly.*

EXAMPLE

Ms. Jones was attempting to decrease Bill's out-of-seat behavior in her classroom. It had been ascertained through systematic observation that Bill received attention from her for out-of-seat behavior. Whenever Bill was out of his seat, Ms. Jones proceeded to yell or otherwise reprimand him. Although Bill was receiving negative attention, his basic needs for attention—positive or negative—were apparently being met in this situation. Bill's inappropriate behav-

ior (being out of his seat) kept increasing as Ms. Jones's behavior (yelling or scolding) kept increasing.

EXAMPLE

Ms. Long was faced with a problem similar to Ms. Jones's—Jerry's out-of-seat behavior. She was reported to have said that she had to dust Jerry's chair every morning because he never used it.

At first, she applied Ms. Jones's technique, that is, yelling. Then she planned a behavior modification intervention. She would totally ignore Jerry's out-of-seat behavior. She would in *no* way reinforce inappropriate behavior. However and whenever Jerry's overactive bottom hit his assigned seat, she would immediately reward him. She would praise him in front of the whole class, if necessary, and pat his shoulder.

As a result of this intervention, Jerry not only learned to sit in his seat but Ms. Long discovered she liked him.

In the second example the approach was effective in bringing about the desired behavior. In the first example, however, Ms. Jones is still yelling and Bill is still grooving on all the attention he is receiving.

In conclusion, Principle 1 suggests that if we desire to modify a specific behavior, we must reinforce *only* that behavior.

Principle 2. The appropriate behavior must be reinforced immediately

The importance of presenting the reinforcer immediately after the appropriate behavior is exhibited cannot be overstressed. This principle is especially true during the initial stages of the behavior change process, when we are attempting to establish a new behavior. Inappropriate and nonfunctional behaviors occur from time to time in every individual's behavioral repertoire. If reinforcers are delayed in a planned intervention program, inappropriate behaviors (rather than the appropriate behavior) may be accidentally or unwittingly reinforced and thus increased.

EXAMPLE

Mr. Flamer was attempting to increase the number of problems Pat completed during math period. He planned to reward Pat immediately after he completed each assigned group of problems. The number of problems in each group would be increased on a weekly basis if Pat responded to the intervention as predicted.

Mr. Flamer was very inconsistent in the presentation of the reinforcer (tokens). As a result, Pat spent considerable time waiting at his desk and waving his hand frantically to gain Mr. Flamer's attention.

After a few weeks it was found that the intervention program was ineffective in changing the number of completed problems. Pat now sat at his desk for much longer periods of time with a bored expression.

Mr. Flamer became aware of Pat's behavior and of his own personal inconsistency. He began to reinforce Pat immediately after Pat had completed each group of problems. Within a short period of time Pat was completing his problems and had doubled his production.

When attempting to establish a new behavior or increase the frequency of an existing behavior, we must reinforce that behavior as soon as it occurs.

Principle 3. During the initial stages of the behavior change process the appropriate behavior must be reinforced each time it is exhibited

If newly acquired behavior is to be sustained at the appropriate frequency rate, the reinforcer must be administered each time the behavior is exhibited. Frequently, beginning behavior modifiers reinforce new, but not yet habituated, behaviors with such inconsistency and so infrequently that the child becomes confused and the desired behavior does not become an established part of the child's behavioral repertoire.

EXAMPLE

Ms. Traber worked several months with Matt, rewarding approximations of a desired behavior (in this case, a complete sentence). Finally, after 6 months Matt said a complete sentence. "I want a candy." Matt was immediately rewarded with a candy, and for the next several weeks he consumed many candies; he was given many opportunities to receive the reward. In addition, during this phase of the behavior change process Matt increased his variety of complete sentences to include "I want a glass of milk," "I want

some juice," "I want some soda," "I want a puzzle," and the like.

EXAMPLE

Russell never requested any materials or assistance in the junior high school classroom without whining or screaming, or both. He would yell, "I want my paper," or "Give me some help." Mr. Hicks had taken about as much of this behavior as he could tolerate. He decided to ignore all whining and screaming from Russell. Russell's initial reaction to being ignored dramatically increased his inappropriate behavior, but Mr. Hicks stuck to the plan.

After 2 weeks of mutual frustration Russell raised his hand one day during social studies. He politely requested Mr. Hick's assistance. He immediately received the assistance, verbal praise, and a pat on the back. Mr. Hicks was very pleased with Russell (and himself). A mutual admiration society developed and continued very consistently for a few days.

Mr. Hicks then focused his attention on the problems of another boy in the class. As a result, Mr. Hicks became an inconsistent reinforcer and Russell began whining and screaming anew.

Mr. Hicks forgot that Russell's inappropriate behavior had been learned over 12 or 13 years and could not be changed overnight, and after only a few successes.

A newly acquired, unconditioned, or not fully habituated behavior cannot be sustained if it is not reinforced each time it occurs. Consistent reinforcement during the initial stages of the behavior change process is extremely important.

Principle 4. When the newly acquired behavior reaches a satisfactory frequency level, it should be reinforced intermittently

Although this principle may appear to be a contradiction of Principle 3, it is not. The behavior modifier must be consistent in the application of inconsistent (intermittent) reinforcement after the appropriate behavior is established. This practice appears to be the only way in which a new behavior can be firmly established and become self-sustaining.

Once a desired behavior has been established at a satisfactory level, the presentation of the reinforcement is changed from continuous to intermittent. This change in the reinforcer presentation increases the probability that the behavior will be maintained at a high level. It appears that if the child whose behavior is being changed does not know exactly when the reinforcer will be given *but does know reinforcement will occur,* the desired behavior will continue at a high level.

EXAMPLE

Ms. Williams wished to increase Phil's frequency of voluntary responses during current events discussions. In this situation poker chips were used as a reinforcer. The chips could be saved and cashed in at the end of the discussion period for a tangible reward from the class store.

Initially Ms. Williams reinforced Phil each time he volunteered a response during the discussion. After several weeks Phil's frequency of responses was at a satisfactory level; that is, it was equal, or nearly equal, to the average frequency of responses of the other members of the discussion groups. At this point in the behavior modification process Ms. Williams changed from giving continuous to intermittent reinforcement.

With intermittent reinforcement Phil's behavior remained at a high level. Phil became aware that he would be rewarded when he responded, but not every time. It also became evident to Ms. Williams that Phil was enjoying his participation in the class discussions.

EXAMPLE

Mr. Jones and Ms. Walker had similar problems in their classroom groups. In Mr. Jones's room Jared would not participate in class discussions. In Ms. Walker's room Herman presented the same problem.

Mr. Jones wished to increase the frequency of Jared's responses during group discussions. He introduced an intervention similar to the one used by Ms. Williams. However, once Jared had attained an acceptable level of performance, Mr. Jones discontinued all reinforcement. Because of the lack of reinforcement, Jared's newly acquired behavior decreased.

Ms. Walker also initiated an intervention program to increase Herman's level of participation. Ms. Walker kept Herman on the continuous reinforcement schedule until he became bored with the tokens and the tangible rewards he could purchase with them. Like Mr. Jones's program, hers was ineffective. Herman's par-

ticipation decreased to its original level. He remained an infrequent participant in group discussions.

The schedules most commonly applied in continuous and intermittent reinforcement are discussed later in this chapter.

Principle 5. Social reinforcers must *always* be applied with tangible reinforcers

All reinforcement, even during the initial phases of the behavior change process, must include the presentation of social and tangible reinforcers simultaneously, if a tangible reinforcer is used. The ultimate goal of the behavior change process is to help the child perform the desired behavior, not for a tangible reward but for the satisfaction of personal achievement.

If tangible reinforcers, such as tokens, chips, candy, stars, smiling faces, or checks, are presented, they must always be accompanied by a social reward, such as a smile, a pat on the back, praise, or a wink. In this way the child associates the social reinforcer with the tangible reinforcer. As the behavior change process progresses, the tangible reinforcer is extinguished (phased out) and the desired behavior is maintained by social reinforcers. If the change process is effective, behavior is maintained by self-satisfaction, occasional unplanned social reinforcers, and delayed tangible rewards.

EXAMPLE

When Ms. Williams was initially attempting to increase Phil's discussion group participation (see example in previous section), she provided Phil with verbal praise and a token each time he exhibited the desired behavior. When Phil was placed on an intermittent schedule, Ms. Williams continued to provide consistent social reinforcement. During the final phase of the behavior change process Phil was provided only intermittent social reinforcement to maintain the desired behavior.

EXAMPLE

Mr. Whiteface wanted to modify George's hand-raising behavior. A Sugar Smack was given to George every time he raised his hand. The reward was delivered by a dispenser affixed to George's desk. Whenever George raised his hand, Mr. Whiteface would push a button to activate the dispenser and release a Sugar Smack.

In this way Mr. Whiteface rewarded George consistently. In addition, he gave George social reinforcers for the new behavior. He would say, "That was very good, George"; "I like the way you are raising your hand, George"; or "Fine," "Great," "Good."

After 6 months on the program George functioned with intermittent social reinforcement only. The dispensing of Sugar Smacks had been terminated, and George's hand-raising behavior remained at a high rate.

Beginning behavior modifiers are cautioned to apply this important principle of reinforcement when using reinforcers: *always apply tangible and social reinforcers simultaneously, if tangible reinforcers are used.*

An extensive list of potentially effective reinforcers, both tangible and social, is presented in Chapter Three.

CONSEQUENCES OF BEHAVIOR

Behavioral consequences (results) have a direct influence on the behavior a child exhibits. Behavior can be modified, that is, increased, decreased, initiated, or extinguished by systematic manipulation of its result. The consequences of human behavior are classified as positive reinforcement, extinction, negative reinforcement, and punishment. Extinction and punishment are also discussed in Chapter Five as methods of decreasing behavior.

In Table 1 are several examples of (1) appropriate and inappropriate behavior, (2) the consequence of that behavior *(not necessarily a planned intervention)*, (3) the probable effect of the consequence on the behavior in the future, and (4) classification of the consequence. The reader is encouraged to study Table 1 carefully.

Positive reinforcement

In positive reinforcement the reinforcer is presented after a behavior has been exhibited. These reinforcers, or consequences of behavior, tend to increase or sustain the frequency with which the original behavior is exhibited in the future. Every human being

Table 1. Behavior: consequence, probable effect, and classification

Original behavior exhibited	Consequence	Probable effect on the original behavior in the future	Classification
Jane cleans her room	Jane's parents praise her	Jane will continue to clean her room	Positive reinforcement
Shirley brushes her teeth after meals	Shirley receives a nickel each time	Shirley will continue to brush her teeth after meals	Positive reinforcement
Jim washes his father's car	Jim's car-washing behavior is ignored	Jim will stop washing his father's car	Extinction
Alton works quietly at his seat	The teacher praises and rewards Alton	Alton will continue to work quietly at his seat	Positive reinforcement
Gwenn sits on the arm of the chair	Gwenn is spanked each time she sits on the arm of the chair	Gwenn will not sit on the arm of the chair	Punishment
Bob complains that older boys consistently beat him up, and he refuses to attend school	Bob's parents allow him to remain at home because of his complaints	Bob will continue to miss school	Negative reinforcement
Elmer puts Elsie's pigtails in the paint pot	The teacher administers the paddle to Elmer's posterior	Elmer will not put Elsie's pigtails in the paint pot	Punishment

receives positive reinforcement throughout each day. The process of positive reinforcement involves increasing the probability of a behavior recurring by reinforcing it with a reinforcer that is appropriate and meaningful to the individual.

EXAMPLE

Kevin has received a superior report card and is praised by his parents and siblings. As a result of the positive reinforcer (praise), the probability of Kevin's continuing to study hard and receive superior report cards in the future is increased. If Kevin's report card were ignored or severely criticized because of one poor grade, the probability of his continuing his efforts and receiving superior report cards in the future would be decreased.

EXAMPLE

Ms. Pompey has identified stars as positive reinforcers with her classroom group. She puts a star on Cynthia's paper because Cynthia has successfully completed her homework assignment. Cynthia enjoys receiving the stars. By placing a star on Cynthia's paper, Ms. Pompey knows she is increasing the probability of Cynthia's completing her homework assignment in the future.

Extinction

Extinction is the removal of a consequence that is sustaining or increasing a behavior. Extinction is an effective method for decreasing undesirable behaviors exhibited by individuals, especially children. Unplanned and unsystematically applied extinction techniques have been naturally applied throughout history. For example, we tend to *ignore* many unacceptable behaviors exhibited by children, such as roughhousing, arguing, and showing reluctance to go to bed, in the hope that these behaviors will decrease in frequency. The ineffectiveness of ignoring as an unplanned intervention is frequently due to the inconsistency of its application rather than its inadequacy as a behavior change technique. We insist that there be no roughhousing or arguing and that the children be in bed at the designated time one day but do not insist on these rules the next day. This behavior on our part tends to confuse children and reinforce the unacceptable behavior.

Extinction involves the removal or withdrawal of the reinforcer responsible for maintaining the inappropriate behavior. In the classroom setting the target behavior will be extinguished once the reinforcer has been withdrawn for a sufficient period of time.

EXAMPLE

Eight-year-old Robin was constantly tattling on every child who committed the slightest transgression within his purview. Robin's teacher, Ms. Fye was unwittingly reinforcing Robin's behavior by responding and attending to him when he tattled on others. Finally, she planned an intervention program employing extinction to decrease Robin's behavior. She would ignore all of his tattling.

Each time Robin approached her to tattle on a classmate, Ms. Fye did one of the following:

Intervened before Robin had an opportunity to tattle and focused his attention on another topic, picture, book, and so on

Turned her back on him and attended to another child who was performing appropriately

Turned her back on him and walked away without any sign of recognition

During the initial phase of the behavior change process, Robin's tattling increased for a brief period of time. As the program continued, the behavior decreased and was extinguished (Fig. 5).

In the extinction process there are two behavior response phases. During the initial phase, immediately after the reinforcer has been removed, the target behavior (the behavior to be changed) usually increases dramatically. During the second phase the target behavior decreases.

The response during the initial phase is a natural, human one that occurs when an individual is suddenly confronted with a situation wherein established methods of gaining desirable goals become nonfunctional. It is natural to become confused under such conditions and continue to try the previously effective method of attaining a goal.

It is during this initial phase that beginning behavior modifiers frequently throw up their hands in frustration and abandon a project.

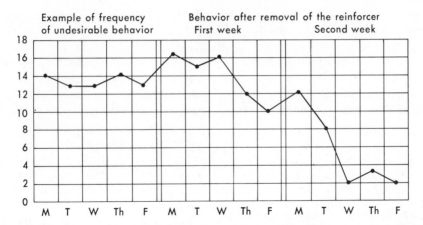

Fig. 5. Frequency of Robin's tattling behavior a week before the removal of the reinforcer and 2 weeks afterward.

However, if they will persist, the behavior will in all probability extinguish.

Robin's rate of tattling before and during the extinction process is presented in Fig. 5. The reader should note that Robin's tattling behavior increased on the first 3 days of extinction, then decreased dramatically during the next 7 days.

The practitioner should be patient and consistent; the behavior will change.

Negative reinforcement

Negative reinforcement is one of the most difficult concepts in the discipline of behavior modification to explain, comprehend, and exemplify. Because negative reinforcement is so frequently misunderstood, several examples of this process are presented below. The reader is urged to study this section and Tables 1 and 2 carefully.

Negative reinforcement is the removal of an already-operating aversive stimulus. As a consequence of the removal of the aversive stimulus, the behavior in question is strengthened.

Axelrod has (1977) described the technique of negative reinforcement in the classroom setting as "an operation in which a student performs a desired behavior and the teacher removes something he dislikes, that is, perceives as unpleasant" (p. 8).

As stated above, negative reinforcement is the removal of an aversive stimulus in an effort to increase the frequency of a desired behavior. In contrast, punishment is the addition of an aversive stimulus in an effort to decrease the frequency of an undesirable behavior.

Axelrod provides two excellent examples.

EXAMPLE

A group of students are working very diligently at their desks *after* the teacher has stated that they will not be required to do homework assignments that evening if their classroom assignments are completed during the alloted time during the school day.

In this example, the homework assignment, which was already given by the teacher, is the aversive stimulus (most students perceive homework as aversive). It is removed, and as a result the students' in-classroom work is increased.

EXAMPLE

Jimmy is in the process of twisting Tommy's arm. This situation is causing Tommy considerable pain. Jimmy says, "Say Uncle Dudley-Do-Good, and I'll let you go." Tommy, in agony, screams, "Uncle Dudley-Do-Good." Jimmy with a smile on his innocent face releases Tommy's arm, and the pain ends.

In this example, the arm twisting, which was already giving Tommy pain (and Jimmy pleasure), is the aversive stimulus. It is removed, and as a result Tommy's comfort level is increased.

The following examples are provided to offer additional clarification of negative reinforcement.

EXAMPLE

The Reynoldses have a 2-year-old daughter, Alice, who wakes up crying (aversive stimulus) in the middle of the night. She wants to sleep with Mommy and Daddy. In an effort to get their sleep and stop Alice from crying, the parents permit her to sleep with them (thus removing the aversive stimulus of crying). By allowing Alice to sleep in their bed, the parents are increasing both their and Alice's sleeping behavior.

However, the parents' method of stopping Alice's crying (allowing Alice to sleep with them) actually reinforces the frequency of the crying.

EXAMPLE

Bobby was absent 141 of 180 days during the school year. He gave no reason for his nonattendance except that he simply did not want to come to school. After several hours of discussion, it was discovered that Bobby remained away from school so his mother would not die, disappear, or become ill. Bobby's mother unconsciously reinforced his staying-at-home behavior. Many times each day she would say, "Bobby, I always feel safe when you're with me," or "I hope I will be here when you get home," or "I am not well, you know."

Bobby, a very sensitive and concerned son of 11 years, applied the following logic to this predicament: "I love my mother and want her to remain with me. If I leave her to go to school, she may die, become ill, or have an accident. Thus, I will not attend school; I will remain with her, and she will be OK."

During the discussion that followed this discovery of why Bobby stayed home, his mother was made aware of her statements and their probable effect. She was asked to cease making these and similar comments (aversive stimulus). After a reasonable time Bobby returned to part-time and eventually full-time attendance at junior high school.

Punishment

Punishment is the most familiar and frequently used behavior change technique. Although it is frequently used on children by a majority of parents and teachers, punishment is perhaps the least effective of the behavior modification interventions discussed in this text. Those using punishment have been reinforced by its immediate result; however, it has been determined that the long-term effects of punishment are limited. Punishment tends to *suppress* the undesirable behavior rather than extinguish it. This suppression is of short duration, and frequently the behavior recurs in the absence of the punisher.

Punishment is viewed by the behavior modification practitioner as two distinct operations. Punishment is accomplished by the *addition* of an aversive stimulus to the environment. Examples of this operation are paddling, electric shock, additional homework, and the like. Punishment may also be seen as the *subtraction* (taking away) of a pleasurable item or activity. Examples of this operation include loss of extracurricular activities, recess, and the like. Punishment is not to be confused with extinction (see following section).

EXAMPLE

Anita, one of Mr. Cooper's fifth-grade pupils, constantly talks in class. She disturbs her classmates when she should be completing her assignments. To stop Anita's inappropriate behavior, Mr. Cooper scolds her, shakes her, and has her stand in the corner of the classroom with a dunce cap on her head.

These techniques are very effective while Mr. Cooper is in the room. However, whenever Mr. Cooper leaves the classroom for whatever reason, the long-term ineffectiveness of punishment becomes apparent. On these occasions Anita goes around the room yelling and screaming, to the glee of her classmates.

EXAMPLE

Joe is in Mr. Dee's junior high school class for the socially maladjusted. Joe enjoys using four-letter words. In addition, he takes great pleasure in the expression on Mr. Dee's face when he tosses a few well-chosen words at him. Mr. Dee believed he could eliminate this behavior via the 3-P method, that is, a punishing paddle on the posterior. He designed the following intervention that he explained to Joe:

"Each time you swear in my presence, you will assume the hands-on-ankle position and receive four swats."

Mr. Dee's intervention has had the following results:

1. Joe's language has improved in Mr. Dee's presence but not in his absence (according to a burnt-eared substitute).
2. Mr. Dee has a very tired arm.
3. Joe continues to use his vocabulary on Mr. Dee to gain attention, especially when there are visitors in the classroom.
4. Others in the class encourage Joe to curse so that they can enjoy the circus.

It can easily be seen that *some punishment will remove some unacceptable behaviors.* However, the punishment must be extremely severe to be minimally effective. Punishments of the severity required are both inhuman and illegal and must under no circumstances be used with children.

It has also been found that when a punished behavior recurs, it usually does so at a rate higher than before the punishment was originally inflicted.

Another concern associated with punishment is its potential and actual effect on the emotional health of the child. In some cases, punishment causes severe emotional problems. The fact that the punished child identifies the punishment with the punisher rather than with the inappropriate behavior should be of great concern to teachers.

The immediate results of punishment are not adequate to justify its continued use as a behavior change agent.

Distinction between punishment and extinction

The basic distinction between punishment and extinction is the consequence of the behavior. The administration of punishment for undesirable behavior only suppresses that behavior and does not, under most conditions, eliminate it. The process of extinction

Table 2. Effects of interventions

	Positive reinforcer	Aversive stimulus
Add	Positive reinforcement (behavior increases)	Punishment (behavior decreases)
Remove	Extinction (behavior decreases)	Negative reinforcement (behavior increases)

is a more scientific and systematic means of eliminating undesirable behavior.

Another distinction concerning the four basic interventions is that positive and negative reinforcement increases appropriate behavior, whereas punishment and extinction decrease inappropriate behavior. Table 2 presents this distinction.

A thorough understanding of the relationships between these four basic interventions is a primary requisite for the effective application of behavior modification techniques. The reader is encouraged to study Table 2 carefully and compare it with Table 1.

SCHEDULES OF REINFORCEMENT

A schedule of reinforcement is the pattern with which the reinforcer is presented (or not presented) in response to the exhibition of the target behavior.

The schedule of reinforcement that is applied has a significant effect on the behavior change process. The four most common types of reinforcement schedules are the fixed ratio (FR), the variable ratio (VR), the fixed interval (FI), and the variable interval (VI).

The primary distinctions among these schedules are related to the timing and frequency with which the reinforcer is presented (or not presented). The ratio schedules, FR and VR, focus on the *completion of*

Table 3. Relationships among four common reinforcement schedules

	Ratio	Interval
Fixed	Child completes 20 problems to receive 10 minutes of free time	Child is rewarded for remaining in seat for 5 minutes
Variable	Teacher rewards child, on an average, every third time child raises hand	Teacher gives child individual attention, on an average, every 15 minutes in response to acceptable behavior during the time period

specific tasks before the reinforcer is presented to the child. Reinforcer presentation on the interval schedules, FI and VI, depend on the exhibition of specific behaviors for *definite periods of time.*

Table 3 summarizes the various schedules discussed in the following sections.

Fixed ratio schedule

When a fixed ratio (FR) schedule is applied, the reinforcer is presented after a specific number of appropriate responses are emitted by the child.

EXAMPLE

Every time John answers 15 social studies questions correctly, he is given 10 minutes to read a comic book. John's schedule has an FR of 15:10.

EXAMPLE

Sheila must read 5 brief passages with 80% accuracy before she is allowed to listen to her favorite record album for 5 minutes. The schedule in Sheila's case is based on an FR of 5:5.

The FR schedule usually results in a high rate of response. Consequently, it is most effectively and appropriately applied during the initial phase of the behavior change process.

Variable ratio schedule

The variable ratio (VR) schedule is designed to sustain the level of response to reinforcement once the acceptable level has been attained by means of the FR schedule. When the VR schedule is applied, the ratio of the reinforcer presentation varies. This

variability is instrumental in sustaining the appropriate level of response.

EXAMPLE

Mr. Davis has Kerry raising his hand and participating in class discussions. He accomplished this via an FR schedule. He now wishes to change to a VR schedule. Kerry is placed on a VR schedule of 5 (the reinforcer is presented around a response mean of 5). Kerry may be reinforced the seventh time he raises his hand, the sixth time, the third, the fourth, or the fifth. If this schedule (7, 6, 3, 4, and 5) is averaged, the response mean or variable ratio is 5. The fact that Kerry does not know when Mr. Davis will call on him to respond (but does know that he will be called on) maintains his hand-raising behavior at a high level.

EXAMPLE

In Las Vegas one-armed bandits (in our experience) operate on a VR schedule. The gambler puts quarters in the slot and is occasionally reinforced with small rewards. This occasional reinforcement keeps the person playing until he or she is broke, but the loser always has the hope that the next pull of the arm will result in the super jackpot.

Inexperienced behavior modifiers are cautioned not to change from an FR to a VR schedule too early in the behavior change process. The desired behavior must be adequately established on an FR schedule before it can be changed to a VR schedule. Many behavior change programs have failed as a result of the practitioner's impatience in making this transition.

Fixed interval schedule

On the fixed interval (FI) schedule a specified period of time must elapse before the reinforcer is presented. The reinforcer is presented immediately *after the first response after* the specified period of time has elapsed. The following examples should clarify this seeming confusion.

EXAMPLE

Debbie does not remain in her seat during language lessons. Mr. Quick has decided to reinforce Debbie on an FI schedule of 10. Thus, every time Debbie remains in her seat for 10 minutes during language lessons, she is rewarded.

EXAMPLE

Most people work on an FI (1 week, 2 weeks, or 1 month) pay schedule. They receive their pay checks after the pay period has elapsed.

With FI schedules it has been found that the longer the time interval between reinforcement, the lower the level of performance. This would suggest that initially during an intervention reinforcers should be presented frequently.

Variable interval schedule

The variable interval (VI) schedule is similar to the VR schedule. However, the presentation of the reinforcer is based on a behavioral response mean. The individual whose behavior is being modified is not aware of when reinforcement will occur. However, the individual does know that he or she will be reinforced for exhibiting a certain behavior.

EXAMPLE

Mr. Quick has decided to place Debbie on a VI schedule of 10. On this schedule Debbie will continue to be reinforced for in-seat behavior. She may be reinforced the first time after only 9 minutes of appropriate behavior, the second time after 4 minutes, the third time after 9 minutes, the fourth time after 15 minutes, and the fifth time after 13 minutes. This is a reinforcement schedule of 9, 4, 9, 15, and 13. It is based on a VI with a mean or average of 10 minutes.

• • •

Again, the behavior modifier should be cautious when changing from FR or FI to VR or VI schedules. If this is done too early or too late in the behavior change process, the newly acquired behavior may be extinguished.

The specific schedule to be applied varies with the behavior being changed. For example, if the concern is to keep an individual in his or her seat for a period of time, an interval schedule would be the most appropriate. However, if the behavior is related to the completion of specific numbers or kinds of tasks, a ratio schedule should be applied. The selection and application of the appropriate schedule is part of the art of behavior modification. Knowing when and how to apply a technique becomes less confusing as the behavior modifier gains experience.

GENERALIZATION

Generalization is the process by which a behavior reinforced in the presence of one stimulus will be exhibited in the presence of another stimulus. The generalization process is an important element of learning. If the process of generalization did not exist, each response would have to be relearned in every specific situation.

EXAMPLE

A young child learns the name of an animal (dog). He calls a specific dog "dog" and will soon generalize the name "dog" to all four-legged animals within this classification. He will at times label other four-legged animals, such as cats, cows, and crawling brothers and sisters, with the name "dog."

EXAMPLE

A toddler is reinforced for calling her father "Daddy." She will generalize and call all male figures "Daddy" at an early stage of her development. She may call the mailman, milkman, and others "Daddy." This may result in considerable stress between husband and wife.

In the above examples we did not intend to imply that generalization is primarily a negative concept. If we wish to function successfully in the environment, we must apply the concepts learned in one situation to many and varied situations. For example, as young children we learn honesty, respect for authority, and the basic principles of computation. Hopefully, each year we can generalize this learning to the completion of our federal income tax returns.

DISCRIMINATION

Discrimination is another important learned behavior. We learn that we act one way in one situation and another way in a different situation. If it were not for the process of discrimination, we would generalize behaviors to a variety of situations in which they would be inappropriate.

EXAMPLE
We behave differently in church than we do at a cocktail party (most of us), and differently in class than we do at a football game (although some classes are stimulating and some football games are boring). Our behaviors in these situations are reinforced by the rewards we receive.

Discrimination is the result of differential reinforcement. Reinforcing a behavior in the presence of one stimulus and not reinforcing it in the presence of another stimulus is differential reinforcement.

EXAMPLE
Teaching a young child to discriminate between the words *cat* and *rat* may be accomplished by listening and reacting to the child's responses. The child is reinforced for the appropriate response only. In this way the child discriminates between the words *rat* and *cat* when they are presented in the future.

SUMMARY

An overview of the basic principles of behavior modification is presented in this chapter followed by a discussion of the concepts of positive and negative reinforcement, extinction and punishment. An understanding of these operations and their effects on behavior is essential for the behavior modification practitioner. To utilize the aforementioned operations, the reader must understand how they are different as well as how they are interrelated.

A discussion of the schedules of reinforcement is also presented. A schedule of reinforcement is the pattern with which the reinforcers are given (or not given) in response to the exhibition of a behavior. Four of the most common types of schedules are fixed ratio (FR), fixed interval (FI), variable ratio (VR), and variable interval (VI). It is essential that the new practitioner of behavior modification have a thorough knowledge of these schedules.

Finally, the concepts of generalization and discrimination are discussed. Generalization increases the probability that a behavior reinforced in the presence of one stimulus will be exhibited in the presence of another stimulus. Discrimination is the process by which we learn to behave differently in different situations.

EXERCISES FOR CHAPTER TWO
Quiz*

1. One of the basic principles of reinforcement states that when building new behavior, the practitioner should reinforce the behavior _____.

2. When the new behavior has been established to a degree of satisfaction, the best schedule of reinforcement to use is a _____ schedule.

3. The decrease in the strength of a response when it is no longer reinforced is called _____.

---

*Turn to Appendix A, p. 174, for answers.

4. The addition of an aversive stimulus or the subtraction of something pleasurable is known as _____ .

5. The process of reinforcing behavior in the presence of one stimulus situation and not reinforcing it in the presence of other stimulus situations is called _____

_____ .

6. _____ is the occurrence of a response in the presence of other stimuli following its response in the presence of one stimulus situation.

7. The process of removing an aversive stimulus is known as _____

_____ .

8. Consequences that strengthen or increase behavior are called _____ .

9. _____ schedules of reinforcement are dependent on the number of responses.

10. _____ schedules of reinforcement are dependent on the passage of time and a specific response.

Projects

1. Describe two examples for each of the following: FR, FI, VR, and VI schedules of reinforcement as they would apply in your teaching situation.
2. Give three examples of discrimination learned through differential reinforcement procedures.
3. Give examples of how positive reinforcement, extinction, negative reinforcement, and punishment can be used to change the behavior of children.
4. List several factors involved in the use of punishment as a behavior change technique.
5. Explain the five basic principles of reinforcement.

REFERENCES

Axelrod, S. *Behavior modification for the classroom teacher*. New York: McGraw-Hill Book Co., 1977.

Bandura, A. *Principles of behavior modification*. New York: Holt, Rinehart & Winston, 1969.

Fargo, G. A., Behrns, C., and Nolen, P. (Eds.). *Behavior modification in the classroom*. Belmont, Calif.: Wadsworth Publishing Co., Inc., 1970.

Sarason, I. G., Glaser, E. M., and Fargo, G. A. *Reinforcing productive classroom behavior*. New York: Behavioral Publications, Inc., 1972.

CHAPTER THREE

Steps in the behavior change process

In this chapter the specific steps and procedures applied during the behavior change process are discussed and exemplified in detail. All practitioners of behavior modification should follow these steps closely. They are (1) selecting a target behavior, (2) collecting and recording baseline data, (3) identifying appropriate reinforcers, and (4) collecting and recording intervention data.

SELECTING A TARGET BEHAVIOR

The initial step in the behavior change process is the identification of the target behavior. The target behavior is the behavior to be changed or modified. A target behavior may be an existing behavior that the practitioner desires to increase or decrease. In addition, the target behavior may be a nonoccurring behavior, that is a behavior that is not observable in the individual's behavioral repertoire but one that the practitioner wishes to develop.

In most classroom situations it is not difficult for the teacher to identify a variety of behaviors needing change (target behaviors). The teacher may recognize that:

1. Percy does not communicate verbally.
2. Jake should increase his reading skills.
3. Mary should stop yelling in the classroom.
4. Joseph needs to learn to listen to instructions before he begins an assignment.
5. Ellis should improve his table manners in the lunchroom.

All of the aforementioned are potential target behaviors that the teacher could identify in the classroom.

Decisions leading to the selection of a behavior for modification should be governed by the following considerations, among others:

Overall number of behaviors needing modification

Frequency of the behavior

Duration of the behavior

Intensity of the behavior

Type of behavior

It should be remembered that whenever an individual or a group is singled out for observation and study for the purpose of initiating a behavior change program, it is inevitable that several individual and group target behaviors will be identified. All children and adults manifest behaviors that are unacceptable to some other individuals or groups of individuals under certain conditions.

It is generally recommended that the beginning behavior modifier not attempt to change more than one individual or group behavior at a time. Implementing several behavior change programs simultaneously frequently results in inefficiency. Consequently, the intervention will be ineffective. Therefore, we advocate that individual and group behaviors needing modification be ranked in priority. The teacher then systematically works down the priority list from the most important to the least important of the potential target behaviors. The importance of a specific behavior should be determined on the basis of its effect on the child's functioning.

EXAMPLE

Peter, an autistic-like child, manifests a variety of unacceptable behaviors. Among the behaviors of greatest concern to his teacher, Mr. Wise, are (1) withdrawal from group activities, (2) unacceptable eating habits, (3) inability to communicate with his classmates and Mr. Wise via speech, and (4) unacceptable gross motor skills.

Mr. Wise recognizes that a program cannot be initiated to modify all of Peter's potential target behaviors at a single time. Because of the nature of the behaviors, the proposed interventions could be in conflict with one another. Mr. Wise must respond to the following question: "Is it more important for Peter, at this time, to participate in the luncheon discussion [behaviors 1 and 3 would be targets] or is it more important to improve his gross motor skills and eating habits [behaviors 2 and 4 would be targets]?"

In response to this question, Mr. Wise develops the following priority list for Peter's program:

First priority: to increase participation in group activities

Second priority: to increase verbalization with others

Third priority: to increase gross motor skills

Fourth priority: to increase acceptance of a variety of foods

With an increase in experience and skill in the behavior change process, the practitioner may desire to program more than one individual or group target behavior simultaneously. However, the beginning practitioner should refrain from multiple programming.

When selecting a target behavior, the practitioner must consider the frequency of the behavior. Some behaviors occur so infrequently that they do not necessitate or respond to a formal behavior modification intervention. Of course, the reverse is also true: some behaviors occur so frequently that they obviously require a behavior change program.

EXAMPLE

Ms. Lochman was very concerned about Martin, a member of her class, and on many occasions she became very angry with him. Six-year-old Martin appeared to be constantly out of his assigned seat. When out of his chair, he would grab other children's work, work tools, and lunches. Using a time-sampling technique (see p. 41), Ms. Lochman collected baseline data on Martin's out-of-seat behavior for 1 hour a day for 5 days. She found that during these observation periods Martin was out of his seat 17 times an hour on an average.

This behavior was so frequent and so obtrusive that it usually brought all productive classroom activity to a halt until Ms. Lochman could corral Martin and return him to his seat.

EXAMPLE

Ms. Derry, like many of her peers, does not approve of chewing gum in school. Johnny, a member of her classroom group, was seen chewing gum on the second day of school this year. Ms. Derry grabbed him, removed the gum from his mouth, and stuck it on his nose, where it stayed for the remainder of the day. Ms. Derry then proceeded to make plans for a formal behavior change program. After several hours of planning she was satisfied with her elaborate scheme for gathering baseline data and applying the chosen intervention. Unfortunately (or fortunately), Johnny never chewed gum in school again (that she observed).

There are many behaviors like Johnny's that appear so infrequently that they do not require a formal behavior change program. Examples of such behaviors are:

George's annual 2-minute tantrum

Barbara's occasional reading reversal

Don's infrequent falling out of his seat

Judy's monthly bus-missing behavior

If a proposed target behavior is both obtrusive and occurs frequently, the teacher should next consider the duration of the behavior.

EXAMPLE

For several weeks Gerald was very nervous in school. His teacher, Ms. Farley, noted that he was frequently out of his seat, irritable, and ready to burst into tears. She had never seen Gerald in this condition. She attempted to discuss the situation with him but was rebuffed.

Ms. Farley decided to establish a formal behavior modification program to decrease the behaviors. However, before initiating the program, she discussed the situation with Gerald's mother. During the conversation the mother indicated that she had observed similar behavior at home and was attempting to help Gerald regain his old composure. She thought the behavior was the result of the recent death of Gerald's grandfather. Gerald and his grandfather had been pals; they had always been together in the evenings. The death left a great void in Gerald's daily life. Gerald's mother said that her husband was rescheduling his evening activities so that he and Gerald could spend more time together.

Ms. Farley decided to hold the intervention program in abeyance for another few weeks. Within a short time Gerald was his normal self. The program was never implemented.

EXAMPLE

Mr. Parker is Maryann's kindergarten teacher. He thoroughly enjoys his work with Maryann and her 16 classmates. The kindergarten is an interesting and exciting learning place for the children.

During the first few weeks of the school year Mr. Parker observed that Maryann, although involved in the classroom activities, seldom if ever spoke to him, the aide, or her classmates. He decided to collect some baseline data on the frequency of Maryann's verbal behavior. In cooperation with the kindergarten aide, an observation schedule was set up to obtain some objective data. Using a time-sampling technique, they observed Maryann's behavior on an average of 1 hour a day for 10 days. Data indicated that Maryann spoke only 4 times a day on an average, while in school. She directed all her verbalizations to one classmate.

Although Mr. Parker was very concerned about the behavior, he did not implement a behavior change program at this time. He had worked with kindergarten children in the past who were shy and quiet and did not begin to interact verbally in the classroom until just prior to Christmas vacation.

The aide continued to collect data 1 day each week until mid-December. No change was noted in Maryann's behavior.

Mr. Parker concluded that the behavior had endured too long and that a behavior change program was needed to help Maryann. He conferred with the school's language therapist, who evaluated Maryann. He also discussed the problem with Maryann's mother, who agree to participate in a home-school behavior change program. The intervention was implemented immediately after the Christmas holidays.

The practitioner must also consider the intensity of the behavior. Some behaviors, although unacceptable, are relatively mild and unobtrusive. They do not generally interfere with the classroom process or the individual child's overall functioning. Of course, other behaviors, although infrequent, are so intense that they are extremely obtrusive. Not only do they adversely affect the individual's overall functioning but they also interfere with the classroom program and group process. Such behaviors must be modified.

EXAMPLE

Keith is 13 years old and in the seventh grade. Occasionally he manifests some behaviors, normal for his age group, that are bothersome, such as know-it-all behavior, bigshotism, and negativism. These behaviors are of minimal intensity. They are manifested by a wise remark at the termination of a conversation, his saying "No, I won't" before beginning a task, and the like. The behaviors are generally ignored by others and have little effect on either the classroom process or Keith's overall functioning.

EXAMPLE

Ricky is 7 years old and in a special class for emotionally handicapped children. Ricky has temper tantrums that are totally unpredictable, frequent, and analogous to all of the Fourth of July fireworks in all the towns of the United States igniting simultaneously. These tantrums involve lying on the floor with feet and arms flying and verbalizations that are interesting but disturbing combinations of four-letter words. The tantrums last up to 45 minutes, averaging about 25 minutes.

These tantrums destroy the classroom program, frighten the other children, and interfere with Ricky's overall functioning. This behavior must be changed.

The final characteristic to be considered in the selection of a target behavior is the type of behavior. Some behavior that is disturbing to some adults and children is really quite normal from a child development point of view. In fact, a child who did not manifest such behavior might be considered abnormal.

EXAMPLE

Paul is a sixth grader and a straight-A student. Whenever he is asked if he likes school, his teacher, or the like, he says "No, I hate it." In addition, he insists on having long hair, wearing jeans and sneakers to school, and other equally "obnoxious" things.

As most teachers realize, these behaviors are quite normal for sixth-grade boys. The behavior manifested by Paul is within normal limits and of a kind that does not necessitate a formal intervention program.

EXAMPLE

Russell is 12 years old and in a junior high school special class. He has an uncontrolled temper and frequently tells his teacher to "go to hell" or "drop dead" (among other things). Russell gets into occasional fights with his classmates. These fights are extremely vicious. On two occasions he has inflicted severe injury on his opponent.

Russell's behavior is of a type that cannot simply be ignored. An intervention must be implemented for both his benefit and the safety of his peers.

After all of these variables have been considered and a behavior selected, the teacher must decide the direction of the behavior change process. There are three possible directions a behavior may follow as a consequence of an intervention. The behavior may (1) increase, (2) decrease, or (3) remain unchanged (be maintained). Table 4 presents these behavior change directions and examples of each.

The majority of behavior change programs are implemented to increase acceptable behaviors or decrease unacceptable behaviors. Teachers can easily select behaviors they wish to increase or decrease. However, the implementation of behavior modification programs to maintain acceptable behaviors has been largely neglected. In most instances the practitioner takes the child's manifestation of acceptable behaviors for granted and does not systematically reward such behaviors. More effort should be made to prevent unacceptable behaviors from developing, via the systematic rewarding and maintenance of existing acceptable behaviors. Such efforts could reduce the need to design interventions to either decrease or increase behaviors in the future.

Two other important characteristics of the target behavior are observability and measurability. The behavior must be readily ob-

Table 4. Behavior change directions

Direction	Example
Increase	Group participation
	In-seat behavior
	Interaction with peers
	Typing skills
	Reading rate
	Number skills
	Visual-perceptual skills
Decrease	Verbal outbursts
	Inattentiveness
	Use of four-letter words
	Food intake
	Smoking
	Talking in study period
	Spelling errors
Maintain	Language skills
	Reading skills
	School attendance
	Independent study habits
	Writing skills
	Motor skills
	Group participation

servable by the teacher or another observer in the environment in which it occurs.

EXAMPLE

Ernest, in Ms. Moral's words, is "an unhappy child." Ms. Moral would like to decrease his unhappiness (and increase his happiness). However, when she attempted to observe and quantify Ernest's unhappiness, she abandoned the behavior change program before the baseline data were collected.

EXAMPLE

Brian seldom participated in organized group activities on the playground. Mr. Spencer wished to increase his level of activity. He recorded Brian's group participation rate on the playground during morning recess. Mr. Spencer easily established Brian's baseline of activity; he could thus directly observe and quantify the frequency and duration of Brian's participation in group activities.

Statements describing the target behavior, the precise intervention, and the criteria for success or acceptability of performance should be written or otherwise communicated in objective and specific terminology. The following objectives are written so that the target behavior and the result of the intervention can be observed, quantified, and evaluated:

Maintain the number of times Jack volunteers to answer questions during class discussions

Increase the number of pages Susan reads during each 15-minute study period

Decrease the number of times Marion yells during the first hour of the morning

Maintain the number of times Ken uses the reference books on the science table

Decrease the amount of time Sharon sucks her thumb during the school day

Increase Benji's skills in recognizing and naming the letters of the alphabet when he sees them

Program objectives should be written as instructional objectives, whether the target behavior is in the cognitive, affective, or psychomotor learning domain. The instructional objective in its written form should respond to the following guidelines:

1. What is the child or group of children whose behavior is being modified expected to do or not to do?
   a. Use action verbs to denote the behavior change process.
   b. List the specific resources and materials to be used by the child during the behavior change process.
   c. Indicate specifically the desired interaction between the child and the environment, including persons and objects.
2. What is the level of performance (in terms of accuracy, duration, and skill) expected of the child?
3. What percentage of time or what percentage of occurrences of the desired behavior is the child expected to perform at the criterion level?
4. How will the anticipated changes in behavior be measured for evaluative purposes? What instrumentation is needed for the evaluation?
5. How long will the proposed intervention program be in force before its effectiveness is evaluated?

Further information on the writing of specific instructional objectives may be found in the books by Gronlund (1970) and Mayer (1962).

The following guidelines summarize the process of selecting a target behavior:

1. Select only one individual or group target behavior to change at a time.
2. Analyze the potential target behavior for its frequency, duration, intensity, and type. The importance and pertinency of these variables vary with the characteristics of the specific target behavior under consideration.
3. Consider the direction or course the behavior is to take during the change process. Is the behavior to be maintained, decreased, or increased?
4. Determine whether the behavior is observable.
5. Determine whether the behavior is quantifiable.
6. Describe the target behavior in precise, descriptive terminology in all verbal and written communications.

The beginning behavior modifier is advised to use the checklist on the opposite page. Additional copies of this checklist are provided in tear-off form at the back of the text.

COLLECTING AND RECORDING BASELINE DATA

Information collected before the behavior change intervention has been implemented is referred to as baseline or preintervention data. Baseline data provide the foundation on which the behavior change process is established. These data are also used to determine the effectiveness of the intervention

Target Behavior Selection Checklist

1. What is the target behavior to be modified? _____

   _____

   _____

   _____

   _____

2. Each characteristic of the behavior that should be considered in the target behavior selective process is listed below. An X should be marked by each characteristic as it is considered. The pertinency of these characteristics varies with the specific target behavior under consideration.

(X)	Characteristic	Comment
( )	1. Frequency	
( )	2. Duration	
( )	3. Intensity	
( )	4. Type	
( )	5. Direction	
( )	6. Observability	
( )	7. Measurability	

3. Restate the target behavior in precise and specific terminology. _____

   _____

   _____

   _____

   _____

during the evaluation phase of the behavior change process.

EXAMPLE

The behavior change program Mr. Dixon selected for Jean concerned increasing the amount of time Jean remained in her seat during history class. Mr. Dixon collected baseline data for 1 week. The data demonstrated that Jean usually remained in her seat an average of 10 minutes at a time before she was up and about the classroom. This information provided Mr. Dixon with the data he needed to determine the kind and characteristics of the reinforcement sched-

ule to be implemented. In order to be sure Jean received immediate reinforcement for staying in her seat, a fixed interval (FI) schedule of 7 minutes was used.

The selection of the FI 7 schedule was not a haphazard choice. It was based on the fact that Jean had demonstrated that she could, on the average, remain in her seat for 10 minutes without interference. Therefore, it was reasonable to select a 7-minute interval because that was a level of performance that Jean could easily attain. Consequently, she could be frequently reinforced for appropriate behavior.

If Mr. Dixon had not collected baseline data but

had proceeded on a hunch, he might have selected an FI schedule of 11 minutes. With this interval there would be a strong possibility that Jean would be infrequently rewarded and that her behavior would not change significantly.

Reinforcement should be initiated at a level of performance below the baseline. In this manner the behavior will be rewarded frequently, and the program will be meaningful to the child.

EXAMPLE

Ms. Waters has a little terror in her class who responds occasionally to the name of Emmet. Emmet is constantly yelling in the classroom, to the annoyance of Ms. Waters and the other members of the group. Ms. Waters initiated a behavior change program but did not collect baseline data, since Emmet appeared to yell constantly. She withdrew attention from Emmet each time he yelled and praised him when he was not yelling.

After 2 weeks, Ms. Waters was convinced that no change had occurred in the frequency of the behavior. Emmet seemed to yell in class more frequently. Ms. Waters concluded that "this behavior modification stuff" only works in textbooks, and she abandoned the project. Emmet is still yelling in class.

It should be stressed here that behavior modification *always* works. The failure of an intervention does not lie in the principles of behavior modification but in the application of those principles by the practitioner. In the preceding example Ms. Waters would have been wise to collect baseline data. She would have been able to evaluate the effectiveness of the behavior change process. Baseline data would have revealed that Emmet yelled in class on an average of 21 times a day. When the intervention was abandoned, the behavior was occurring only 18 times a day (Fig. 6). The behavior was, in fact, changing in the desired direction. However, without appropriate data, 18 yells a day sound very much like 21 when you are immersed in a situation, as in the case of Ms. Waters.

There are a variety of methods for observing and recording behavior. The efficiency

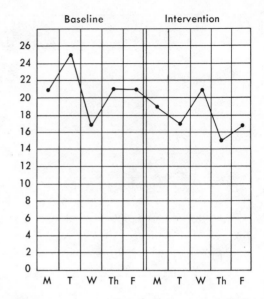

Fig. 6. Frequency of Emmet's yelling behavior before and during the intervention.

of a particular technique depends in large part on the expertise of the practitioner.

Among techniques available to teachers are (1) analyzing anecdotal records; (2) analyzing cumulative records; (3) interviewing an adult (parent or teacher) about the child; (4) interviewing the child; (5) using observation data collected by somebody else, such as an aide, parent, supervisor, or diagnostician; and (6) directly observing the child, using a time-sampling technique.

To obtain meaningful baseline data, the behavior modifier must engage in two activities: counting the behavior and charting the behavior. Counting the behavior means enumerating the number of times the behavior occurs in a given period of time. Charting the behavior means preparing a visual display of the enumerated behavior in graphic form.

These two processes are of paramount importance in the behavior change process. When the number of occurrences or the average duration of the occurrences of a be-

Table 5. Baseline data: Joshua's hitting behavior

Time	Day					Time total
	Mon.	**Tue.**	**Wed.**	**Thur.**	**Fri.**	
9:00–9:10	/	/		/	/	4
9:30–9:40	/	/	//	/	/	6
10:00–10:10	//	///	/	//	/	9
10:30–10:40	///	/	////	///	//	13
DAY TOTAL	7	6	7	7	5	32

havior in a temporal framework are known, the behavior modifier can select an efficient reinforcement schedule before implementing an intervention. Equally important is the application of the baseline data to the intervention evaluation process. By comparing baseline data with intervention data, the teacher can determine the effectiveness of the reinforcer and the reinforcement schedule. Judgments can be made regarding the responsiveness of the target behavior to the intervention; that is, is the behavior increasing, decreasing, or being maintained?

Generally, the recommended method of collecting baseline data is direct observation of the child in the environment in which the behavior occurs. The beginning behavior modifier is well advised to obtain observation data by means of a time-sampling technique.

A trained observer realizes that it is impossible to observe *all* of the behavior occurring within the environment; neither is it possible to efficiently observe all of the occurrences of a single behavior over an extended period of time.

With the time-sampling technique the teacher first selects the behavior to be observed and then selects the periods of time that can be devoted to observing that behavior each day during the baseline phase. Each occurrence of the target behavior during the observation period is tallied or recorded.

EXAMPLE

Joshua's teacher, Mr. Cates, wished to modify Joshua's hitting behavior during the 2-hour language arts period. With all his other teaching duties, he could not observe Joshua the full 2 hours for the 5 days required to collect reliable baseline data. Thus, Mr. Cates used a time-sampling technique; he observed Joshua's behavior during two 10-minute periods for each hour of the language arts period for 5 days. He designed a behavior-tallying sheet to record his observations. (Table 5).

Mr. Cates noted several things as a result of his data-collecting efforts:

1. Joshua hit other children a total of 32 times during the observation periods.
2. Mr. Cates only observed one third of the total language arts period, that is, 20 minutes out of each 60 minutes. Thus, in all probability, Joshua hit others approximately 96 times during language arts that week.
3. Joshua hit others, on an average, approximately 6 times a day. However, he hit others less on Friday than on any other day of the week.
4. Joshua hit others more frequently with the passing of each observation period of the day.

During the intervention phase of the behavior change program, Mr. Cates would isolate Joshua for 2 minutes each time he hit another child.

Before initiating the intervention, Mr. Cates transferred the baseline data to a graph to improve his visual image of the behavior (Fig. 7).

Mr. Cates first made a chart for a 2-week period. His baseline data were entered in the section of the chart reserved for the first week. The remainder of the chart would be used for intervention data; he would enter the number of occurrences of hitting behavior during his observations each day of the intervention phase.

Mr. Cates used the horizontal axis of the chart for the days of the week and the vertical axis for the fre-

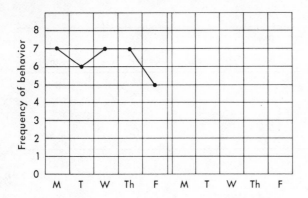

Fig. 7. Joshua's hitting behavior (frequency).

Table 6. Bucky's tantrums (duration and frequency)

Time		Total minutes	Comments
Begin	End		
9:31	9:38	7	End of reading
11:03	11:12	9	Beginning of science
12:07	12:17	10	Lunchtime
2:30	2:39	9	Preparing-to-go-home time

Total occurrence for day: 4.
Average duration: 9 minutes.
Day: Monday.

quency of the behavior. He plotted the behavior and drew lines between the daily occurrences.

Although the same basic methods of counting and charting behavior are applied in all cases, certain modifications may be necessary, depending on the behavior under consideration.

In the example of Joshua's hitting behavior, we were primarily concerned with the frequency of the behavior. The behavior itself was instantaneous; thus the duration of the occurrences was not germane to the primary objective of the behavior change program.

However, if we were concerned with the duration of Bucky's tantrums, for example, we would focus our observation on both the frequency of occurrence and the duration of each occurrence. In this case we would collect raw observation data in the manner shown in Table 6.

Table 6 is a tally log for Monday only, but the tally logs for the remaining 4 days of the baseline period are similar. The teacher, Mr. Wagner, is interested in decreasing both the frequency of the behavior and the duration of the behavior when it does occur.

Mr. Wagner has noted in the comments column that the tantrums occur when a change in group activity is taking place, such as at the end of reading period, at the beginning of science, at the beginning of lunchtime, and when it's time for preparing to go home.

The planned intervention is:

1. Intervene before an activity change and

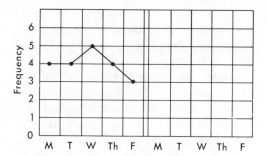

Fig. 8. Bucky's tantrums (frequency).

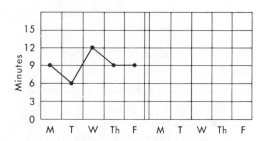

Fig. 9. Average duration of Bucky's tantrums.

assist Bucky through the potential tantrum period.

2. If a tantrum does occur, isolate Bucky immediately until 2 minutes after the tantrum ceases.

As a result of this data-collecting procedure, Mr. Wagner designed two graphs to visually display the behavior. Fig. 8 is concerned with the number of tantrums a day. Fig. 9 represents the average duration of the tantrums.

Regardless of the specific target behavior being charted, the practitioner should remember that the ordinate points are generally located on the vertical axis of the chart and the abscissa points, on the horizontal axis. Ordinate points represent the behavior's frequency, duration, and percent of occurrence. Abscissa points represent the hours, days, and sessions of observation (Axelrod, 1977).

The methods of counting and charting behavior presented in this section are the ones used most frequently in the field, probably because of the ease with which the practitioner can visually perceive and evaluate the data and thus determine the status of the behavior at a given point in time. We recommend that practitioners of behavior modification practice these methods until they have gained experience. Several practice charts are provided in tear-off form at the back of the text.

IDENTIFYING APPROPRIATE REINFORCERS

A behavior modification intervention is only as effective as its reinforcer. Regardless of the intervention applied in any behavior change program, if the exhibition of the desired behavior is not rewarded, the individual exhibiting that behavior will in all probability not continue to exhibit it. In a behavior change program all factors may be carefully planned and the intervention precisely implemented, but if the child is not reinforced by the result of this behavior, little probability exists for a permanent behavior change.

Remember, a reinforcer is not necessarily a desirable consequence for a child merely because the child's teacher or mother believes it should be. Likewise, a reinforcer is not necessarily desirable to John simply because it is desirable to Mary, Herm, or Lucinda. The *only* true test of the effectiveness of a specific reinforcer with a specific child is implementation.

How can the practitioner identify potential reinforcers for the child whose behavior is to be modified? There are several procedures recommended for identifying reinforcers having a high probability of changing behavior in the desired direction. Among the available procedures are (1) use of reinforcement preference scales, (2) use of reinforcement lists, (3) a direct interview with the child, (4) a parent or teacher interview about the child, and (5) direct observation.

Use of reinforcement preference scales

Commercially available reinforcement preference scales are designed to assist the practitioner in eliciting and ranking the child's reward preferences. By means of pictures and questions the practitioner presents the child with a variety of potentially desirable objects and activities, both tangible and social. The child selects from these reinforcers. The practitioner systematically guides the child through the process of selecting, comparing, and ranking the desired rewards. With these materials, however, the possibility exists that the child will not respond to the selected reinforcers during the behavior change process. The child's interpersonal characteristics may prohibit communication of the child's real desires to the evaluator. It is also possible that the reinforcers suggested in the scale are not desirable to the child or are not appropriate for the child's age. Of course, the possibility always exists that the child does not know or simply cannot articulate what is desirable to him or her.

Another problem with commercially prepared materials is that they are both costly and time consuming to administer.

Use of reinforcement preference lists

Reinforcement lists, such as the one presented on this page, are frequently helpful to the practitioner who is having difficulty thinking of rewards for children. The list may be used in a manner similar to the reinforcement preference scale. The disadvantages of the reward list are similar to those of the preference scale.

The reinforcement list's greatest practical value to the practitioner is that it stimulates consideration of a broad spectrum of potential reinforcers; new reinforcers can be added to the list as the teacher becomes aware of them.

Sample tangible and social reinforcers. The rewards listed are suggestions for classroom use. Each child has unique personal likes and dislikes. The reinforcers must be selected and decided on in consultation with and by observation of the child whose behavior is to be modified.

Consumable food reinforcers
    Apples
    Grapes
    Oranges
    Raisins
    Crackers
    Cookies
    Popcorn
    Potato chips
    Peanuts
    Gumdrops
    Jelly beans
    Small candies
    Mints
    Juice
    Kool-Aid or Kool-Aid with lemonade ("bug" juice)
    Milk
    Soda
    Ice cream
    Lollipops
    Gum

Reinforcing activities in relation to the above-listed consumables
    Distributing reinforcers
    Cleaning the area after reinforcers have been distributed
    Popping popcorn
    Scooping ice cream
    Baking cookies
    Preparing snacks

Tangible reinforcers other than food
    Tickets to games, movies
    Personal grooming supplies

Toys, games, and so on, from the class store

Special materials, such as colored chalk, pencils, or felt-tipped pens.

Token reinforcers

Check marks and points

Happy faces and stars

Behavior and achievement charts

Individual behavior and achievement cards and bankbooks

Rubber stamp marks of various designs

Gold stars next to child's name on the class chart

Trading stamps

Conservation stamps

Good citizen tags and certificates

Game activity reinforcers

Checkers

Dominoes

Puzzles

Dot-to-dot

Color-print-draw

Blockhead

Spill and Spell

Throw and Add

Coloring books

Tip-It

Beanbags

Jacks

Bingo

Blocks

Lincoln Logs

Lego

Dolls and dollhouses

Matchbox cars

Frisbees

Gliders

Jump ropes

Kites

Marbles

Modeling clay

Monopoly

Tops

Yo-yos

Tinker Toys

Chess

Sorry

Jump-in

Tiddlywinks

Cards

Life

Word games

Number games

Crossword puzzles

Number puzzles

Circle games

Reinforcing activities

Reading books, magazines, and comic books

Writing on the chalkboard with white or colored chalk

Getting free time for self-selected projects

Making things, such as kites, model cars, and airplanes

Participating in creative drama

Participating in creative dance

Making bead jewelry

Playing in water or sand

Singing

Finger-painting

Playing with puppets

Drawing with colored pens, pencils, or paints

Reading with a friend

Being captain or leader

Bringing pets to school

Studying with a friend

Tutoring younger children

Eating lunch at a restaurant

Being excused from a test

Decorating a designated area of the room in own style

Taking field trips

Going on outdoor walks

Watching a movie

Watching television

Listening to music

Doing a project of own interest

Using the tape recorder or phonograph

Roller skating
Having access to the playroom
Getting extra recess
Going home early
Taking a class pet home for the weekend
Going on a trip to a fair or museum
Using a typewriter
Doing "special," "the hardest," or "impossible" teacher-made arithmetic problems
Reading the newspaper
Reading or drawing a road map
Listening to the radio with an earplug
Going to the library
Doing a science experiment
Weighing or measuring various objects in the classroom

Social reinforcers

Receiving verbal praise
Having photograph displayed
Getting personal time with the teacher, aide, counselor, or principal
Participating in small-group discussions
Having work and projects displayed
Participating in show and tell
Demonstrating a skill
Clapping and cheering by others when successful
Being leader or organizer of an event
Getting a hug, handshake, or pat on the back
Sitting next to the teacher at lunch
Playing with a classmate of choice
Sitting and talking with a friend (child or adult)

Job reinforcers

Conducting an auction in class
Passing out paper, pencils, and so on
Taking a note to the office
Erasing the chalkboard
Helping the teacher with a project
Conducting a class raffle
Being teacher for a lesson
Managing the class store
Shopping for the class store

Being messenger for the day
Helping in the cafeteria
Assisting the custodian
Cleaning the erasers
Watering the plants
Running the ditto machine
Stapling papers together
Feeding the fish or other animals
Giving a message over the intercom
Picking up litter on the school grounds
Cleaning the teacher's desk
Taking the class roll
Carrying messages to other teachers
Serving as secretary for class meetings
Raising or lowering the flag
Emptying the wastebasket
Carrying the wastebasket while other children clean out their desks
Distributing and collecting materials
Operating a slide, filmstrip, or movie projector
Using the overhead projector
Recording own behavior on a graph
Teaching another child
Helping the librarian
Telling the teacher when it is time to go to lunch
Sharpening the teacher's pencils
Opening the teacher's mail
Sweeping the floor of the classroom
Adjusting the window shades

Direct interview with the child

Interviewing a child to determine what is desirable as a reward is frequently productive. The interview should be structured, and the reinforcement list may be used to stimulate discussion. The child is encouraged to express and discuss desires; he or she is asked questions such as "What kinds of things do you like to do?" "What are your favorite toys?" "What do you like to do more than anything else?" The child's responses will be of great help in attempting to pinpoint those items and activities to be used as reinforcers.

Also, the interviewer has an opportunity to thoroughly explain the behavior change program and answer the child's questions.

There is evidence to indicate that when a child is involved in decision making concerning important ingredients of his or her program, the overall quality and rate of the program is enhanced. Thus involving the child in the selection of reinforcers enhances the probability that the intervention will be successful.

The use of the interview technique provides the child with an opportunity to learn to select reasonable and positive reinforcers. Many children initially have difficulty making reasonable selections because of a lack of experience in decision making. In this situation, the interview is in itself a learning experience for the child.

The interview technique can be used with small groups as well as individual children. The disadvantage of the technique is that it is time consuming and its success is dependent on (1) the child or group's ability to communicate with the interviewing adult and (2) the adult's skill an as interviewer.

In the interview situation the following steps should be used as guidelines (Shea and others, 1974a, 1974b):

1. Establish rapport with the child or group.
2. Explain the purpose of the meeting.
3. Define and explain the meaning of individual and/or group reinforcers.
4. Elicit suggestions for individual and/or group rewards.
   a. Ask the child or group what rewards could be used as individual reinforcers. Record these suggestions. If working with a group, ask the individuals which suggested rewards could be used as group rewards.
   b. Give the child or group an opportunity to add to the list of rewards.
   c. Request that the child or each member of the group choose three rewards and rank them according to their desirability. If working with a group, determine the group's ranking of the rewards. Have the members vote to decide on the reward.
   d. Make arrangements for another meeting at which the child or group may choose to add to or change the reinforcers.

It is useful to record the reinforcers suggested by the child or group on the chalkboard.

Parent or teacher interview about the child

The parent or teacher interview can also be used in an effort to obtain and rank the child's desired reinforcers. Although less desirable than a direct interview with the child, the parent or teacher interview can be helpful in determining what reinforcers have been applied successfully and unsuccessfully by others. It may also be used to determine the range of successful reinforcers within the child's response repertoire.

The parent or teacher interview is especially valuable to the behavior modification consultant who is trying to determine the level of understanding and acceptance of behavior modification techniques by the individuals who work directly with the child.

The obvious disadvantage in applying this technique is that the parent's or teacher's level of sophistication as an objective observer is unknown. It should be recognized that the parent or teacher may not be of real assistance in the selection of potent rewards, because of a distorted perception of the child's likes and dislikes. However, the use of the technique can be an excellent learning experience for parents and teachers; frequently it can sensitize them to the importance of meaningful rewards for children.

This topic is discussed in detail in Chapter Six.

Direct observation

The most productive strategy for identifying effective reinforcers is direct observation of the child. According to an old saying, "If you want to see a person do something well, observe him doing something he enjoys."

Direct observation requires the teacher to observe the child's self-selected activities in a variety of situations, such as on the playground, in the classroom, during structured time, and during free time, and to list those activities the child chooses without direction from others. These self-selected activities and items can be utilized during the intervention as rewards.

EXAMPLE

Ms. Maron observed that Marvin liked to congregate with his friends during recess to trade baseball cards. She decided to allow the boys to have an additional trading time after they finished their arithmetic lesson. The total arithmetic period was 40 minutes. After 20 minutes the boys who had finished the assignment could go to a special area of the room and quietly trade cards. The longer Marvin took to complete the lesson, the less time he had to trade cards.

EXAMPLE

Mr. Dee knew that all 8-year-old boys like to play baseball. Mr. Dee wished to improve Jamie's performance in spelling. Mr. Dee told Jamie that each day that he got 80% of his spelling words correct, he could play for 20 minutes on the playground. Mr. Dee was astonished when Jamie did not respond to this reward.

There were several reasons why Jamie did not respond, and Mr. Dee had failed to take them into consideration. Jamie had not only a visual-perceptual handicap but also a gross motor handicap, and these problems interfered with his skill in large muscle activities. It was far more difficult to play baseball than to flunk spelling. Mr. Dee's fundamental error was that he did not include Jamie in the reinforcer selection process.

Additional suggestions

Different children value different consequences. It is nearly impossible to identify any event or item that will serve as a positive reinforcer for all children.

In the end, the potency of a reinforcer selected as a result of using any of the techniques described can only be determined by implementation. Many reinforcers, thought to be highly potent, fail to be effective with some children; whereas some reinforcers, discovered only on a teacher's hunch, prove to be most powerful in modifying behavior.

A few additional suggestions for the selection and use of positive reinforcers may be useful.

1. Except for a few basic items such as food and water, no item or activity can be identified with certitude as an effective reinforcer before it has been demonstrated to be effective for a specific child. What is highly reinforcing for one child may not be for another.

2. When satiation occurs, even the most powerful reinforcer will lose strength and must be replaced. The teacher should provide a variety of reinforcers, not only to prevent satiation but also to satisfy the individual and his ever-changing preferences. Many teachers provide a "menu of reinforcers" for their children. On any given day a variety of items or activities are available to satisfy the diverse needs and interests of the children. They are permitted to select from this menu.

3. The task of observing the effects of existing reinforcers and searching for new reinforcers is a continuous process. A good reinforcement system is an ever-changing blend of established reinforcers and potential but untried reinforcers.

4. Reinforcers should not be thought of only in terms of candy and other tangible items. There are many activities and privileges that are potent reinforcers. Frequently teachers use a tangible reinforcer (with a social reinforcer such as praise) initially during the behavior change program. Later, they change the reward from the tangible re-

inforcer to a special activity or privilege (always keeping the social reinforcer). In the final stages of the behavior change process, the social reinforcer used alone should be adequate.

Phasing out reinforcers

As stated previously, a goal of the behavior change process is to train an individual to respond to appropriate and occasional social reinforcers *only*. Consequently, it is necessary that the behavior modification practitioner focus particular attention to phasing out the reinforcers over a period of time. This difficult task is accomplished primarily by changing from a fixed interval or ratio reinforcement schedule (FI or FR) to a variable interval or ratio reinforcement schedule (VI or VR) and by the systematic attenuating of the average frequency of reinforcer presentation.

It must be remembered that a social reinforcer is always presented concurrently with a tangible reinforcer, if tangible rewards are used.

The reinforcement fading process may be perceived as follows:

Step 1: Social and tangible reinforcers are presented simultaneously to the individual on a fixed reinforcement schedule. This statement assumes that tangible reinforcers are needed in the particular situation.

Step 2: Social reinforcers are presented on a fixed reinforcement schedule, and tangible reinforcers are presented on a variable reinforcement schedule. Tangible reinforcers are attenuated over time and are finally extinguished. Social reinforcers are always presented simultaneously with tangible reinforcers during this step.

Step 3: Social reinforcers are presented on a variable reinforcement schedule. They are attenuated over time and are finally extinguished as the formal behavior change program is terminated.

Conclusion

Although several methods for identifying reinforcers are discussed in this section, the two procedures most recommended for use by the new practitioner of behavior modification are direct observation and a direct interview with the child. Both of these procedures have proved effective for identifying desirable rewards (Karraker, 1977).

The fact that a child is turned-on by a specific reinforcer today does not necessarily mean the child will response to that particular reinforcer next week. The skillful practitioner is sensitive to the ever-changing influence of a specific reward.

A change in performance may be the signal to initiate a new reward. The fact that Lisa correctly completed 25 addition problems on Monday to play with a puzzle, 27 problems on Tuesday to play with a puzzle, and 28 problems on Wednesday for the same privilege does not mean she will respond in a similar fashion on Thursday. To avoid this situation, a reward menu, as discussed in Chapter Four, is recommended. The schedule allows the practitioner to systematically vary the rewards a child can work for on different days. With proficiency gained through practice in the techniques for modifying behavior, the practitioner can predict when it is time to change reinforcers.

Schedules of reinforcement are discussed in Chapter Two; however, it should be re-emphasized that the schedule on which the reinforcement is administered has considerable influence on the behavior change process.

COLLECTING AND RECORDING INTERVENTION DATA

Intervention data involve information collected on the effects of the intervention dur-

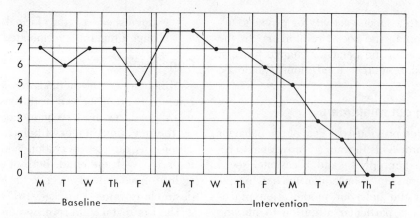

Fig. 10. Frequency of Joshua's hitting behavior before and during the intervention.

ing the implementation phase of the behavior change process. Equally as important as baseline data, intervention data provide a yardstick for comparing baseline behavior with new behavior. By comparing baseline data with intervention data, the teacher can determine the changes that have occurred as a result of the intervention. Fig. 10 presents a comparison of Joshua's hitting behavior before and during the intervention.

In this graph the target behavior shows an increase during the initial 2 days of the intervention phase. The behavior then decreases to zero over the remaining 8 days of the program.

The initial increase in the unacceptable behavior (days 6 and 7) was probably due to Joshua's testing of the teacher's response to his original behavior. In all probability, Joshua was confused by the fact that his previously effective response was no longer effective. Of course, this increase might also have been a result of the initial inefficiency of either the reinforcer or the practitioner. However, the initial increase in unacceptable behavior, as discussed in Chapter Two, is normal and should be anticipated during the beginning days of the intervention program.

The importance of continuing to count and chart the target behavior during the intervention can be readily seen on Joshua's graph. This procedure provides the practitioner with a visual image to be used in comparing the baseline and intervention behaviors. The availability of such data alerts the teacher to the child's response to the intervention and thus to the overall effectiveness of the program at a particular point in time.

Once the new behavior has been established at the acceptable level, the practitioner may question whether the observed changes were a result of the intervention or of an unknown intervening variable. This query cannot be responded to with exactitude. However, there is a procedure to test the effectiveness of the intervention. This is the process of extinction, or of reestablishing the baseline (Baseline 2). The process of reestablishing the baseline in this situation is as follows: If a behavior is thought to be maintained at a specific level by a reinforcer, the practitioner can evaluate the effectiveness of the reinforcer by withdrawing it.

EXAMPLE

Mr. Curtain had established Shirley's hand-raising behavior at an acceptable level. He then wondered

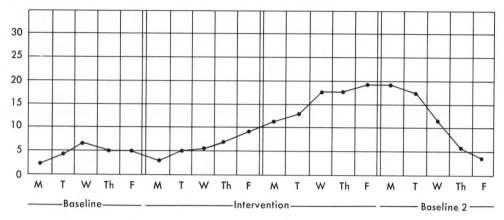

Fig. 11. Frequency of Shirley's hand-raising behavior before and during the intervention, and as a result of reestablishing the baseline (Baseline 2).

if the reinforcer applied in the intervention phase was *the factor* that had resulted in her change in behavior. The reinforcer was a smile and verbal praise each time Shirley raised her hand in class.

To check the potency of the reinforcer, Mr. Curtain withdrew it; that is, he ceased smiling at Shirley and praising her when she raised her hand in class. Within a few days, as demonstrated in Fig. 11, Shirley's hand-raising response began to be extinguished. Because of the decrease in Shirley's hand-raising behavior, Mr. Curtain could assume that the reinforcer (smiles and verbal praise) was instrumental in increasing the hand-raising behavior.

Reestablishing the baseline is not always an effective means of evaluating the potency of a reinforcer. If a behavior has been firmly habituated into the child's behavioral repertoire, it will not respond to extinction.

Establishing and extinguishing a behavior is *not* a standard procedure applied in the behavior change process. However, this technique may assure new practitioners of behavior modification that their efforts are effective in changing behaviors.

The use of Baseline 2 in an intervention program is at the discretion of the practitioner. However, once a practitioner has determined that the reinforcer was instrumental in the behavior change program, it

would be a disservice to the child not to reinstate it, or not to return to the intervention state. The desired behavior will rapidly return to the previous level when the reinforcer is reinstated.

SUMMARY

In this chapter four steps for changing behavior are discussed. They are (1) *selecting a target behavior,* (2) *collecting and recording baseline data,* (3) *identifying appropriate reinforcers,* and (4) *collecting and recording intervention data.*

When selecting a target behavior, the new practitioner should choose only *one* individual or group behavior to modify at a time. The practitioner should analyze the potential target behavior in relation to its frequency, duration, intensity, and type; determine the direction the behavior is to take (whether it is to increase, decrease, or be maintained); determine whether the behavior is observable and quantifiable; and finally, describe the behavior in precise, descriptive terminology.

The collecting and recording of baseline data allows a scientific analysis of the changes in behavior that occur during the intervention phase. Some techniques used to collect baseline data are analysis of anecdotal records, analysis of cumulative records, an interview with parents, an interview with the child, and direct observation. We have found direct observation to be the most reliable of these procedures.

A list of tangible and social reinforcers for application in the classroom and school are presented. Consideration is given to consumable rewards, tangible and token rewards, games, activities, social rewards, and jobs.

The two most effective methods of identifying appropriate reinforcers for a child are direct observation and an interview with the child in which the child is asked to name desirable rewards.

Comparison of baseline and intervention data provides the practitioner with an evaluation technique for determining changes occurring in the target behavior as a result of intervention.

It is highly recommended that the new practitioner of behavior modification carefully follow each step in the behavior change process presented in this chapter.

EXERCISES FOR CHAPTER THREE
Quiz*

1. The steps in the behavior change process are:

    a. Selecting a _____ behavior.

    b. _____ and _____ baseline data.

    c. Identifying _____ reinforcers.

    d. Collecting and recording _____ data.
2. Decisions concerning the selection of a target behavior should be governed by the following four characteristics of the behavior:

    a. _____   c. _____

    b. _____   d. _____
3. The directions a behavior may take as a result of an intervention are:

    a. _____   c. _____

    b. _____
4. List three of the techniques available for collecting baseline data.

    a. _____

    b. _____

    c. _____
5. a. Counting means enumerating the _____ that the behavior occurs.

---

*Turn to Appendix A, p. 174, for answers.

    b. _____ means presenting a visual display of the enumerated behavior in graphic form.

6. Three techniques for obtaining a list of potential reinforcers are:

    a. _____

    b. _____

    c. _____

7. The best method available to demonstrate with certitude the effectiveness of a reinforcer

    is _____.

8. Collecting and charting procedures should continue throughout the _____

    _____ phase.

9. Immediately after the implementation of an intervention to decrease a behavior, the behavior modifier can anticipate a brief dramatic _____ in the behavior in most cases.

10. One method of evaluating the effectiveness of a reinforcer during the behavior change process is to withdraw it. This is the process of _____.

Projects

1. Select five potential target behaviors and observe them. After observing the behaviors, discuss their characteristics in terms of frequency, duration, intensity, and type.
2. Collect and record accurate baseline data on two of the behaviors observed.
3. List 25 reinforcers that may be useful in modifying the behavior of children in your present teaching situation. Classify these as tangible or social reinforcers. At least 12 of the 25 reinforcers should be classifiable as social rewards.
4. Observe a child and develop a list of potential reinforcers for this child. Observe the child in a variety of situations.
5. a. As outlined in the text, interview the same child and develop another list of reinforcers.
   b. Interview the child's parent or teacher (if applicable) as outlined in Chapter Six and develop a third list of reinforcers.
6. Conceptualize and write a detailed description of an intervention to be applied to one of the behaviors observed in Project 1.

REFERENCES

Axelrod, S. *Behavior modification for the classroom teacher.* New York: McGraw-Hill Book Co., 1977.

Gronlund, N. E. *Stating behavioral objectives for classroom instruction.* New York, Macmillan Publishing Co., Inc., 1970.

Karraker, R. J. Self versus teacher selected reinforcers in a token economy. *Exceptional Children*, April 1977, 43(7), 454-455.

Mager, R. F. *Preparing instructional objectives.* Palo Alto, Calif.: Fearon Publishers, Inc., 1962.

Shea, T. M., Whiteside, W. R., Beetner, E. G., and Lindsey, D. L. *Psychosituational interview.* Edwardsville: Southern Illinois University, 1974. (a)

Shea, T. M., Whiteside, W. R., Beetner, E. G., and Lindsey, D. L. *Selecting reinforcers.* Edwardsville: Southern Illinois University, 1974. (b)

CHAPTER FOUR

Methods of increasing behavior

The four most common techniques applied in behavior modification interventions for increasing a desired behavior are (1) shaping, (2) modeling, (3) contingency contracting, and (4) the token economy. These basic methods should be of assistance to the beginning practitioner attempting to establish acceptable behaviors in children. The techniques are applicable to both individual and group behaviors.

SHAPING

To initiate an intervention for the purpose of increasing behavior, the practitioner need only wait until the desired behavior is emitted by the child. When the behavior occurs, it must be immediately rewarded with a potent reinforcer.

However, suppose a situation arises in which the level of performance of the desired behavior is at zero or near zero. What can the practitioner do to establish the desired behavior? There are two alternatives:

1. Wait an undetermined length of time (in some cases, forever) for the behavior to naturally occur.
2. Utilize a behavior-shaping technique.

Shaping is the systematic, immediate reinforcement of successive approximations of the desired behavior until the desired behavior is established. It is primarily used to establish behaviors that have not been previously manifested in the individual's behavioral repertoire. Just as the sculptor shapes and molds an object of art from clay, the behavior modification practitioner shapes and molds a new behavior from an undifferentiated behavioral response (Neisworth and others, 1969).

The behavior-shaping process includes the following steps:

1. Selecting a target behavior
2. Obtaining reliable baseline data
3. Selecting potent reinforcers
4. Reinforcing successive approximations of the desired behavior each time they occur
5. Reinforcing the newly established behavior each time it occurs
6. Reinforcing the behavior on a variable reinforcement schedule

Many of these steps are explained in Chapters Two and Three. However, some of them require additional comments here for clarification.

The behavior selected for shaping must be carefully specified. This rule is especially true when the behavior of severely handicapped children with restricted behavioral repertoires is being shaped. The practitioner must be positive that the selected behavior is meaningful to the child in terms of the child's present life situation and developmental level.

If the performance level of the desired behavior is at zero, the practitioner must initiate the shaping process from the child's undifferentiated behavioral manifestations.

EXAMPLE

Tommy's teacher, Ms. Allen, wishes to establish intelligible verbal responses in Tommy's behavioral repertoire. However, the child emits no understandable words. His entire verbal behavior consists of vocal noises, such as screeches, howls, and gutteral sounds. The teacher must begin the shaping process with the manifested behavior, that is, vocal noise. She must reinforce successive approximations of intelligible verbal responses.

EXAMPLE

Jeff, a severely handicapped child, was having great difficulty interacting appropriately on the playground during circle or ball games requiring running from one specific location to another. Whenever he was required to engage in a game of this type, he ran about at random, dashing here and there, jumping up and down, and in general confusing himself and his playmates.

Mr. Speer, the physical education teacher, wished to modify this behavior. He realized he had to start the change process with the behavior presently being manifested by Jeff. He determined that Jeff did attend to the action of the game and attempted to play by the rules. In his effort to help Jeff, Mr. Speer, modified the rules of the game; he established a "new rule" in which all team members ran hand-in-hand in pairs from one location to another. Jeff was Mr. Speer's partner until he was conditioned to the new running pattern. The game was played by the traditional rules after Jeff developed acceptable skills.

In some educational settings there is a resistance to the use of tangible rewards, such as food and drink. However, teachers working with children who lack a broad reward menu may have to resort to the use of tangible reinforcers when initiating a behavior-shaping program. Of course, as previously stated in this guide, tangible rewards should always be presented simultaneously with social rewards.

During the behavior-shaping process, the practitioner reinforces only those behavioral manifestations that approximate the desired behavior.

EXAMPLE

Mr. Jackson designed a shaping intervention to increase the number of assigned math problems that Robert would successfully complete in his workbook during independent study. Robert never completed the 20 problems given for practice. However, baseline data revealed that Robert consistently solved the first 9 problems successfully in each practice section. He simply did not attempt the remaining 11 problems.

During the shaping process, Mr. Jackson reinforced Robert for *any improvement* over his baseline of 9. Robert was rewarded for successfully completing 10 problems, 11 problems, 12 problems, and so on. Robert was *never* rewarded for completing a quantity of problems below his highest level of accomplishment. Within a short time, Mr. Jackson's intervention data confirmed the fact that Robert was consistently completing the 20 problems successfully. The reinforcer was phased out.

Reinforcing less than the existing baseline results in rewarding behavior in a direction of change that is the reverse of the proposed direction. Remember, *only* the *highest* approximation of the desired behavior should be reinforced.

Another important consideration in the shaping process is the practitioner's knowledge of how long to provide reinforcement at one level of performance before moving on to the next level. Such a movement increases the demands on the child. Determining when to move on is the practitioner's greatest dilemma. If reinforcement continues too long at a given performance level, the child's behavior will become so rigidly established that further progress will be difficult. However, if the practitioner insists that the child progress too rapidly from one level to the next, there is a great possibility that the new behavior will be extinguished.

Knowing when to progress from one level of performance to the next is of utmost importance. Unfortunately, this knowledge is part of the skill needed for behavior modification, and developing it is not easy. The practitioner develops this needed sensitivity and skill only with practice and experience in behavior shaping and through knowing the individual child.

The following two examples are presented to clarify the steps in the behavior-shaping process.

EXAMPLE

Ms. Simpkins wished to increase Jim's letter identification skills. Jim could identify 7 of the 26 letters of the alphabet consistently. Before implementing a shaping intervention, Ms. Simpkins determined that gumdrops were an effective reinforcer for Jim.

During the intervention phase of the behavior change program Jim was exposed to one new letter of the alphabet at a time. He was to learn each new letter before another letter was presented. Jim was only reinforced with a gumdrop if he identified the new letter and all previously identified letters. The new letter was always presented last in the daily sequence of letters. After he had learned a letter, it was presented randomly with all the other previously learned letters in the daily session.

This procedure was continued until Jim successfully identified all the letters in the alphabet.

EXAMPLE

Mr. Behe wished to increase Barry's in-seat behavior. Baseline data revealed that, on an average, Barry remained in his seat approximately 6 minutes. Mr. Behe had determined through observation that Barry enjoyed listening to story records. This activity was selected as a reinforcer for acceptable in-seat behavior.

During the intervention a timer was placed on Barry's desk. He was told that each time he remained in his seat until the timer bell sounded, he would be allowed to go to the reinforcement area of the classroom and listen to his favorite story record for a specified number of minutes. The reinforcement schedule Mr. Behe utilized to shape the in-seat behavior is presented in Table 7.

Barry's behavior was shaped with little difficulty. However, during the 20-minute interval between reinforcement Barry became bored. As a consequence, he remained at the 20-minute interval longer than the teacher had anticipated. At Barry's suggestion, Mr. Behe changed the reinforcer from story records to jigsaw puzzles.

According to Panyan (1972), there are two distinct types of behavior-shaping interventions: progressive and chain.

In the progressive shaping intervention, the child is required to engage in a series of

Table 7. Reinforcement schedule for in-seat behavior

Minutes of in-seat behavior	Minutes in reinforcement area
5	2
5	2
7	2½
8	2½
10	2½
15	3
20	3
25	3
30	3½
45	4
60	4
90	5
120	7½
150	10

steps, each of which is a continuation and progression of the previously learned step or steps. Examples of this intervention are bathing, handwashing, putting on a sweater or socks, and so on. (See also the example of Marie—following page.)

A chain intervention is composed of two or more separate and distinct steps or skills that are learned and combined sequentially to complete a specific task. Examples of this intervention are tying shoes, polishing shoes, eating, buttoning clothing, and the like.

Children often need special assistance during the steps of the behavior-shaping intervention. This special assistance may be manual or verbal and is frequently called "prompting." Prompts may include such activities as guiding a child's hand or foot in the completion of a task, moving the child's head to gain his or her attention, talking a child through a task by repeated precise verbal instruction, providing a verbal model for imitation, and providing printed or three-dimensional material that structures a task. Prompts are used to increase the probabilities of success in a task. They have proved to be effective in both types of shaping interventions.

Although prompts of various kinds may be a necessary component of the behavior-shaping intervention initially, they must eventually be eliminated; the child must learn to complete the task independently. The gradual elimination of prompts is called "fading" (Panyan, 1972). Fading includes the reduction of the amount and quality of manual guidance, verbal assistance, and/or printed or three-dimensional material used to structure an activity.

EXAMPLE

Marie, a 6-year-old child, was enrolled in a motor therapy program in an effort to remediate her physical coordination problems. One of the activities in the motor therapy program was walking a 10-foot balance beam without assistance.

During the therapy program's assessment phase, Marie fell off the balance beam seven times in her effort to walk its length unaided. It was decided that during the initial stages of her motor therapy Marie would be manually guided by a therapist. He would hold her right hand as she walked the beam.

With manual guidance Marie learned to walk the 10-foot beam with efficiency within a few days. The therapist decided to fade the prompt (manual guidance) and applied the following schedule during the fading process:

1. The therapist reduced the firmness of his grasp on Marie's right hand.
2. The therapist grasped only one finger of Marie's hand.
3. The therapist positioned his hand in progressive steps approximately 6, 9, and 12 inches from Marie's right hand.
4. The therapist walked beside Marie with his hands at his side.
5. The therapist withdrew to the position he normally assumed to observe a person's efficiency on the balance beam.

An example of the use and elimination of a prompt can also be seen in the previous example of Jeff (p. 55).

To summarize this discussion of the behavior-shaping process, the following example and conceptual model are presented.

EXAMPLE

Five-year-old Stephen was nonverbal. His speech teacher selected the initiation of verbal exchanges with his preschool teacher as the target behavior. Baseline data revealed that Stephen's only verbal behavior consisted of babbling, yelling, and screaming. This behavior was frequent when he was in the company of known adults. However, he did not consistently emit this behavior in response to queries from others.

Behavior-shaping model (Stephen's verbal behavior)

Direction of desired behavior →			
Initiates verbal exchange with teacher	10	← Desired behavior
Initiates verbal exchange with therapist	9	
Initiates two or more–word exchanges	8	
Initiates one-word exchange	7	
Gives two or more–word responses	6	
Gives one-word response	5	
Gives second-level approximations	4	
Gives first-level approximations	3	
Emits undifferentiated consistent verbal noise	2	
Emits undifferentiated inconsistent verbal noise	1	← Baseline behavior

Stephen was observed by the speech teacher, who determined that he consistently responded to four tangible reinforcers: pickles, potato chips, prunes, and Popsicles.

The behavior-shaping intervention was initiated on a daily basis for 30 minutes during the preschool sessions that Stephen attended at a local school. The effectiveness of the intervention was to be evaluated by means of direct observation of the behavior-shaping sessions and the boy's activities in the preschool classroom with his teacher and playmates.

Shaping began with undifferentiated, inconsistent verbal responses. Within 1 school year Stephen had progressed to initiating some verbal exchanges with others in both the shaping sessions and the preschool class. By the end of the year he would ask his teacher for milk, juice, cookies, toys, and the like. Although he seldom played with his classmates, he did verbally object to their attempts to confiscate his toys and snacks.

Stephen's ascent up the behavior-shaping ladder is presented on p. 57. The steps of the ladder are self-explanatory with the possible exception of Steps 3 and 4. During these steps Stephen consistently used specific verbal noises in place of words. For example, "ah" was used for the word "milk," "eh" was used for the word "no," and the like. Emphasis here was put on converting these emissions into meaningful words.

MODELING

One of the most common forms of human learning is accomplished through the processes of observation and imitation. All parents and teachers can relate a variety of acceptable and unacceptable behaviors exhibited by their children and students that are imitations of their own (the adults') personal acceptable and unacceptable behaviors. This form of learning at various times and by various theorists and practitioners has been called modeling, observational learning, identification, copying, vicarious learning, social facilitation, contagion, role playing, and so on (Bandura, 1969). In this text the term modeling is used to describe learning by observation and imitation.

As a behavior change method, modeling is the provision of an individual or group behavior to be imitated by the child. This is one of the oldest and most frequently applied methods of changing behavior.

Mothers and fathers, husbands and wives, and teachers and principals have been suggesting models to their sons, daughters, spouses, and students for generations.

"Be a good boy like your brother John."

"Why can't you be like George, an excellent father, a great lover, and a good provider?"

"Mary, can't you be a good student like Eileen?"

"Why can't you behave like the other boys and girls?"

"Well, Marilyn Monroe did it. Why can't you?"

Several state and national organizations exist for the sole purpose of providing handicapped and other children with an acceptable social model. These organizations provide children with either the direct services of a live model or an abstract model inherent in their program and printed materials. Among these organizations are Big Brother and Big Sister, Boy Scouts and Girl Scouts, 4-H, and Little League.

According to Bandura (1969), Bandura and Walters (1963), and Clarizio and Yelon (1967), exposure to a model has three effects:

1. Modeling effect or observational learning. Children may acquire behavior from a model that was not previously a part of their behavioral repertoire. In this situation the model performs a behavior that is imitated by the child in substantially identical form. Examples of the modeling effect are teaching a nonverbal child to verbalize in imitation of a model and teaching a child signing skills as a method of communication.

2. Inhibitory and disinhibitory effects. Modeling is not confined exclusively to the learning of new behaviors, as in the modeling effect above. Modeling includes imitating a model for the pur-

pose of disinhibiting or inhibiting a behavior. For example, a child may observe and imitate a peer who is positively reinforced for exhibiting a behavior. Or the child may observe and *not* imitate a peer who is punished or ignored for exhibiting a behavior. In these situations the child may be said to be experiencing the peer's behavior and its consequences vicariously.

3. Eliciting or response facilitation effect. In this situation the model's behavior is employed to facilitate the occurrence of a previously learned but dormant behavior from the child. For example, a child may know that it is appropriate to say "Thank you" when given a cookie at snack time. However, this child may not say "Thank you" as a matter of common practice. Appropriate social responsiveness may be facilitated if all the children who receive cookies previous to this child during snack time say "Thank you."

Before implementing a modeling intervention, the practitioner should consider the following factors:

1. Is the child able developmentally and cognitively to imitate the model? Practitioners must be cognizant of the fact that some children are simply not ready to utilize modeling.

2. Will the child be rewarded for imitating the model? Some children are simply not intrinsically rewarded by performing behaviors that others consider acceptable. This problem may be caused by a variety of group and cultural factors of which the practitioner is unaware.

3. Is the model "good"? Caution must be taken when a model is being selected for a child. Remember, what the model does in science class may be quite different from what this individual does in

English, shop, on the playground, at home, or behind the barn.

4. Is the model acceptable to the child? A model who is too good, too bright, too fast, or just plain obnoxious will be rejected by the child.

Modeling techniques can be effectively applied by teachers in an effort to change behavior only when consideration is given to these factors.

EXAMPLE

Ms. Simpson is a resource teacher of educable mentally handicapped children. Dave and Carl work with Ms. Simpson in the resource room for 1 hour each day. Until recently, Dave would usually attempt his assigned tasks, whereas Carl would seldom attempt his assigned work.

It was determined by Ms. Simpson that both boys were reinforced by her attention. Therefore, she decided to use her attention as a reward they received for completing their work. Dave was reinforced by Ms. Simpson's attention. She praised him each time he did his class work, attended to the appropriate stimulus, or completed an assigned task; she ignored Carl's inappropriate behavior.

After several sessions during which Dave's appropriate behavior was rewarded, Carl began to imitate Dave to receive Ms. Simpson's attention. She immediately reinforced Carl whenever he exhibited the appropriate behavior.

The result of this intervention was a dramatic change in Carl's behavior. He is now completing his work and doing other things to gain approval from Ms. Simpson.

EXAMPLE

Mr. Cohen is an instructor of three boys and one girl in a class for behaviorally disordered children. The students' names are John, James, Charles, and Shirley. Of the four students, Charles is the most troublesome. Charles constantly moves about the room, exhibiting feelings of indignation at assignments and disrupting the activities of Mr. Cohen and his classmates. This behavior occurs throughout the school day. Originally when the behavior occurred, the other children remained busy at their seat. On these occasions, Mr. Cohen would chase after Charles or provide him with attention for the unacceptable behavior he was exhibiting. The acceptable behaviors manifested by Shirley, John, and James were ignored. Lately, Shirley, John, and James have begun to move about the room and exhibit behaviors that disturb

Mr. Cohen. They are imitating the behavior of Charles.

One can conclude that Shirley, John, and James are modeling Charles's behavior for the purpose of receiving attention from their teacher.

In both of these examples the procedure of modeling is effective; modeling is effective in developing both appropriate and inappropriate behaviors. The consequence of behavior is again the key factor. Teachers should be aware that they are models to some children; their behavior is effective in establishing new behavior in some children.

In too many classrooms appropriate behavior is taken for granted. Modeling is perhaps the most potentially effective preventive technique among the behavior modification practitioner's long list of techniques.

CONTINGENCY CONTRACTING

When one considers contemporary emphasis on deferred payment purchasing and organized crime in the American communications media, one feels that every child should have some idea of the meaning of a contract. A contract is an agreement, written or verbal, between two or more parties, individuals, or groups that stipulates the responsibilities of the parties concerning a specific item or activity. Contingency contracting in behavior modification parlance was well defined by Becker (1969) when he stated, "Arrange the conditions so that the child gets to do something he wants to do following something you want him to do."

We are all parties to contracts in our everyday life. Some of us are fortunate enough to have a written contract stating the terms of our employment. This contract explains what duties we are to perform, for what period of time, and for what compensation. If we perform as specified in the contract, we cannot be fired under normal circumstances. A verbal contract exists between husband and wife. The terms of the contract state that each will love, honor, and respect one another until death (or divorce) do they part.

There are many lesser contracts in American society, such as home loans, loans on new automobiles, boats, and the like. Contracts such as these are indispensable to the efficient operation of the American business system.

There are some contracts, seldom written, that we often take for granted but that nevertheless are indispensable in a complex urban society. Among these unwritten contracts are trust arrangements with the sanitation service that the rubbish will be collected on certain mornings, the lights will go on when we turn a switch, or the water will flow when we open a faucet.

The use of contingency contracting as a behavior modification technique is based on a principle developed by David Premack in 1959. Premack's principle is: "A behavior that has a high rate of occurrence can be used to increase a behavior with a low rate of occurrence." What Premack stated was in reality a very ancient and frequently used principle. For centuries people have applied this principle to raising their children, teaching their students, and supervising their employees. *If you do X, then you can do or get Y.* This principle has often been referred to as "Grandma's law." Most of us remember the power of this law from childhood:

"Eat your spinach; then you can have some ice cream."

"Clean your room; then you can go to the movies."

"Cut the lawn; then you can use the car."

This same principle carries over to adult life:

"Write 27 articles and 10 books; then you will be promoted to professor."

"Don't join the union; then you will retain your job."

"Don't make waves on the bureaucratic sea of calm; then you will be granted tenure."

Table 8. X, then Y, statements

X	Then	Y
Sit in your seat 2 hours		Get a 10-minute recess
Complete your term paper		Get an A
Be a "good" student		Receive a good report card
Volunteer for the football team		Receive recognition from the coach and cheerleaders
Learn a letter of the alphabet		Immediately receive a gumdrop

Table 8 presents a series of *X* and *Y* statements found in the classroom.

Within the last two decades teachers and parents have recognized the significance of individual differences caused by such factors as maturation, general knowledge, locus of control, and experience. Various instructional programs have been developed in response to these differences. Contingency contracting is one method that can be used to individualize instruction and behavior control to respond to the child's interest, needs, and abilities; it can be applied to the cognitive, affective, and psychomotor domains of learning.

The advantages of contingency contracting are many. The method is positive; that is, the child takes an active role in deciding the type and amount of work required. Consequently, personal responsibilities are understood by the child. At regular intervals the contract is reviewed for the child's reaffirmation. Accountability factors are built into this intervention. The teacher collects empirical data that indicates where the child was, where the child has progressed to, and the child's current needs. The teacher can use this information to develop the program, instructional objectives, and developmental objectives with the child.

The teacher serves as contract manager, providing facts and explaining the principles. The teacher encourages the child to choose realistic goals and desirable reinforcers and keeps the ratio of task to reinforcer within realistic limits. The teacher ensures that both the task and the reinforcer are fair to both parties of the contract (child and teacher).

When contingency contracting is first utilized with a child, small tasks and small reinforcers are most effective since they encourage frequent reinforcement. Lengthy or complex tasks and small reinforcers are unfair and defeat the motivational factors inherent in this intervention. If the task is more demanding than the reinforcer is desirable, the learner is not sufficiently motivated to perform. Likewise, the reinforcer should not be greater than the task warrants. Otherwise, the instructional objective established for the child is difficult to obtain.

Initially, contracts may encourage and reward approximations of desired behavior. Short work periods are desirable because they permit frequent reinforcement. Low-achieving children usually require immediate reinforcers; consequently, short-term contracts (daily) are appropriate. Higher achieving children can usually delay reinforcements; therefore, long-term contracts (1 or 2 weeks) are feasible.

Some educators believe it is beneficial to separate the locations for task performance and reinforcer delivery. In this way the learner equates the task performance as a means to a desirable end, that is, going to the reinforcement area. This also broadens the type and variety of reinforcers that can be made available to the students. Teachers are encouraged to establish a reinforcement area in their classroom. The establishment of reinforcement areas is discussed later in this chapter.

The teacher must encourage the child to adhere to the contract for the designated period of time. The child should be cautioned that if the agreed-on task is not performed, the child will not receive the reinforcer. However, if the original contract is too difficult, a new contract must be written for the learner to perform successfully. However, every effort should be made to ensure the success of the original contract.

The underlying principle of contingency contracting is constant: the learner, by making decisions concerning personal productivity, develops critical thinking skills, self-control, and the independence that increases this productivity.

There are two types of contracts applicable in the classroom setting: verbal and written. Educators have generally found verbal contracts more useful than written contracts. The following are examples of verbal contracts that can be utilized in the classroom:

"John, when you have completed 8 addition problems correctly, you may play with the puzzles."

"Mary, if you remain in your seat for 5 minutes, you may work in your coloring book."

"James, if you come to school on time tomorrow, you may be first in line for lunch."

"Tom, if you don't hit anyone this morning, you may have an extra milk at lunch."

"Mike, if you complete your seat work, you may watch "Sesame Street" on television."

Verbal contracts such as these are made daily in the classrooms. They work effectively for both the teacher and the child.

Written contracts are more elaborate than verbal contracts. The elaborateness of written contracts should depend on the sophistication of the child for whom it is designed. Contracts frequently lose their effectiveness when they include pseudolegal jargon such as "the parties of the first part," "the party of the second part," or "henceforth and forevermore."

It is recommended that the practitioner use the contract format on the opposite page or a similar one. Additional copies of this contract are provided in tear-off form at the back of the text.

Homme and associates (1969) have suggested ten basic rules for writing a contract for classroom use. These rules are:

1. The contract payoff (reward) should be immediate.
2. Initially contracts should call for and reward approximations of desired behavior.
3. The contract should provide for frequent rewards in small amounts.
4. The contract should call for and reward accomplishments rather than just obedience.
5. The performance should be rewarded after it occurs.
6. The contract must be fair to both parties.
7. The terms of the contract must be clear.
8. The contract must be honest.
9. The contract must be positive.
10. Contracting must be used systematically as an integral part of the on-going classroom program.

In addition to the above rules, the practitioner should consider the following factors when developing and implementing a contract:

1. The contract must be negotiated and freely agreed on by both the child and the teacher.
2. The contract must include the desired achievement or production level.
3. The reinforcer must be consistently delivered in accordance with the terms of the contract.
4. The contract must include the date for review and renegotiation.

One of the major functions of contingency contracting is to get children to the level of development at which they will initiate a con-

Date _____

Contract

This is an agreement between _____
Child's name

and _____. The contract begins on
Teacher's name

_____ and ends on _____. It will be re-
Date   Date

viewed on _____ .
Date

The terms of the agreement are:

Child will _____

_____

_____

_____

Teacher will _____

_____

_____

_____

If the child fulfills his or her part of the contract, the child will receive the agreed-on reward from the teacher. However, if the child fails to fulfill his or her part of the contract, the
rewards will be withheld.

Child's signature _____

Teacher's signature _____

tract instead of waiting for a suggestion from the teacher.

The key to successful contracting is a negotiation session during which (1) the system of contracting is explained and discussed, (2) the contract is written, and (3) the contract is signed by the child and the teacher.

Negotiation should be systematic and precise. The tacher, as manager, has an obligation to ensure that these sessions are pro-

ductive. It is recommended that the new practitioner use the following negotiation procedure (Shea, and others, 1974):

1. Teacher establishes and maintains rapport with the child.
2. Teacher explains the purpose of the meeting by saying something like, "I know you've been working hard on your schoolwork [reading, writing, spelling, arithmetic], and I'd like to help you."

3. Teacher gives a simple definition of a contract, explaining that a contract is an agreement between two people.
    a. Teacher gives an example of a contract, such as: "When your mother takes your TV to the repair shop, the clerk gives her a ticket. The ticket is a contract between your mother and the repairman. He will repair and return the TV, and your mother will pay him."
    b. Teacher asks the child to give an example of a contract.
    c. If child cannot respond, the teacher gives another example.
4. Teacher explains to the child that they are going to write a contract.
5. Teacher and child discuss tasks.
    a. Child suggests tasks for the contract.
    b. Teacher suggests tasks for the contract.
    c. Child and teacher discuss and agree on the task.
6. Teacher and child discuss reinforcers.
    a. Teacher asks the child what activities the child enjoys doing and what things he or she likes. The teacher may also suggest reinforcers.
    b. Teacher writes a menu of child-suggested reinforcers.
    c. Child selects reinforcers for which he or she would like to work.
    d. Teacher and child rank the desired reinforcers in the child's order of preference.
7. Teacher and child negotiate the ratio of task to reinforcer.
8. Teacher and child agree on the time to be allotted for the child to perform the task; that is, the child works 10 addition problems in 15 minutes to receive the reinforcer, or the child completes a unit of science and does the laboratory experiments in 2 weeks to receive an A.
9. Teacher and child identify the criterion for achievement; that is, the child will work 10 addition problems in 15 minutes with at least 80% accuracy.
10. Teacher and child discuss evaluation procedures.
    a. Teacher discusses different types of evaluations with the child.
    b. Teacher and child agree on a method of evaluation.
    c. Teacher asks the child to explain the method of evaluation. If the child appears confused, the teacher restates and clarifies the evaluation procedure.
11. Teacher and child negotiate delivery of the reinforcer. The reinforcer must be delivered according to the terms written in the contract.
12. Teacher and child agree on a date for renegotiation.
13. Teacher or child writes the contract. If feasible, the child should be encouraged to write it. Teacher gives a copy of the contract to the child.
14. Teacher reads the contract to the child as the child follows on his or her own copy.
15. Teacher elicits the child's verbal affirmation to the terms of the contract and also gives own affirmation.
16. Child and teacher sign the contract.
17. Teacher congratulates the child for making the contract and wishes the child success.

A properly conducted negotiating session is complex and time consuming, particularly if the teacher has not previously introduced the concept of contracting in the classroom. As an aid to reducing confusion on the part of the teacher or the child and in an effort to facilitate the negotiation process, a contract work sheet is provided (see pp. 65 and 66). Additional copies of this work sheet are provided in tear-off form at the back of the text.

Contract Work Sheet

Child _____

Teacher _____ Date _____

(X)	Tasks	Comments
( )	1. Establish and maintain rapport.	
( )	2. Explain the purpose of the meeting.	
( )	3. Explain a contract.	
( )	4. Give an example of a contract.	
( )	5. Ask the child to give an example of a contract; if there is no response, give another example.	
( )	6. Discuss possible tasks.	
( )	7. Child-suggested tasks: _____ _____ _____ _____	
( )	8. Teacher-suggested tasks: _____ _____ _____ _____	
( )	9. Agree on the task.	
( )	10. Ask the child what activities he or she enjoys and what items he or she wishes to possess.	
( )	11. Record child-suggested reinforcers.	
( )	12. Negotiate the ratio of the task to the reinforcer.	

Continued.

Contract Work Sheet—cont'd

(X)	Tasks	Comments
( )	13. Identify the time allotted for the task.	
( )	14. Identify the criterion or achievement level.	
( )	15. Discuss methods of evaluation.	
( )	16. Agree on the method of evaluation.	
( )	17. Restate and clarify the method of evaluation.	
( )	18. Negotiate the delivery of the reinforcer.	
( )	19. Set the date for renegotiation.	
( )	20. Write two copies of the contract.	
( )	21. Read the contract to the child.	
( )	22. Elicit the child's verbal affirmation and give your own affirmation.	
( )	23. Sign the contract and have the child sign it.	
( )	24. Congratulate the child (and yourself).	

The left-hand column of the work sheet should be checked as the teacher and child complete each of the specified tasks. The tasks to be accomplished are specified in the middle column. The tasks are presented in logical order. It is strongly recommended that the order of presentation be followed during the session. The right-hand column of the work sheet is reserved for teacher comments and notations.

The following are three examples of contracts drawn from classroom experience.

Date _____February 3, 1980_____

Contract

This is an agreement between _____Bob Wellrock_____ and _____Mr. Bare_____. The contract
Child's name Teacher's name

begins on _____2/6/80_____ and ends on _____2/10/80_____. It will be reviewed on _____2/9/80_____.
Date Date Date

The terms of the agreement are:

Child will _____spell with 90% accuracy the 20 assigned spelling words for Friday._____

Teacher will _____provide a ticket good for admission to the school movie on February 10,
1980._____

If the child fulfills his or her part of the contract, the child will receive the agreed-on
reward from the teacher. However, if the child fails to fulfill his part of the contract, the rewards will be withheld.

Child's signature _____

Teacher's signature _____

Date _____April 5, 1980_____

Contract

This is an agreement between _____Russell Palmer_____ and _____Mr. Davis_____. The contract
Child's name Teacher's name

begins on _____4/8/80_____ and ends on _____4/12/80_____. It will be reviewed on _____4/10/80_____.
Date Date Date

The terms of the agreement are:

Child will _____not engage in any fights during the school day for the period of the contract._____

Teacher will _____take the child to a Golden Gloves boxing match at the local arena._____

If the child fulfills his or her part of the contract, the child will receive the agreed-on
reward from the teacher. However, if the child fails to fulfill his part of the contract, the rewards will be withheld.

Child's signature _____

Teacher's signature _____

Date _____ *March 7, 1980* _____

Contract

This is an agreement between ___ *Tom Hawk* ___ and ___ *Mr. George* ___. The contract

Child's name   Teacher's name

begins on ___ *3/10/80* ___ and ends on ___ *3/30/80* ___. It will be reviewed on ___ *3/27/80* ___.

Date   Date   Date

The terms of the agreement are:

Child will ___ *participate in a teacher-prescribed physical education program for 30 minutes a day during the period of the contract.* ___

Teacher will ___ *provide one out-of-town basketball trip and admission to the game.* ___

If the child fulfills his or her part of the contract, the child will receive the agreed-on reward from the teacher. However, if the child fails to fulfill his part of the contract, the rewards will be withheld.

Child's signature _____

Teacher's signature _____

TOKEN ECONOMY

When most of us think of learning, we recall our participation in formal educational systems, which involved the acquisition of knowledge by listening to teachers, having discussions, taking tests, and the like. This symbolic or verbal learning is essential to our development, but it is not the only kind of learning in which we participate. Human nature permits us to learn directly from experiences in our environment. It is through learning that we develop habitual ways of working our environment for our reinforcers, that is, to obtain and sustain pleasure and to avoid discomfort and pain.

Although they differ in some ways, all learning environments are similar in that they are worked for reinforcers. Reinforcers may be defined as stimuli that induce changes in the person. These are positive reinforcers if they induce a pleasant state and negative reinforcers if they induce an aversive or painful state. Generally, we work our environment to acquire positive reinforcers and to avoid or escape negative reinforcers. Learning occurs by discovering behaviors that produce rewards and then repetitively working the environment to continue to obtain the desired reward. In general, the strength of a reinforcer is judged by the magnitude of the change it produces in the individual. The stronger or more desirable the reinforcers, the more quickly and easily the individual learns.

Learning environments generally provide feedback process cues that predict the presentation of delayed reinforcers. The immediacy of feedback, whether it is reinforcement per se or a process cue predictive of later reinforcement, is an important determinant of the rate of learning. In general, learning occurs more easily and more rapidly when feedback is immediate.

Learning environments vary in the consistency of feedback that they provide for the individual. The more consistent the feedback, the more quickly and easily the individual learns. Learning environments also vary in the degree to which individuals are allowed to set their own work rate. In other words, some environments allow individuals more freedom to work at a self-selected rate than others. Individuals learn more easily and quickly when they are free to set their own pace in working the environment for the desired reward.

Many children are not able to function appropriately if they must wait an extended time for their reward. In addition, there are some children who have not developed to the level at which social rewards alone are satisfactory reinforcers. In these cases, the use of a token economy has proved to be an effective behavior change intervention.

The tokens are usually valueless to the children when originally introduced to them. Their value becomes apparent as the children learn that tokens can be exchanged for a variety of rewards, such as being first in the lunch line, getting 10 minutes of free time, listening to phonograph records, watching television, purchasing a favored toy, and so on. This versatility makes the token system superior to most interventions.

It is an accepted fact that the child who is first in line for lunch today may not wish to be first in line next week. A properly administered token economy adjusts to this human tendency by providing a variety of rewards.

When the teacher "sells" admission to a movie, use of Play-doh, or the like, the tokens rapidly take on value for the children. When the teacher states the price and asks a child to count out the needed quantity of tokens, they are engaged in a token economy.

In this manner, the tokens become potent reinforcers. They can be awarded over a period of time for acceptable academic and non-academic work. The system allows the teacher to structure the learning environment for positive reinforcement and to provide immediate feedback to the children via tokens. Hence, a moderately well run token exchange can promote direct learning regardless of the content of the activity.

We are all exposed to and use tokens daily. The most common form of token exchange is the use of currency to purchase various items and services. It is generally agreed (especially in today's economy) that money itself has no value; only the objects for which it is exchanged have real value. In the classroom, the token takes on the same meaning as currency has in the marketplace.

The classroom token economy suffers the same problems as the marketplace economy, that is, loss, theft, and counterfeiting. Some of these problems can be prevented by not using poker chips and other readily available objects for tokens.

For instance, what would you do if Joel came to your classroom every morning with his pockets filled with poker chips? Not only is Joel selling the chips to his classmates but they are constantly dropping them on the floor, a very distracting practice.

Items that could be utilized instead of poker chips include:

Check marks
Points
Stars
Smiling faces
Point cards
Point tally forms
Conservation stamps
Trading stamps
Animal stickers
Fairy tale character stickers
Teacher-made tokens
Play money

These tokens have several advantages over tokens made of rigid, hard materials such as metal, plastic, and wood. They are made of soft, flexible materials, that is, paper, vinyl, or simple pen and pencil markings. They are less distracting to have in the classroom atmosphere because they neither rattle nor make noise if dropped on a hard surface. These characteristics eliminate much potential and actual distraction and confusion in the classroom. The tokens are easily glued to a paper, desk top, record card, or chart. They can be permanently affixed to various surfaces to minimize the incidence of misplacement, loss, or theft. However, they must be sufficiently distinctive to prohibit unauthorized duplication.

There are ten basic rules to be applied when one is establishing a token economy system for the classroom:

1. Select a target behavior. This topic is thoroughly discussed in Chapter Two and does not warrant further elaboration here.
2. Conceptualize and present the desired behavior to the child or group. It is a well-known fact that an emphasis on "what you can do" is more palatable to children than an emphasis on "what you cannot do." Many unsuccessful behavior modification practitioners have determined their own failure by introducing a program by saying, "Now you boys and girls are going to stop that noise and fooling around in here. I have this new . . . [and so on]." The children are immediately challenged; they prepare to defeat the teacher and defend their personal integrity.
3. Select an appropriate token.
4. Establish rewards for which tokens can be exchanged.
5. Develop a reward menu and post it in the classroom. The children should be permitted to thoroughly discuss and consider the items on the menu. They should be encouraged to make their selections from among the items available. The children should not be permitted to debate the cost (number of tokens) of the various rewards after prices have been established.
6. Implement the token economy. Introduce the token economy on a limited basis, initially. A complex sophisticated system as an initial exposure confuses and frustrates the children. *Start small and build on firm understanding.* Explain the system to the children with great clarity and precision. Be patient and answer all the children's questions. It is better to delay implementation than create confusion and frustration.
7. Provide immediate reinforcement for acceptable behavior. The children will lose interest in the program if the process for obtaining the tokens is more effort than the reward is desirable. Many systems fail because the teacher neglects to dispense tokens at the appropriate time. Rewarding the children immediately reduces frustration and overconcern with the system. When the children are sure they will receive the tokens at the proper time, they can ignore the delivery system and concentrate on their work or behavior.
8. Gradually change from a continuous to a variable schedule of reinforcement. As discussed in Chapter Two, quick, unpredictable, or premature changes in a reinforcement schedule can destroy the program.
9. Provide time for the children to exchange tokens for rewards. If the token economy is a legitimate class program, time during the school day

should be made available for the exchange. Time should not be taken from the children's recess, lunch, or free time.

10. Revise the reward menu frequently. Children, like adults, become bored with the same old fare day after day.

The token economy has worked very effectively in the classroom. Two reasons for its success are its lack of emphasis on competition with others and the fact that the reward menu provides sufficient variety to prevent boredom.

Table 9 is an example of a reward menu for classroom use.

The menu need not be lengthy or elaborate but should contain at least ten items and activities. The children should cash in their tokens daily; they should not be allowed to take them home. If they are deferring their rewards and saving tokens for long-range ones, their tokens should be collected and recorded each day.

The number of tokens earned may be recorded on a point card or tally form. The teacher can affix the card or form to each child's desk and then either record or circle the points earned by the child. The points are totaled at the end of each day. The child may either delay the reward or accept it immediately.

Examples of the point card and tally form to be used for specific behaviors are presented below and on p. 72.

The teacher, with little difficulty, may plan

Table 9. Reward menu

Reward	Time	Cost (points)
Getting free time	10 minutes	20
Watching television	30 minutes	45
Reading comic books	5 minutes	15
Listening to records	10 minutes	20
Cutting and pasting	5 minutes	10
Purchasing modeling clay	—	55
Purchasing crayons	—	45
Purchasing coloring books	—	50
Fingerpainting	12 minutes	25
Playing with toys	10 minutes	25
Borrowing a book	48 hours	35
Borrowing a game	48 hours	50

Point Card*

Child's name _____ Date _____

1	2	3	4	5	6	7	8	9	10
11	12	13	14	15	16	17	18	19	20
21	22	23	24	25	26	27	28	29	30
31	32	33	34	35	36	37	38	39	40
41	42	43	44	45	46	47	48	49	50
51	52	53	54	55	56	57	58	59	60
61	62	63	64	65	66	67	68	69	70
71	72	73	74	75	76	77	78	79	80
81	82	83	84	85	86	87	88	89	90
91	92	93	94	95	96	97	98	99	100

*Teacher circles the cumulative total.

Point Tally Form

Child _____ Date _____

Monday												
Tuesday												
Wednesday												
Thursday												
Friday												

TOTAL

Monday	
Tuesday	
Wednesday	
Thursday	
Friday	
Week	

Point Card for Multipurpose Token Economy

Child _____ Day _____ Date _____

Work period	Readiness	Social behavior	Work effort	Work success	Teacher comments
9:00-9:15			⋆	⋆	
9:15-10:00					
10:00-10:30					
10:30-10:45			⋆	⋆	
10:45-11:30					
11:30-12:00					
12:00-1:00			⋆	⋆	
1:00-1:30					
1:30-2:45					
2:45-3:00			⋆	⋆	

⋆Points for work effort and work success are not available during these periods due to the nature of the activity: opening exercises, recess, lunch, and closing exercises.

and implement a multipurpose token economy in the classroom. In this situation the children earn tokens for a variety of appropriate social behaviors as well as academic effort and academic success.

Tokens or points can be presented to the child for any or all of the following behaviors:

Being present at the work station on time

Having appropriate work tools available for use

Attending to the instructor's directions

Exhibiting appropriate social behavior during the work period (raising hand for attention, remaining at the work station, not talking without permission)

Engaging in the assigned work task during the work period (that is, showing effort)

Correctly or satisfactorily completing the assigned work task

Returning or storing work tools to their appropriate place

Tokens can be presented for various appropriate behaviors and withheld for inappropriate and unacceptable behaviors.

A point card for a multipurpose token economy is presented on p. 73. Additional copies of each of the forms for recording points in a token economy are provided in tear-off form at the back of the text.

A special area should be set aside in the classroom to serve as a reinforcement area. This area should be selected before the token economy is implemented and should contain those items needed to provide the rewards. Among the items may be:

A table and chairs

A rug

Reading material (books, comics, magazines)

Art materials (clay, paint, paper, crayons)

Games (bingo, checkers, chess, cards)

Listening equipment (record player, tape deck)

Viewing equipment (television, slide or filmstrip projector)

Obviously, the furnishings, materials, and equipment in a reinforcement area must be selected in response to the age, physical size, developmental levels, and interests of the students using the area.

Fig. 12 is an illustration of a classroom with a reinforcement area.

EXAMPLE

Mr. Newman, a junior high school math teacher, was having difficulty with Charlie, who had developed the habit of counting and computing aloud while doing math assignments. At first, this behavior was not a serious problem, but then it began to distract many of the other students.

Mr. Newman decided to implement a token economy system to modify Charlie's behavior. He discussed the system with the class, established a set of rules, and developed a reward menu before implementing this intervention.

The reward menu is presented in Table 10.

The token economy was used with the entire class and effectively modified the behaviors of Charlie and his peers.

Tokens were initially presented on a fixed interval (FI) schedule: as the group progressed, however, a variable interval (VI) schedule was introduced. Throughout the program Mr. Newman consciously paired social rewards with the tokens.

EXAMPLE

Two physical education teachers were having problems with student participation in PE class. They were being bombarded with complaints such as headaches, back pains, sore toes, and sore ears. After discussing the token economy system of behavior modification between themselves and with their students, they decided to initiate a program to increase participation. A student delegation aided the teachers in developing the reward menu shown in Table 11.

In these two examples the economy system proved to be effective in increasing participation. In both cases the teachers changed the reward menu frequently in cooperation with their students throughout the duration of the program.

The token economy is an effective and usable intervention for changing behavior.

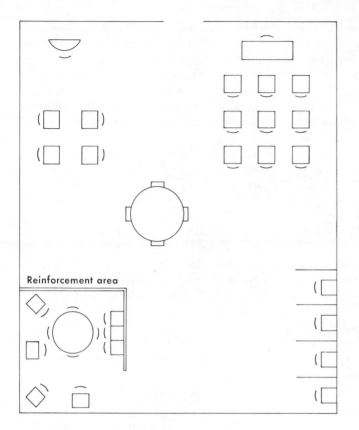

Fig. 12. Classroom with reinforcement area.

Table 10. Mr. Newman's reward menu

Reward	Time (minutes)	Cost (points)
Checkers	10	15
Cards	10	15
Puzzles	15	20
Magazines	18	25
Chess	12	30
Model car kits	10	20
Comic books	5	10
Bingo	15	25
Quiet conversation	10	30

Table 11. PE class reward menu

Reward	Time (minutes)	Cost (points)
Getting free time	15	50
Using trampoline	10	40
Shooting baskets	5	30
Acting as activity leader	—	25
Talking with friend	10	40
Playing badminton	10	30
Using trapeze	15	50
Sitting out an activity	—	100

SUMMARY

In this chapter the practitioner of behavior modification is provided with an overview of the four most common techniques utilized to increase appropriate behavior: (1) shaping, (2) contingency contracting, (3) modeling, and (4) the token economy.

Shaping is the reinforcement of successive approximations of the desired behavior. It is primarily used to establish behaviors that have not been previously manifested in the individual's behavioral repertoire. The steps in behavior shaping are (1) selecting a target behavior, (2) collecting baseline data, (3) selecting a reinforcer, (4) reinforcing successive approximations of the desired behavior, (5) reinforcing the approximations continuously and immediately, and (6) changing to a variable reinforcement schedule.

Modeling, one of the oldest and most frequently applied methods of behavior change, has been very effective in developing appropriate behaviors in children. Modeling is the provision of an individual or group behavior to be imitated by the child.

Contingency contracting involves the completion of X before you will be able to do Y. This process is actively utilized in day-to-day living. Contracts may be verbal or written. Verbal contracts are commonly used in schools, but written contracts are more appealing to the reluctant learner. When developing a contract, the practitioner should know the level of sophistication of the child or children with whom the contract is being negotiated. Contracting is more effective when the child is allowed to share in its development.

A token economy is a system of exchange. Children earn tokens that are exchanged for specific rewards. The tokens themselves are valueless; their value lies in the rewards for which they can be exchanged. There are a number of objects that can be used as tokens, such as checkmarks, points, smiling faces, stars, and other similar items. An important component of a token economy is the reward menu, which should be developed with the child or group.

EXERCISES FOR CHAPTER FOUR
Quiz*

1. The four most common techniques used to increase behavior are _____, _____, _____, and _____ .

2. The process of providing an example of behavior for imitation is known as _____ _____ .

3. Contracts may be either _____ or _____ .

4. Another term for rewarding successive approximations of appropriate behavior is _____ .

5. A schedule of rewards is referred to as a reward _____ .

6. A method of increasing behaviors that provides an exchange system of reinforcers is the _____ .

7. Mr. K. O'Shea tells his son, Tim, that when he cleans his bedroom, he can go outside to play. This is an example of a _____ .

8. Mr. Johnson has been rewarding Jim for his good attending behavior. He also rewards Martha, whose previously poor attending behavior has started to improve. He is using an intervention called _____ .

---

*Turn to Appendix A, p. 174, for answers.

9. Mr. Walker is constantly out-of-sorts and slapping his wife about the house. His son, Joshua, was reprimanded by the principal yesterday for slapping a classmate. Joshua is using his father as a _____ .

10. When Mary's mother says, "Mary, when you eat your spinach, you can have ice cream," she is making a _____ with Mary.

Projects

1. Select a desired behavior change and describe how you would implement each step of shaping the behavior.
2. Write two examples of modeling as a technique for increasing behaviors.
3. Develop and implement a contract for (a) an individual child in a class and (b) an entire class.
4. Develop a reward menu for your class.
5. Develop a token economy system.

REFERENCES

Bandura, A. *Principles of behavior modification*. New York: Holt, Rinehart & Winston, 1969.

Bandura, A., and Walters, R. H. *Social learning and personality development*. New York: Holt, Rinehart & Winston, 1963.

Becker, W. C. Introduction. In L. Homme and others (Eds.), *How to use contingency contracting in the classroom*. Champaign, Ill.: Research Press, 1969.

Clarizio, H. F., and Yelon, S. L. Learning theory approaches to classroom management: Rationale and intervention techniques. *Journal of Special Education*, 1967, *1*, 267-274.

Homme, L., Csanyi, A. P., Gonzales, M. A., and Rechs, J. R. *How to use contingency contracting in the classroom*. Champaign, Ill.: Research Press, 1969.

Neisworth, J. T., Deno, S. L., and Jenkins, J. R. *Student motivation and classroom management: A behavioristic approach*. Newark, Del.: Behavior Technics, 1969.

Panyan, M. C. *New ways to teach new skills*. Lawrence, Kan.: H & H Enterprises, Inc., 1972.

Premack, D. Reinforcement theory. In D. LeVine (Ed.), *Nebraska symposium on motivation: 1965*. Lincoln: University of Nebraska Press, 1965.

Shea, T. M., Whiteside, W. R., Beetner, E. G., and Lindsey, D. L. *Contingency contracting in the classroom*. Edwardsville: Southern Illinois University, 1974.

CHAPTER FIVE

Methods of decreasing behavior

During the course of a single school day a teacher may observe a number of behaviors that may either be decreased in frequency or eliminated. Examples of behaviors he may observe are:

Rusty's incessant talking

Richard's constant bullying

Mary's endless complaining

Barbara's inability to keep her hands off things and people

Martin's thumb sucking

In this chapter six methods of decreasing and eliminating behavior are discussed and exemplified. The suggested methods are (1) extinction, (2) time-out, (3) satiation, (4) punishment, (5) reinforcement of incompatible behaviors, and (6) desensitization.

EXTINCTION

The discontinuation or withholding of the reinforcer of a behavior that has previously been reinforcing it is called extinction. (This process is also discussed in Chapter Two.)

EXAMPLE

Timmy was constantly attempting to obtain Mr. Calm's attention in class by jumping up and down in his seat, frantically waving his hand and whispering in a loud voice, "Mr. Calm, Mr. Calm, me, me, I know."

Mr. Calm knew he would have to change his name to Mr. Storm if this behavior did not stop or at least decrease in frequency. In an effort to retain his compo-

sure and aid Timmy, he commenced to study the situation.

Baseline observation data indicated that Timmy exhibited the target behavior an average of 8 times per day, or 40 times during the 1-week baseline data–collecting phase. During this phase Mr. Calm also collected data on his personal overt reactions to the unacceptable behavior. He discovered that 90% of the time he responded to the behavior by either permitting Timmy to answer the question, telling the child to be quiet and sit still, or signaling his disapproval nonverbally. Regardless of his specific reaction, Mr. Calm realized that he was *attending* to Timmy's attention-getting behavior.

Mr. Calm devised an intervention whereby he *would not* reinforce the behavior with his attention and would thus extinguish it. He would only respond to Timmy when he was exhibiting acceptable behavior in response to questions directed to the class.

As indicated in Fig. 13, the behavior was extinguished within 2 weeks, although there were brief periods of regression thereafter.

Timmy's behavior (attempts to obtain attention) increased during the days immediately following the implementation of the intervention. This increase in the target behavior appeared to be an attempt by the child to defend his method for obtaining attention against the loss of effectiveness. This phenomenon is discussed in detail in Chapter Two, and the reader is referred to that section for further clarification.

As demonstrated in the case of Timmy, extinction techniques, when properly applied, result in a gradual decrease in the target behavior and its eventual elimination.

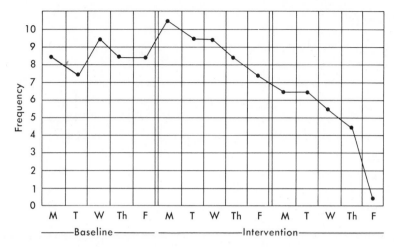

Fig. 13. Frequency of Timmy's attention-getting behavior before and during the intervention.

Extinction is only as effective as the practitioner is consistent and persistent in implementation of the intervention.

TIME-OUT

Time-out is the removal of a child from an apparently reinforcing setting to a presumably nonreinforcing setting for a specified and limited period of time. Such removal can effectively decrease a target behavior.

EXAMPLE

Benji is a hyperactive child in first grade. The boy was having great difficulty remaining in his seat and refraining from impulsive grabbing of persons and objects near him. He was also appropriating and ingesting his classmates' lunches. Benji's teacher realized that these behaviors were interfering with his classroom progress and that of his classmates. She attempted several procedures to help Benji control the behavior. Among these were verbal reprimands, ignoring the inappropriate behavior and reinforcing appropriate behavior, and peer pressure. Observation data revealed that none of these interventions were effective, although her efforts were sufficient.

A behavior management consultant observed Benji and recommended time-out as a potentially effective intervention. Together, the teacher and the consultant decided that *each time Benji left his seat, he was to be timed-out for 2 minutes.*

This intervention necessitated defining and specifying several factors:

1. Out-of-seat behavior was defined as any time Benji's posterior was not in contact with his chair.
2. When the unacceptable behavior did occur, the teacher's aide was to escort Benji to the time-out area. Benji was to remain in time-out for 2 minutes; during this time he had to be quiet and seated.
3. After the time-out period Benji would return to the group. There would be no discussion or reprimand.
4. Benji's desk and chair were relocated in the classroom to ensure that he could not participate in unacceptable behavior such as grabbing people and lunches without leaving his seat.
5. A time-out area with a chair was arranged in the corner of the classroom. The time-out area was constructed by rearranging two five-drawer filing cabinets. A chair was provided outside the area for the aide, who was to monitor Benji whenever he was in time-out.

The intervention was imposed, and although the behavior did not decrease immediately, significant progress was observed during the first months, as indicated in Figs. 14 and 15.

Benji's out-of-seat behavior was brought under control within a period of several months. However, it remains an occasional problem; therefore, time-out procedures remain in effect.

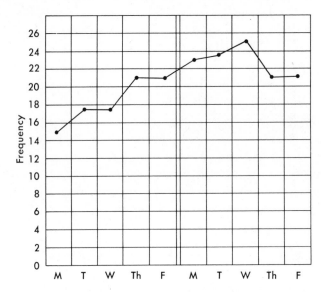

Fig. 14. Frequency of Benji's out-of-seat behavior before and during the first week of intervention.

The time-out intervention should include the reinforcement of acceptable behavior. A child who is performing or approximating the desired behavior in the classroom should be reinforced for these efforts.

The effectiveness of time-out as an intervention is contingent on several factors:

Characteristics of the individual child

Teacher's consistent application of the intervention

Child's understanding of the rules of time-out

Characteristics of the time-out area

Duration of time-out

Evaluation of the effectiveness of the intervention

Characteristics of the child

The practitioner must know the characteristics of the individual child before implementing a time-out intervention. For the acting-out, aggressive, group-oriented child, time-out may be very effective. Such children personally want very much to be with the group and attended to by the teacher.

Consequently, the time-out area is not a rewarding place. However, for a withdrawn, passive, solitary child who is prone to daydreaming, the time-out area may be rewarding, and this intervention would be contraindicated. These children may engage in their own little world while in the time-out area.

EXAMPLE

Cheryl, a 6-year-old girl, is in Mr. Roy's class for behaviorally handicapped children. Cheryl is quiet, shy, and withdrawn; she frequently engages in daydreaming.

Mr. Roy read about a new technique for behavior problems in a popular magazine. This technique was time-out. He decided to impose the intervention on Cheryl in an effort to force her to participate in class discussions and activities. He planned to put her in time-out each time she was inattentive in class.

Cheryl appeared to enjoy the opportunity to go to time-out for 3 minutes. Her rate of inattentiveness increased dramatically immediately after the intervention was implemented. She evidently appreciated the opportunity to legitimately participate in her dream world.

This example is a stark illustration of an abuse of time-out by its use with a child

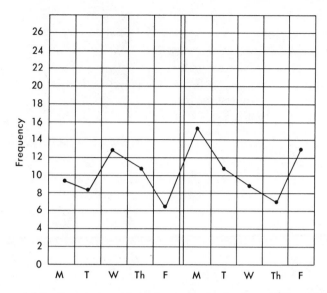

Fig. 15. Frequency of Benji's out-of-seat behavior during the fourth and fifth weeks of intervention.

whose unacceptable behavior was reinforced by the intervention.

EXAMPLE

Richard, an 11-year-old boy in Ms. Jone's physical education class, was constantly arguing and fighting with his teacher and classmates about the rules of a game or how an activity should be conducted. This behavior occurred particularly when he was losing. Observation indicated that Richard truly enjoyed the activities and the company of his peers and Ms. Jones. However, the behavior was obtrusive and had to be eliminated for the sake of the group.

Ms. Jones selected time-out as a potentially effective intervention. Before the technique was imposed, it was decided that each time Richard started to argue or fight during PE he was to be timed-out. The time-out area was out of view but not out of hearing of class activities. Under these conditions Richard's disruptions were eliminated very rapidly.

Time-out in this situation was effective because Richard preferred to be with his classmates and teacher rather than in the less stimulating time-out area.

Teacher's consistency of application

If time-out is to be applied as an intervention with a particular child, it must be uti-lized with consistency over a predetermined period of time. Frequently, teachers are inconsistent in their application of time-out. As a result, the child becomes confused and the target behavior is unwittingly reinforced. This situation is analogous to the confusion that results when a child is forced on Monday, Wednesday, and Friday to eat green vegetables under pain of death at the hands of Father; but on Tuesday and Thursday Father is not so insistent; and on the weekend at Grandma's house, the child does not have to eat green vegetables at all.

Child's understanding of the rules

Children should know specifically what behaviors are not acceptable in their classrooms. In addition, they should know the consequences for exhibiting the forbidden behaviors. If time-out is to be used as an intervention, the rules for time-out should be communicated to the children; they should be posted and reviewed frequently. The rules will assist the teacher in trying to remain consistent and fair in the application of the intervention.

Time-out should never be used whimsically with children; that is, one day a child is timed-out for talking in class, the next day for chewing gum, the next day for not completing a homework assignment, and so on. Such misuse will confuse the child and reduce the effectiveness of the intervention.

When time-out is imposed on the behavior of very young children or severely emotionally disturbed children, the teacher is often confronted with an additional problem. Frequently it is impossible to verbally communicate to such children the rules governing time-out and its imposition. In this situation it is necessary to initiate the program and demonstrate the intervention through implementation.

Whether the reason is communicated verbally or by demonstration, children should understand why they are being placed in time-out.

Time-out is not a technique that includes lecturing, reprimanding, or scolding before, during, or after the intervention. These techniques, although frequently used in everyday classroom exchanges, can provide unwanted reinforcement to the child. Time must be taken to explain why time-out is warranted, but the explanation should be brief and explicit. Going to time-out should not be a matter for debate between child and teacher. As the program continues, these explanations need only be reminders of the rules and consequences of exhibiting certain behaviors.

EXAMPLE

Ms. Smith selected time-out as an intervention to decrease Elmo's talking in class. Each time Elmo talked out of turn in class, Ms. Smith would grab him by the arm and drag him to the time-out area. There she would proceed to babble at him (rather incoherently) for about 10 minutes. She would always conclude with the statement, "Now, shut up for 2 minutes." She would then proceed to stare at Elmo for 2 minutes. At the end of that time she would say, "Now, get back to your seat."

Ms. Smith's intervention is an example of the im-

proper use of timeout. The results were as expected:

1. Elmo continued to talk out in class because, although he was not particularly interested in Ms. Smith's lectures, he was pleased with his classmates' reactions to her behavior.
2. Ms. Smith's classroom group certainly enjoyed the circus.
3. Ms. Smith suffered from nervous tension.

Characteristics of the time-out area

Care must be taken in the selection of the time-out area. Teachers should avoid selecting an area that may appear nonreinforcing but is in effect reinforcing to a particular child. For instance, placing a child in the corridor for time-out may be extremely reinforcing. In the hallway the child has an opportunity to communicate with everyone who passes. In addition, the child is provided with a legitimate opportunity to get out of the classroom and assignments.

Another commonly used but generally ineffective area for time-out is the principal's office. The office has been demonstrated to be one of the most stimulating and reinforcing areas in the school for the majority of children. In the office the child has an opportunity to observe peaked parents, out-of-sorts mailmen, and anxious administrators in their natural human state. In addition, the child has opportunities to pick up the latest school news and gossip for dissemination among peers and teachers.

Many administrators do not understand the concept of time-out, and on occasion, the child is given various clerical tasks to perform in the office, such as stapling, folding, carrying messages, and making announcements. The timed-out child just happens to be available when a body is needed to do something; the reason for the child's presence in the office is not considered when the task is assigned.

An investigation of the use of the office for time-out would probably reveal that it is a far more attractive alternative for the child than sitting in the classroom reading, writing, or doing math problems.

The time-out area should be as nonreinforcing to the child as possible. The area should be devoid of all visual and aural stimulation, and in the case of severely disturbed children, tactile variations.

In most classroom settings it is not necessary to construct a time-out room, although this practice is followed in many special classes for severely emotionally disturbed children. A chair in an out-of-the-way corner of the classroom is adequate. In some rooms room dividers, screens, filing cabinets or the backs of bookcases can be arranged to construct the walls of the time-out area. It is necessary to ensure that the area is supervised, safe, properly lighted, and ventilated. A chair may be placed in the time-out area. However, many children, especially young children, prefer to sit on the floor, and this practice should be permitted.

The area selected should be (1) away from high traffic, (2) away from doors and windows, (3) out of the other children's view, and (4) within view of the observer-supervisor.

It is recommended that a chair be placed outside the area for the observer-supervisor. A teacher's aide can serve as observer-supervisor if properly instructed. However, in cases where an aide is not available for this duty, the area must be in a location that permits the teacher to observe it from his or her teaching station. Fig. 16 is a diagram of a time-out area in a classroom.

Duration of time-out

Time-out loses its effectiveness as an intervention if a child is left in the setting for too lengthy or too brief a period of time. Time-out should be limited to approximately 2 minutes after the child has quieted. Four or 5 minutes in time-out should be maximum except under extraordinary circumstances. Never should a child remain in time-out for

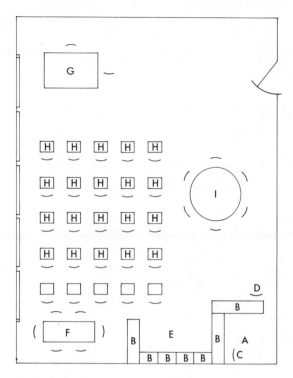

Fig. 16. Classroom with time-out area. *A*, time-out area; *B*, bookcase; *C*, child's chair; *D*, supervisor's chair; *E*, library; *F*, science or game area; *G*, teacher's station; *H*, students' desks; and *I*, discussion center.

more than 10 minutes. It is strongly recommended that the practitioner use a bell-type or inexpensive egg timer to ensure that the time limit of time-out is not violated. The timer alerts both the teacher and the child to the exact moment the time-out period expires. In addition, it reassures the child that the teacher is being fair in the application of the intervention.

Evaluation of effectiveness

Records of time-out incidents should be collected and analyzed by the practitioner. Teachers should prepare a log such as the one on the following page. Additional copies of this log are provided in tear-off form at the back of the text.

Time-out Log

Child _____

Supervisor _____

Date _____

Time		Behavior before time-out	Behavior during time-out	Behavior after time-out
Enters	Leaves			

The log should include (1) the time the child was sent or escorted to the time-out area, (2) the time the child returned to the activity, (3) any incidents during the time-out period, (4) the activity taking place just prior to the child's being timed-out, and (5) the activity to which the child returned after time-out.

The log should be posted on the exterior wall of the time-out area. The practitioner evaluates the overall effectiveness of the technique by studying the child's time-out record. In addition, the records, if closely analyzed, provide clues as to why time-out is an effective or ineffective intervention in a particular case.

EXAMPLE

Mr. Sherman was recently called to a day school for severely disturbed boys to consult on the case of Hector, a 14-year-old student with a behavior problem. When Hector enrolled in the school 2 years ago, he was exposed to time-out as a behavior control intervention. During the following 2 years time-out was effective in modifying much of Hector's behavior.

The boy had progressed to a point of being timed out on an average of only once each day. However, he had never progressed beyond this point. His daily disruption prohibited his integration into a regular classroom.

Fortunately, at the day school precise time-out records were maintained for all children and were available for study. An analysis of Hector's log indicated that he was timed-out each day immediately after the teacher announced that it was time for math. Although math time varied, it was discovered that Hector's disruptive time varied with it.

Mr. Sherman suggested that for Hector, time-out was more reinforcing than math; that is, it was the lesser of two evils. In an effort to test this hypothesis, Hector's math period was eliminated; Hector no longer went to time-out.

Hector's skill in math has progressed acceptably under the guidance of a tutor. The tutor assists him individually during regular math periods.

It is highly recommended that the child return to the task that was interrupted by the time-out intervention. Of course, the feasibility of the child's returning to the inter-

rupted task will vary with the structure of the class schedule and activities.

If the child is returned to and held responsible for the task being engaged in prior to time-out, the child learns that time-out cannot be used as a means of avoiding assignments he or she finds difficult or simply dislikes. This recommendation assumes that the assigned task is appropriate to the child's learning level and competency.

The following examples will further clarify the process of time-out.

EXAMPLE

Ms. Drake was confronted with the problem of Donald striking other children in the stomach. She was so distressed by this behavior that she was about to reciprocate in kind. Ms. Drake had tried every intervention she knew to change the behavior (and a few she didn't know she knew), but they only increased it.

At an in-service workshop time-out as a technique to decrease inappropriate behavior was described. After absorbing the available knowledge about time-out and becoming somewhat comfortable with the concept, Ms. Drake implemented it in her classroom.

First, a set of "classroom rules of behavior" were presented to the children. Next, a time-out area was designed, and the concept of time-out was introduced and explained to the group.

The new rules included "Do not strike other children." Persons exhibiting this behavior would be timed-out for 3 minutes in an area located in a corner of the classroom. The area was screened off, devoid of visual stimuli, and unfurnished with the exception of a chair. A child in time-out could neither see nor be seen by classmates (Fig. 16). After the rules were communicated and apparently understood by all the members of the class, time-out was implemented.

When Donald struck another child, he was quietly escorted to the time-out area for 3 minutes. After sitting quietly in the area for that period of time, Donald was asked why he was timed-out. If his response indicated that he understood the reason, he was instructed to return to his regular seat. However, if his response indicated that he did not understand the reason for being sent to time-out, it was briefly explained to him. He was then instructed to return to his seat. After several repetitions of the time-out routine (appropriate behavior was reinforced), both Donald and Ms. Drake became aware of the potency of the intervention.

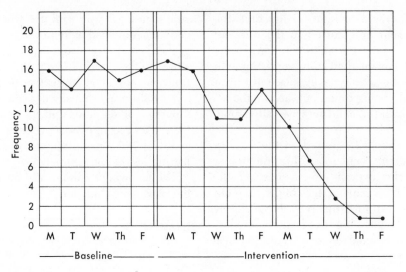

Fig. 17. Frequency of Donald's striking behavior before and during the intervention.

Donald's baseline and intervention data are presented in Fig. 17.

EXAMPLE

Mr. Seltz had used every method possible to decrease Shauna's unacceptable burping behavior in the classroom. Finally, time-out was used as a technique to eliminate this behavior. Shauna was told that each time she burped in class she was to go to the time-out area for 2 minutes. Mr. Seltz reinforced Shauna with attention and praise whenever she performed appropriately in the class. The baseline and intervention data for the behavior are presented in Fig. 18. The data clearly indicate that Shauna preferred to cease burping rather than be timed out.

As indicated in the examples, time-out can work effectively if it is properly applied. When implementing a program, the new practitioner of behavior modification should adhere closely to the suggestions in this section.

SATIATION

Satiation is the decreasing or elimination of an unacceptable behavior as a result of continued and increased reinforcement of the behavior.

Satiation is a more common occurrence than is generally realized. Because it is so common, we are frequently unaware of its effect on our behavior.

Many of us engage in certain sports and recreational activities (golf, baseball, camping, cards, and the like) with such frequency and regularity that we become satiated; that is, we discontinue the activity.

Some of us smoke, often in excess. Mr. Don, a book editor, was a 2- or 3-pack-a-day smoker. He honestly and sincerely wished to stop smoking. His self-selected intervention was to smoke continuously until he was satiated. He made himself ill and as a result stopped smoking (the hard way but perhaps for him the only way).

Bobby loved (not just liked, but loved) chocolate ice cream. He would snitch it from the freezer any time of the day or night. His wife, Louise, scolded and deprived him in an effort to decrease his intake. One day, with great ceremony Louise presented Bobby with 2 gallons of chocolate ice cream. He was given ice cream at every opportunity, day and night, until he became ill. Bobby now prefers gelatin.

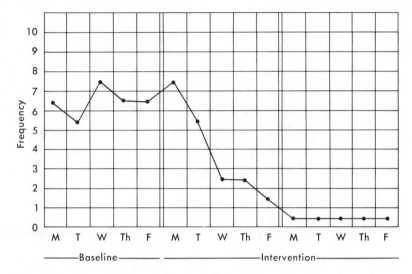

Fig. 18. Frequency of Shauna's burping behavior before and during the intervention.

We all have remembrances from our college days of the class hero who wished to gain immortality in the books on world records. This individual is the one who today hates bananas, pizza, blueberry pie, goldfish, raw eggs, frankfurters, and a score of other edibles.

Perhaps everyone reaches the point of satiation in relation to some behavior. Grandma used to call this phenomenon "getting too much of a good thing."

The continued and increased reinforcement of a behavior can result in a decrease in that behavior. The central factor that influences the effectiveness of satiation as an intervention is the reinforcement schedule.

As discussed in Chapter Two, a variable reinforcement schedule is more resistant to satiation than a fixed reinforcement schedule. Consequently, the key to successful application of satiation as an intervention is a *fixed reinforcement schedule*.

The following example will clarify the application of a satiation intervention in the classroom.

EXAMPLE

Charles, a student in Ms. Barker's classroom, stole paper from his teacher's and classmates' desks. Ms. Barker wanted to decrease this behavior. She tried techniques such as reprimanding, parent counseling, and having Charles counseled by the school psychologist. Nothing appeared to work. The school psychologist suggested trying a satiation procedure. Ms. Barker was impressed and willing to try any technique that might prove successful. She decided to implement the satiation program.

She placed a ream of paper on her desk at the beginning of the school day. After the children had arrived and morning exercises were completed, Ms. Barker gave Charles 3 sheets of paper. Four minutes later she returned to Charles's desk and gave him 3 more sheets of paper; 4 minutes later Charles received 3 more sheets of paper and so on throughout the day. This process continued day after day until Charles's possession of paper lost its value to him. Charles began to tell Ms. Barker that he did not need or want any paper; he had more than he could use to complete his assignments for the next 6 months. Fig. 19 presents the baseline and intervention data for Charles's stealing behavior.

Charles's behavior was placed on a fixed reinforcement schedule. The behavior rapidly decreased because of satiation.

The process of satiation can be a very helpful tool in decreasing certain inappropriate

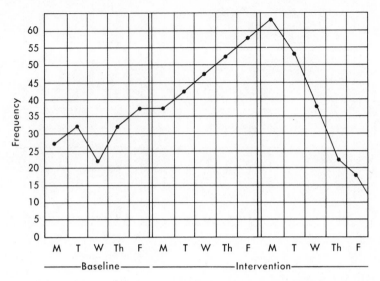

Fig. 19. Frequency of Charles's stealing behavior before and during the intervention.

classroom behaviors, such as pencil sharpening, putting paper in the wastebasket, getting drinks of water, and constantly requesting the time.

PUNISHMENT

Briefly discussed in Chapter Two, punishment is perhaps the most misunderstood and emotionally explosive of the behavior modification techniques. It is an intervention used to decrease or eliminate an unacceptable behavior.

There are two distinct forms of punishment that the practitioner can consider for application with students. As commonly understood and applied by parents and teachers, punishment is the *addition* of an aversive stimulus as a consequence of an unacceptable behavior. Punishment of this form can be either physical or psychological. Examples are a spanking (physical punishment) or a scolding, extra work, after school detention, or an undesirable additional task (psychological punishment).

The other form of punishment is the *subtraction* of something the child perceives as desirable. Examples are the taking away of television privileges, late bedtime hours, freedom to leave the house, or tokens and points.

The subtraction of previously earned tokens or points in the token economy intervention presented in Chapter Four is called response-cost. In this situation students are informed that not only can they earn points for privileges and goods but if they exhibit specific unacceptable behaviors, they can lose points. A specific number of points are subtracted from the total for each transgression. In a word, the child is punished for exhibiting specific unacceptable behaviors.

Punishment by deprivation or response-cost is generally considered less harmful to the child and a more effective intervention than the addition of physical or psychological aversive stimuli.

The short-term effectiveness of punishment for decreasing unacceptable behaviors is difficult if not impossible to dispute. Punishment *is effective* for obtaining short-term goals. However, other interventions such as extinction and ignoring the behavior are probably more effective for attaining permanent long-range changes.

Clarizio and Yelon (1967) have presented several logical reasons for avoiding the use of punishment:

1. It does not eliminate but merely suppresses the behavior.
2. It does not provide a model for the acceptable behavior to be emitted.
3. Aggression on the part of the practitioner presents an undesirable model.
4. The emotional results of punishment may be fear, tension, stress, or withdrawal.
5. The child's resulting frustration may result in further deviation.

In addition, physical punishment may result in physical harm to the child, even though such harm may be unplanned.

Punishment in the perception of the punished child is frequently associated with the punisher rather than with the unacceptable behavior. As a result, the punished child's reactions may be avoidance and dislike of the punisher rather than a change in behavior. Teachers who acknowledge that they are in effect behavioral models for their students will avoid assuming the role of punisher.

It may be helpful at this point to clarify some of the punishments that are frequently applied in school and homes. The following is a list of commonly used punishments:

Denying participation in scheduled activities (games, field trips)

Denying snacks (milk, cookies, candy)

Physical punishment (paddlings, spankings, slaps)

Verbal punishment (scoldings, reprimands, sarcasm, derogation, curses)

Having the child stand apart from the others (in the corner, hallway)

Having the child wear a sign ("I am a bad boy.")

As members of the teaching profession, we seem to be very efficient in developing and applying harsh physical and psychological punishment of a negative nature. However, a variety of other methods of behavior management are available for the teacher's use. Punishment, especially harsh physical and psychological punishment, should be a last resort if it is used at all.

If punishment is to be used, the practitioner should adhere to the following guidelines:

1. Specify and communicate the punishable behavior to the children by means of classroom rules for behavior.
2. Post the rules where the children can see them, and review them with the group frequently.
3. Provide models of acceptable behavior.
4. Apply the punishment immediately.
5. Apply the punishment consistently, not whimsically.
6. Be fair in using the punishment (what is good for Peter is good for Paul).

The following are examples of the misuse of punishment.

EXAMPLE

Paul, an 11-year-old boy in Ms. Wood's classroom, was constantly punching other boys during recess. Ms. Woods told Paul he would receive two swats with the paddle each time he hit another child.

Paul went to morning recess and within 10 minutes had punched three children and the playground supervisor. Paul was returned to the classroom. Nothing was said or done about his behavior.

About 2:30 PM, Mr. Brinks, the assistant principal, arrived at the classroom door. Paul was called into the hallway. Mr. Brinks struck him eight times with the paddle (two swats for each person). Ms. Woods observed the punishment as a witness.

After accomplishing this task, Mr. Brinks returned to his office without comment; Ms. Woods returned to the classroom without comment; Paul returned to his seat, crying and confused.

The absurdity of this example is that it happened at all and continues to happen.

EXAMPLE

Mr. Sayers is a master at applying sarcasm and degradation. He is quick and devastating with his tongue, much to the discomfort of his students. His favorite epithets are "stupid," "dumbbell," "idiot," "meathead," and "dink."

One day Rosemary was fooling around in English class. This behavior greatly disturbed Mr. Sayers. He grabbed 17-year-old Rosemary by the arm, shook her, and called her a "dink." The girl was very embarrassed and began to cry. Encouraged by her reaction, Mr. Sayers added a few more names to the list and caused the other students to laugh.

This is an example of a teacher losing self-control and perhaps causing psychological damage to a student. Mr. Sayers was unaware, or so he claimed, of the contemporary meaning of "dink." However, Rosemary and her peers were very aware of its meaning.

We are irrevocably opposed to the use of corporal punishment, whether it is paddling, slapping, spanking, or using a cattle prod or electric wand. We are also opposed to psychological punishment, which at minimum can erode the already fragile self-concept of the developing child.

There are many logical reasons to avoid the use of physical and psychological punishments. The following are adapted from the Committee to End Violence (1974):

1. It is unnecessary. Other, as effective and more effective, behavior management techniques are available.
2. It can physically and psychologically damage the child.
3. It creates in the child resentment and dislike of the punisher. Many nonpunishing teachers suffer strained relationships with many children because the children have, after a harsh experience, classified all teachers as punishers.
4. It teaches the child that might is right. After so many years of national and world disorder, the citizenry in all probability is aware that many contemporary social problems are a result of the inappropriate models provided to our children.
5. It teaches the child that it is better to be dishonest and evasive because to be caught or even to be wrong results in punishment.
6. It is inconsistent with the national

view of the child as a precious national resource and an individual worthy of respect and dignity.

7. It is a violation of the individual human and constitutional rights of the child.
8. It is damaging to the image of the individual teacher and all persons within the teaching profession.
9. It frequently destroys present and future opportunities to develop positive communication with the child.
10. It encourages aggressive behavior in the child.
11. Slaps or spankings may escalate to the battering of a child.
12. It can result in psychological pathology.
13. It increases anxiety in the punished child and the other children in the environment.
14. It negatively affects the child's ability to concentrate on positive and meaningful academic and nonacademic activities.

REINFORCEMENT OF INCOMPATIBLE BEHAVIORS

At times it is necessary or desirable to decrease a behavior by systematically reinforcing a behavior that is in opposition to or incompatible with the target behavior. This intervention is called the process of reinforcing incompatible behaviors.

For instance, a teacher has two students in the classroom who are constantly bickering with each other. After analysis of the situation, it is proposed that the behavior would decrease if one of the students' seats were relocated to the opposite side of the room. The students are separated, and the behavior decreases.

The assumption underlying the intervention in this example is that the distance between the seats is incompatible with the bickering.

The effectiveness of this intervention is heavily dependent on the selection of the two incompatible behaviors (sitting apart and bickering).

EXAMPLE

For a major part of the school year Mr. Weber had been trying to decrease Wallace's random walking about the classroom. All efforts appeared to have been in vain. It seemed that the more effort Mr. Weber put forth to modify Wallace's out-of-seat behavior, the more frequent it became. Evidently, the attention Wallace received from Mr. Weber for being out of his seat was reinforcing.

As a last resort, Mr. Weber decided to attempt the technique of reinforcing incompatible behaviors. To remain in one's seat would be incompatible with walking about the classroom. Mr. Weber decided to positively reinforce Wallace's in-seat behavior and ignore his out-of-seat behavior. Initially, Wallace resisted the program. However, after a short time the out-of-seat behavior decreased and was eventually eliminated. Fig. 20 represents the data collected on Wallace's behavior.

There is no known explanation for the recurrence of Wallace's out-of-seat behavior on the sixteenth and seventeenth days of the intervention. One possible explanation is that since the target behavior had not been exhibited for 2 days, Mr. Weber acted as though the behavior had been eliminated. He may have altered his response to either the behavior he was reinforcing or the behavior he was ignoring.

The classroom teacher could probably think of a number of other situations wherein reinforcing an incompatible behavior might decrease a target behavior.

DESENSITIZATION

Desensitization, the process of systematically lessening a specific, learned fear or phobic reaction in an individual became a popular therapeutic technique in the second half of the 1970s. It was developed by Wolpe during the 1950s and 1960s.

The desensitization method consists of presenting to the imagination of the deeply relaxed patient the feeblest item in a list of anxiety-evoking stimuli repeatedly, until no more anxiety is evoked. The next item of the list is presented, and so on, until eventually, even the strongest of the anxiety-evoking stimuli fails to evoke any stir of anxiety in the patient. It has consistently been found that at every stage a stimulus that evokes no anxiety when imagined in a state of relaxation will also evoke no anxiety when encountered in reality.*

---

*From Wolpe, J. The systematic densitization treatment of neuroses. *Journal of Nervous and Mental Diseases,* 1961, *132,* 189-203, © 1961, The Williams & Wilkins Co., Baltimore.

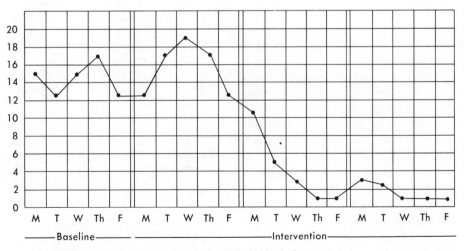

Fig. 20. Frequency of Wallace's out-of-seat behavior before and during the intervention.

As indicated by Wolpe, the process of desensitization has been demonstrated to be an effective technique when applied to individuals with fears and anxieties related to public speaking, school attendance, participation in large groups, water, animals, heights, flying, test-taking, and the like.

The process of systematic desensitization, according to Wolpes, involves three phases or steps:

1. Training the subject in deep muscle relaxation
2. Constructing an anxiety-evoking hierarchy of stimuli
3. Counterposing relaxation and the anxiety-evoking stimuli

The importance of these three phases can not be overemphasized; they are interdependent.

The new practitioner of behavior modification is *not* encouraged to apply systematic desensitization on the basis of the information provided in this text alone. The practitioner should study other sources and obtain the services of a behavior therapy consultant before implementing a desensitization intervention.

The following reports of research are presented to clarify the procedures and effects of systematic desensitization under various conditions with a variety of problems.

Kravetz and Forness (1971) reported an experiment with a 6½-year-old boy who was unable to verbalize in the classroom. Psychiatric and medical reports did not reveal any known reason for his not talking in the classroom. The child's school progress was poor; however, test results indicated that he had above-average potential. A desensitization intervention of 12 sessions (2 per week) was implemented to reduce the child's fear of speaking in class.

The anxiety-evoking stimulus hierarchy used in this study is presented here:

1. Reading alone to investigator;
2. Reading alone to roommate;
3. Reading to two classroom aides (repeated);
4. Reading to teacher and classroom aides (repeated);
5. Reading to teacher, classroom aides, and small group of classroom peers (repeated);
6. Reading to entire class.
7. Asking question or making comment at weekly ward meeting when all patients, teachers, and staff were present.*

The reader should note that Steps 3, 4, and 5 were repeated during the behavior change process.

This desensitization program, combined with positive reinforcement, was successful in helping the boy overcome his fear of verbalizing in the classroom.

Deffenbacher and Kemper (1974) applied systematic desensitization in a program to reduce test-taking anxiety in 28 junior high school students. The group was composed of 12 girls and 16 boys. All of the students had been referred by either a counselor, their parents, or a teacher. The test-taking anxiety-evoking stimulus hierarchy used with these students included:

You are attending a regular class session.
You hear about someone who has a test.
You are studying at home. You are reading a normal assignment.
You are in class. The teacher announces a major exam in two weeks.
You are at home studying. You are beginning to review and study for a test that is a week away.
You are at home studying, and you are studying

---

*Reprinted from The special classroom as a desensitization setting by R. Kravetz and S. Forness, *Exceptional Children*, 1971, 37, 389-391, by permission of The Council for Exceptional Children; copyright 1971 by the Council for Exceptional Children, 1920 Association Drive, Reston, Va. 22091.

for the important test. It is now Tuesday and three days before the test on Friday.

You are at home studying and preparing for the upcoming exam. It is now Wednesday, two days before the test on Friday.

It is Thursday night, the night before the exam on Friday. You are talking with another student about the exam tomorrow.

It is the night before the exam, and you are home studying for it.

It is the day of the exam, and you have one hour left to study.

It is the day of the exam. You have been studying. You are now walking on your way to the test.

You are standing outside the test room talking with other students about the upcoming test.

You are sitting in the testing room waiting for the test to be passed out.

You are leaving the exam room, you are talking with other students about the test. Many of their answers do not agree with yours.

You are sitting in the classroom waiting for the graded test to be passed back by the teacher.

It's right before the test, and you hear a student ask a possible test question which you cannot answer.

You are taking the important test. While trying to think of an answer, you notice everyone around you writing rapidly.

While taking the test you come to a question you are unable to answer. You draw a blank.

You are in the important exam. The teacher announces 30 minutes remaining but you have an hour's work left.

You are in the important exam. The teacher announces 15 minutes remaining but you have an hour's work left.*

The desensitization treatment consisted of eight sessions (one per week) in groups of two to five students. The intervention effectively reduced test-taking anxiety.

Another interesting experiment with students having test-taking anxiety was conducted by Beck (1972). The investigator provided videotaped scenes for application in the densensitization process. The videotaped stimulus hierarchy included:

1. Scene of a typical place of study with books and papers in disarray on the desk.
2. Scene of person tossing and turning in bed the night before the examination is to be given.
3. Scene of person nervously awakening and trying to get ready for class. He is experiencing increasing anxiety as the time for the examination is nearing.
4. Scene of person gathering together his books and leaving for class while trying to recall everything studied the night before.
5. Scene of a typical classroom with students talking nervously before class. The instructor enters carrying the examination.
6. In the same classroom the instructor picks up the pile of examinations and commences to distribute them to the students.
7. Scene of students receiving the examinations with close-up shots of an examination paper being nervously rustled by anxious student.
8. Close-up of time slipping by as anxious student writes frantically on examination paper.
9. Time running out as the last of the students finish the examination and begin leaving the classroom. Instructor waiting impatiently for the last student to finish. Close-up of student feverishly trying to finish and becoming more nervous as he tries harder.*

---

*From Deffenbacher, J., and Kemper, C. Systematic desensitization of test anxiety in junior high students. *The School Counselor*, 1974, *21*, 216-222. Copyright 1974, American Personnel and Guidance Association. Reprinted with permission.

*Reprinted with permission from *Journal of Behavior Therapy and Experimental Psychiatry*, *3*, T. Beck, Videotape scenes for desensitization of test anxiety, Copyright 1972, Pergamon Press, Ltd.

This self-administered videotaped desensitization intervention was effective in reducing test-taking anxiety.

Parrino (1971) applied systematic desensitization to reduce the frequency of the grand mal seizures of a 36-year-old man. It was determined by observation that the seizures were triggered by specific anxiety-provoking situations such as:

Socializing with fellow patients

Meeting persons in authority

Initiating conversations with acquaintances

Interacting with female patients who were harassing him

Hearing family-related material such as his wife's or his child's name

The desensitization sessions, which lasted for 15 weeks, focused on the following anxiety-evoking stimulus hierarchy:

A person you recognize appears in the unit.

The acquaintance is having a conversation with a staff member.

The acquaintance looks in your direction.

The acquaintance and you make eye contact.

The acquaintance smiles at you from across the room.

The acquaintance starts walking towards you.

The acquaintance is getting very close to you.

The acquaintance extends his hand to you.

You shake hands with the acquaintance.

You engage in conversation with the acquaintance.*

The subject of this therapeutic intervention returned to full-time employment and remained free of seizures.

Marzagao (1972) reported a case study of a 24-year-old woman with a 12-year history of kleptomania. Kleptomania was used by the woman to reduce anxiety in specific situations, such as being left alone in a strange setting. A total of 17 desensitization sessions were conducted with the subject during the treatment process. She imagined herself in the following situations:

1. Chatting with girl-friend and making an appointment to study in home of one of her friends.
2. Arriving at friend's place, alone.
3. Going into her friend's study and finding her alone.
4. Chatting with the friend while awaiting other students.
5. Noticing her friend's handbag on the bed.
6. Being invited by the friend to go to the dining room to have some snacks.
7. Refusing the invitation and asking the friend to bring the snacks to the study.
8. Being alone in the study and making sure of being unobserved.
9. Picking up the handbag.*

During follow-up sessions the first, second, fourth, and tenth month after treatment, it was determined that the target behavior had not recurred.

These experiments by Parrino and Marzagao focused on adult patients. They have been presented here because similar problems occur among children in the classroom setting.

There have been several applications of desensitization techniques in cases of school phobia. Two studies especially worthy of notation are those of Ayllon and others (1970) and Garvey and Hegrenes (1966).

Ayllon and others (1970) applied desensitization techniques in the case of Valerie, an 8-year-old with school phobia. Valerie had average school attendance during kindergarten and first grade. However, during the sec-

---

*Reprinted with permission from *Journal of Behavior Therapy and Experimental Psychiatry*, 2, J. Parrino, Reduction of seizures by desensitization, Copyright 1971, Pergamon Press, Ltd.

*Reprinted with permission from *Journal of Behavior Therapy and Experimental Psychiatry*, 3, L. Marzagao, Systemic desensitization treatment of kleptomania, Copyright 1972, Pergamon Press, Ltd.

ond grade she was absent all but 4 days. Whenever an attempt was made to take Valerie to school, she would engage in a violent temper tantrum.

After a 70-day desensitization program, Valerie's attendance was returned to normal.

Garvey and Hegrenes (1966) reported a similar study concerning Jimmy, a 10-year-old with school phobia. During treatment the therapist eliminated the child's fear of school by having him approach the school accompanied by the therapist and by proceeding with the following anxiety-evoking stimulus hierarchy:

1. Sitting in the car in front of the school;
2. Getting out of the car and approaching the curb;
3. Going to the sidewalk;
4. Going to the bottom of the steps of the school;
5. Going to the top of the steps;
6. Going to the door;
7. Entering the school;
8. Approaching the classroom in a certain distance each day down the hall;
9. Entering the classroom;
10. Being present in the classroom with the teacher;
11. Being present in the classroom with the teacher and one or two classmates;
12. Being present in the classroom with a full class.*

After 20 consecutive daily treatments Jimmy resumed a normal school routine. No return of the phobia was noted during a 2-year follow-up study.

Before the implementation of this intervention Jimmy had participated in 6 months of traditional psychotherapy without apparent success. Desensitization is an effective

---

*From Garvey, W. P., and Hegrenes, J. R. Desensitization techniques in the treatment of school phobia. *American Journal of Orthopsychiatry*, 1966, *36*, 147-152. Copyright 1966. American Orthopsychiatric Association, Inc. Reproduced by permission.

technique that can conserve both time and money.

We have found desensitization to be a potent intervention that can be applied in a modified form by the teacher in the classroom. However, if desensitization is to be applied in the classroom, the following conditions must exist:

1. The teacher must have a positive interpersonal relationship with the child. The phobic child must trust the teacher and be free to express fears in the teacher's presence.
2. The teacher must construct an anxiety-evoking stimulus hierarchy.
3. The teacher must be willing (and have adequate time) to accompany the child in the progression from the least to the most anxiety-evoking stimulus in the hierarchy.

Under normal classroom conditions the desensitization process is time consuming. The practitioner must be consistent and patient in the application of this intervention. It may be necessary to repeat some of the specific anxiety-evoking situations until their effect on the child has been eliminated.

EXAMPLE

David, a 5-year-old boy in Ms. Philly's class for children with behavior problems, was afraid of dogs. Whenever the boy saw a dog, he would crawl under the nearest object or person and scream until the animal disappeared from view.

This behavior made it impossible for David to go out on the playground during recess with his peers, to walk to and from school, or to play outdoors in his neighborhood.

Desensitization was suggested as a possible intervention. Ms. Philly thought it was an excellent idea but suggested that implementation be deferred until she knew David better. A stimulus hierarchy was constructed, but the intervention was held in abeyance until 3 months after the beginning of the school year.

The following anxiety-evoking stimulus hierarchy was used to reduce David's fear of dogs:

1. Pictures of dogs were hung on the walls of the classroom. The pictures were initially placed as far away from David's desk as possible. As de-

sensitization continued, they were moved nearer to David.

2. Pictures of dogs were observed by David in motion pictures and filmstrips.
3. Pictures of dogs were affixed to David's desk and notebook covers.
4. David observed dogs playing in the school yard from his classroom window.
5. David observed dogs playing in the school yard from the door of the school.
6. David observed dogs playing in the school yard as he stood at a distance that was systematically decreased.
7. David permitted dogs to walk past him in the school yard.

At *no time* during the desensitization process was David encouraged to touch or pet a dog. This precaution was taken simply because *some* dogs do bite *some* children.

During the desensitization process, Ms. Philly removed David from an anxiety-evoking situation whenever he manifested the slightest discomfort. The lessening of David's fear permitted him to tolerate dogs and to increase his interactions with his peers in the school yard and neighborhood.

EXAMPLE

Keith, an 8-year-old third-grade student, was enrolled in summer camp. Keith had a fear of water. Swimming lessons were a part of the camp program. Although swimming was not mandatory, it was encouraged. At the first suggestion of swimming or going to the pool, Keith would have a temper tantrum of considerable magnitude.

It was decided that Keith should overcome this irrational fear. The staff concluded that systematic desensitization would be an effective intervention.

The following stimulus hierarchy was constructed and applied during desensitization:

1. Swimming was announced to the group and discussed with Keith's peers. Keith did not attend swimming lessons but watched his peers, who were very happy and excited, get on the bus and depart for swimming.
2. Keith rode the bus to the pool and waited outside the building.
3. Keith rode the bus to the pool and waited outside the locker room.
4. Keith entered the locker room, put on his trunks, and remained in the locker room.
5. Keith, in trunks, observed the lesson from the pool observation room.
6. Keith observed the lesson from the poolside (approximately 10 feet from the water).
7. Keith observed the lesson from the edge of the pool.
8. Keith observed the lesson while sitting on the edge of the pool with his feet in the water.
9. Keith stood in the pool with his hands on the edge of the pool.
10. Keith walked in the shallow end of pool with his hands on the edge of the pool.

Throughout this procedure Keith was accompanied by his counselor, who provided positive reinforcement. As a result of this process and within 3 weeks, Keith began his swimming lessons. After 3 years it was noted that the fear had not returned. Keith is an excellent swimmer.

SUMMARY

In this chapter some techniques to decrease behaviors are demonstrated.

Extinction is the discontinuation or withholding of the reinforcer of a behavior that has previously reinforced that particular behavior. Extinction is the most frequently used and least complex of the techniques suggested for decreasing behaviors. The technique is based on the principle that if you take away the reward, you decrease the probability of the recurrence of the behavior.

The second technique recommended, time-out, appears to be the most frequently misunderstood behavioral intervention. Time-out is the removal of a child from an apparently reinforcing setting to a presumably nonreinforcing setting for a specified and limited period of time. Six factors related to the effectiveness of time-out are (1) the characteristics of the individual child, (2) the consistency of application by the teacher, (3) the child's understanding of the rules, (4) the characteristics of the time-out area, (5) the duration of time-out, and (6) the evaluation of the effectiveness of the intervention.

Satiation is the decreasing or elimination of an inappropriate behavior as a result of continued and increased reinforcement of that behavior. This intervention is effective for decreasing behaviors such as "borrowing" materials, stealing, and dominating time.

Punishment, the most familiar of the interventions discussed, is the addition of an aversive stimulus or the subtraction of a desired reinforcer or privilege as a consequence of behavior. There are a number of serious concerns associated with the use of punishment. The major problem with the use of punishment to modify behavior is that punishment does not eliminate inappropriate behavior; it only suppresses the behavior. Punishment should be used very infrequently, if ever, in the school.

The reinforcement of incompatible behaviors involves systematically reinforcing a behavior that is in opposition to or incompatible with the target behavior. The effectiveness of this technique depends greatly on the pairing of incompatible behaviors.

Desensitization is the process of systematically lessening a specific fear in an individual.

EXERCISES FOR CHAPTER FIVE
Quiz*

1. The six most common methods of decreasing behavior are:

    a. _____   d. _____

    b. _____   e. _____

    c. _____   f. _____

2. _____ is the process of discontinuing or withholding the reinforcer of a behavior that has previously reinforced that particular behavior.

3. Time-out is the removal of a child from an apparently _____ setting to

    a presumably _____ setting for a specified and limited period of time.

4. List at least three of the factors that a behavior modifier should consider when designing a time-out intervention.

    a. _____

    b. _____

    c. _____

5. When selecting a time-out area within the classroom, what four factors should a practitioner consider?

    a. _____

    b. _____

    c. _____

    d. _____

6. _____ is the decreasing or elimination of an unacceptable behavior as a result of continued and increased reinforcement of the behavior.

---

*Turn to Appendix A, p. 174, for answers.

7. _____ should only be used to decrease or eliminate behaviors as a last resort.

8. Reinforcing incompatible behaviors is accomplished by _____

_____

_____ .

9. _____ is the process of lessening an individual's particular fear.

10. Three of the logical reasons presented by Clarizio and Yelon (1967) for avoiding the use of punishment are:

a. _____

_____

b. _____

_____

c. _____

_____

Projects

1. Joanie, a girl in Ms. Jewel's classroom is constantly asking, "What time is it?" She requests the time about 15 times per day. The teacher considers this to be an attention-getting behavior and wishes to eliminate it. She usually responds to Joanie's request by telling her the time. Using this example, design four interventions for eliminating the behavior, using the processes of:
   a. Extinction
   b. Time-out
   c. Satiation
   d. Reinforcement of incompatible behaviors
2. Write a brief essay (250 words or more) emphasizing the pros and cons of the use of corporal punishment in the school.

REFERENCES

Ayllon, T., Smith, D., and Rogers, M. Behavioral management of school phobia. *Journal of Behavior Therapy and Experimental Psychiatry*, 1970, *1*, 125-138.

Beck, T. Videotape scenes for desensitization of test anxiety. *Journal of Behavior Therapy and Experimental Psychiatry*, 1972, *3*, 195-197.

Clarizio, H. F., and Yelon, S. L. Learning theory approaches to classroom management: Rationale and intervention techniques. *Journal of Special Education*, 1967, *1*, 267-274.

Committee to End Violence Against the Next Generation, Inc. We oppose corporal punishment because. *The Last Resort*, 1974, *2*(5).

Deffenbacher, J., and Kemper, C. Systematic desensitization of test anxiety in junior high students. *The School Counselor*, 1974, *21*, 216-222.

Garvey, W. P., and Hegrenes, J. R. Desensitization techniques in the treatment of school phobia. *American Journal of Orthopsychiatry*, January 1966, *36*, 147-152.

Kravetz, R., and Forness, S. The special classroom as a desensitization setting. *Exceptional Children*, 1971, *37*, 389-391.

Marzagao, L. Systematic desensitization treatment of kleptomania. *Journal of Behavior Therapy and Experimental Psychiatry*, 1972, *3*, 327-328.

Parrino, J. Reduction of seizures by desensitization. *Journal of Behavior Therapy and Experimental Psychiatry*, 1971, *2*, 215-218.

Wolpe, J. The systematic desensitization treatment of neuroses. *Journal of Nervous and Mental Diseases*, 1961, *132*, 189-203.

Wolpe, J. *The practice of behavior therapy* (2nd ed.). New York: Pergamon Press, Inc., 1973.

CHAPTER SIX

Parent training and home-school behavior management

After studying the literature on parent education and training from a variety of theoretical and methodological perspectives, Clements and Alexander (1975) concluded: "Extensive research demonstrates unequivocally that children learn more, adjust better, and progress faster when parent training is effected" (p. 7).

Parent education and training is an integral part of a successful school management program.

The primary purposes of this chapter are to present a systematic methodology designed to facilitate (1) the effectiveness with which parents manage their children's behavior in home and community settings, (2) cooperation between the parents and teacher in the implementation of effective behavior management interventions in behalf of the child for whom they have a shared responsibility, and (3) the teacher's efforts to plan and conduct a parent program in the classroom and school or other work setting.

The parent education and training perspective presented here—a behavior modification approach—is but one of many discussed in the literature. Extensive references to other approaches, such as those developed by Auerbach (1968), Barsch (1969), Dinkmeyer and McKay (1973), Dreikurs (1958), Gordon, T. (1970), Homan (1977), and Webster (1977), as well as references to several

other methods of conducting parent education and training, are presented at the end of the chapter. The reader should find these chapter references an excellent point of departure for a comprehensive study of parent education and training.

The following are discussed in the chapter:

The need for and desirability of parent education and training

The reactions, problems, and needs of parents of children having behavioral deviations and handicapping conditions

An overview of the purposes and objectives of parent education and training and the specific objectives of the program presented in this chapter

Assessment techniques used to aid parents in selecting a target behavior

A list of potentially effective reinforcers available in the home

An eight-session behavior modification training course for parents

Several aides to facilitate home-school communication and thus the effectiveness of cooperative behavior management programs

NEED FOR AND DESIRABILITY OF PARENT EDUCATION AND TRAINING

There is among present-day regular and special education teachers, as well as educational administrators, skepticism concerning the need for and desirability of school-sponsored programs for parents. Our experience, however, as parents and educators, indicates that parent education and training is a necessary component of a comprehensive school service program.

Clements and Alexander (1975) agree:

It is unnecessary to revisit the already proven axiom that parents are effective change agents in the lives of exceptional children. It is, perhaps, equally as extravagant to indulge in outlining the boundaries of social and academic learning and perpetuate the pseudoissue of who governs which set of constructs when, in reality, these are shared and interactive responsibilities. We must instead face an important issue in the third quarter of the twentieth century; parents are moving both physically and intellectually back into the mainstream of American education. (p. 1)

The question is not whether parent education and training is needed but how educators can effectively and efficiently conduct parent programs for the ultimate benefit of all children. Clements and Alexander suggest that the teacher is the school-based professional primarily responsible for parent services. All teachers, of regular and special classes, must acknowledge this responsibility and take steps to provide appropriate programs for parent education and training.

As part of the Rutland Center's Early Childhood Project, Wood (1975) and her associates offer a parent program with two primary goals: to provide parents with information relative to the needs of their exceptional children and to assist them in practical ways in their efforts to meet their children's needs.

Gardner (1974) maintains that cooperative home-school endeavors are more effective in responding to the needs of behavior-disordered children than are school endeavors only. He states that parents require the assistance of school personnel in efforts to manage their children's behavior:

Many parents do need assistance in recognizing that what they are doing may create additional problems for the child. Many could benefit from guidance in modifying the manner in which they interact with or respond to their children. They do not need the teacher to place blame on them or to lecture them on what they have done wrong or how they have created the child's problem. They do require information, guidance, and support. They need information about how specific and general problems can be approached and how their day to day interactions with their child can contribute to the child's development. They do not need generalities about being a good parent. They do need specific, concrete, and practical suggestions about how they can best promote optimal adjustment for their child. (p. 316)

The Pathfinder School (Susser, 1974) perceives parents and educators as partners. According to Susser, success in the classroom is lasting only if there is 24-hour-a-day follow-through: the approach of school and home, teacher and parent, must be consistent.

Karnes and Zehrbach (1972) have suggested that programs for handicapped children can be significantly improved if parents are meaningfully involved in them.

Opinions relative to the need for and desirability of programs for parents are not exclusively the domain of professionals. Many parents are aware of their need for education and training. In *Heartaches and Handicaps: An Irreverent Survival Manual for Parents,* Stigen (1976) writes repeatedly of her need for assistance through meaningful education and training. She discusses, sometimes with a laugh, sometimes with a cry, the inadequacy of the guidance and supportive services for parents offered by hospitals, schools, clinics, and other social service agencies.

Kratoville (1975a, 1975b) and Jogis (1975), both parents of a handicapped child, have described their need for sensitive, practical assistance in their role as primary therapist for their children. These parents noted a lack of meaningful assistance and understanding of their problems by professionals in hospitals, schools, clinics, and community agencies. They discovered the obvious lack of training and sensitivity of professionals toward parents.

The opinions of the parents and professionals cited above and those of many others, including parents and teachers involved primarily with nonhandicapped children, lead us to the following conclusions:

1. Both parents and professionals recognize the need for parent education and training.
2. Parent programs are desirable because they not only respond to the needs of the parents but also have a significant positive effect on the children.
3. The teacher, a specialist in instructional processes and behavior management techniques, is the logical professional to coordinate and conduct parent programs in the schools.
4. Children benefit most when the behavior management approaches of the home and school are consistent.
5. Parent programs must be practical, concrete, specific, and meaningful to the parents.

Although the literature cited is primarily concerned with children administratively classified as handicapped, the conclusions drawn from that literature are relevant to all children and their parents. "Normal" children also have problems and are frequently a behavior management concern to their parents.

PARENTS' REACTIONS, PROBLEMS, AND NEEDS

The parents of a child with a problem are first and foremost human beings; and like all human beings, they react as individuals to the problems of loved ones. A particular parent's reaction is in large part determined by personal characteristics, life experiences,

education and training, expectations, socioeconomic circumstances, and a variety of other variables. The parent's reaction is influenced by the characteristics of the child and the specific problem and, to some degree, by the professional practitioner's reaction to the problem.

The practitioner should keep in mind that parents with problem children are not necessarily "problem parents" (Denhoff, 1960). They do not necessarily need personal counseling. The majority are normal people who are responding in a normal manner to unanticipated trauma.

Ross (1964) discussed parental reactions to the birth or diagnosis of a child with exceptionality from a psychoanalytic perspective. The recognition of a handicap in a child causes an increase in the parents' level of anxiety. This anxiety appears to be caused by recognition of the unanticipated discrepancy between the parents' expectations for the child and the way the child is in reality. In their efforts to control anxiety, the parents employ one or more of a broad range of defense mechanisms. These defenses are utilized to regain emotional equilibrium, which has been threatened by the crisis (or perceived crisis). Although the defense mechanisms are applied for positive reasons—that is, the regaining of emotional equilibrium— they may be distructive to the individual parent and child if they are overused or if they become habitual. According to Ross, counseling and similar supportive therapeutic services are required to aid these parents in dealing with their initial anxiety and consequent defensive reactions.

A crisis reaction to a child's problems is not the exclusive province of parents of children classified as deviant, special, exceptional, or handicapped (Gordon, S., 1976). Emotional reactions to problems with a child are a natural human response for any parent confronted with a crisis or perceived crisis. Also, all parents do not employ the same defense mechanisms. Parental reactions are as varied as the individual parents confronted with a crisis situation (Gordon, S., 1976).

Among the defense mechanisms parents may apply in response to their recognition of a problem with a child are:

Self doubt: The parents may react to the child's problem with self-doubt. They may doubt their worth as human beings and as parents. Their self-worth may be in doubt because of a perceived inability to give birth to or raise a child according to their expectations and the expectations of society.

Unhappiness and mourning: The parents may react to the child's handicap with extreme unhappiness. The child's problem is perceived as so severe that the parents' joy of life is gone. It is impossible for them to smile, laugh, converse, or take an active part in any of life's common pleasures. In the extreme, this parental reaction is similar to the mourning that occurs after the death of a loved one.

Guilt: Because of the uncertain etiology of their child's problem, many parents feel guilty. They believe that the child's problem is their fault. Many times parents will go to extreme lengths to find a reason for the child's difficulty and may discover some small insignificant personal behavior or incident in the past on which to place personal blame.

Denial: The parents may react to the child's problem by denying its existence. They reason that if the existence of the problem is denied, they do not have to concern themselves with it.

Projection: Many parents who recognize the existence of a problem blame it on another person. They may blame the child's difficulty on a physician, nurse, caseworker, counselor, baby sitter, or teacher. Occasionally, they will project blame onto their spouse or other children.

Withdrawal: The parents may react to the child's problem by withdrawal, believing that they can find a solution if they give the problem sufficient time and personal consideration. In some cases such withdrawal leads to depression requiring professional attention to restore normal functioning.

Avoidance and rejection: To some parents the birth or diagnosis of an exceptional child is so traumatic that they avoid contact with the child; they are unable to feed, clothe, or play with the child.

Embarrassment and social isolation: Many parents of handicapped children are embarrassed by them. In some cases, this embarrassment leads to social isolation. Neither parent nor child leaves the home for shopping, walks, visits, or entertainment. These parents choose to avoid embarrassment by not participating in social situations that may result in curious stares or questions concerning the child.

Hostility: Some parents report feelings of hostility and, on occasion, overt anger toward others who stare or ask questions about the child. The object of this hostility and anger may be anyone: a passenger on a bus, a man in the street, a friend, a neighbor, or a relative.

Over-dependency and helplessness: The parents may react with over-dependency on their spouse, a child, a relative, or a professional. They are helpless to make any decision concerning the child's future.

Confusion: Most parents are confused by the child's problem. They are confused about the etiology of the problem, its normal course, and its treatment. Such confusion appears to be largely due to a lack of factual information and guidance from professionals responsible for providing such services.

Frustration: Many parents who have decided on a course of action that is appropriate for their child become frustrated in their efforts to obtain services. They are confronted with insensitive and inadequately trained professionals. Many parents are frustrated by the lack of appropriate services in the community.

The practitioner must recognize that many of the foregoing emotional reactions are not under a parent's conscious control. Parents must be aided in dealing with their emotional reactions before they can fully participate in and benefit from an educational program.

Effective parent educators realize that they need a variety of counseling and instructional skills. They must *listen* to the meaning behind the parents' words, as well as the words themselves (Lichter, 1976). They must be sensitive to the parents' feelings. They must be able to empathize with the problems confronting the parents and child. Although parent educators must approach their task with honesty and forthrightness, they must not be cruel; give the impression that the parents, child, and problem are hopeless; or indicate that they have all the answers. Parent educators must have sufficient confidence in their teaching ability to permit parents to develop confidence in them—and through them, in themselves.

PURPOSES AND OBJECTIVES OF PARENT EDUCATION AND TRAINING

McDowell (1976) has classified parent programs under three headings: (1) informational, (2) psychotherapeutic, and (3) training.

The informational program is designed primarily to present knowledge to parents about a variety of topics. Among the focuses of such informational programs are: (1) child-raising techniques; (2) child development; (3) educational program designs, objectives, and procedures; (4) the causes, effects, and treatment of handicapping conditions; and (5) techniques of behavior management. The primary purpose of these parent programs is the transmission of information. It is assumed that information will change a parent's behavior.

The psychotherapeutic strategy is employed to assist parents in their efforts to deal with personal feelings and conflicts resulting from the child's problem. It is assumed that parents must adjust to the emotional crisis before they can plan and implement an action program.

Parent training programs are designed to assist parents' efforts to effectively interact with and manage the behavior of their children. These programs can be exemplified by several contemporary parent training programs. Parent effectiveness training (Gordon, T., 1970) focuses primarily on assisting parents in establishing effective and positive communications with children. The C-Group strategy (Dinkmeyer and McKay, 1973) focuses on training parents to solve practical child management problems. Both programs are action oriented. They necessitate parental involvement and commitment. In these programs it is assumed that once parents have learned appropriate and effective problem-solving skills and have made them a habit, they will continue to apply them in the management of child behavior.

The program for parent-teacher cooperation in child management presented in this chapter can be classified as a parent training program. It focuses primarily on training parents in behavior modification techniques as an effective and efficient means of managing behavior. As a consequence of this focus, the program is limited in its effectiveness with those parents in need of psychotherapeutic or basic informational services.

Objectives of the parent training program

The specific objectives of the parent training program presented in this chapter are:

To increase the parents' knowledge of the techniques of behavior modification

To increase the parents' skills in the application of behavior modification techniques in the management of their children's behavior

To provide both the parents and the teacher with a common perspective of child behavior management and facilitate cooperative child behavior management efforts

These objectives are attained by instructing the parents in behavior modification techniques and by assisting the parents' application of these techniques in home and home-school behavior management programs.

The steps in the behavior change process applied in the parent training program are identical to those presented in Chapter Three. However, in the parent training situation the teacher is generally once removed from direct observation of the child's behavior in the home setting; thus, the teacher must rely on the parents' observations and reports. Consequently, assessment strategies must be implemented by the teacher to facilitate the parents' selection and objectification of a target behavior.

In addition, the reinforcers that may be applied in the home setting differ from those available and applicable in the school; thus, attention is given to the parents' recognition and application of home reinforcers.

SELECTING THE TARGET BEHAVIOR: ASSESSMENT TECHNIQUES

To be of practical assistance to parents wishing to improve their behavior management skills, the teacher must obtain specific information. The information needed by the teacher includes (Blackham and Silberman, 1975):

The history of the problem

Specific areas of conflict

A description of the behavior that makes it receptive to direct observation and measurement

The identity of the person or persons present when the behavior occurs

Reinforcers that appear to maintain the behavior

The roles and responsibilities of the parents and other family members in the child's life

Parental expectations and behavior requirements and the reasonableness of these expectations and requirements

Methods presently used to deal with the behavior

Rewards that are available or that can be made available in the home

Observational data on the rate of the behavior

Blackham and Silberman have suggested four methods for obtaining data on parent-child interactions and problem areas:

1. Direct observation of the child and other family members in the home
2. Direct observation of the child and other family members in the clinic or school setting
3. Parental observation of the child's interaction within the family at home and the reporting of the resultant data to the teacher
4. A personal interview with the parents and child

In large part because of the nature of the public school organization, the first two methods proposed by Blackham and Silberman are not feasible; that is, the teacher is usually unable to spend the needed time observing parent-child interaction in either the home or the school. The third and fourth methods appear to relate to the psychosituational assessment interview.

Psychosituational assessment interview

The psychosituational assessment interview is primarily an information-gathering technique. It is not a therapeutic intervention designed to elicit and facilitate the analysis of the parents' personal feelings or their feelings about the child. The interview focuses primarily on obtaining from the parent or parents descriptive data about the child's behavior and the circumstances surrounding it.

The psychosituational assessment interview is not a conversation between parents and teacher.

A conversation is a two-way exchange of information in which all parties involved may contribute equally or alternately to the flow of the communication. The implicit rules of a social conversation state that all parties have a responsibility for keeping the exchange from coming to a standstill, periods of silence are avoided, "personal" topics are generally taboo, and the content of the conversation may range widely as the participants introduce new topics in association to something another may have said. (Ross, 1964, p. 76)*

The assessment interview is

. . . a specialized pattern of verbal interaction—initiated for a specific purpose, and focused on some specific content area, with consequent elimination of extraneous material. Moreover, the interview is a pattern of interaction in which the role relationship of interviewer and respondent is highly specialized, its specific characteristics depending somewhat on the purpose and character of the interview (Kahn and Cannell, 1957, p. 16)

*From Ross, A. O. *The exceptional child in the family: Helping parents of exceptional children.* New York: Grune & Stratton, Inc., 1964. Reprinted by permission.

The psychosituational assessment interview technique was designed by Bersoff and Grieger (1971). The purpose of the interview is to analyze the unacceptable behavior and uncover the antecedents and consequences that elicit, reinforce, and sustain it. This information about the child is elicited from the parent or parents and contributes to decisions concerning interventions to modify the behavior.

The model of behavior applied in this technique is a departure from the predominant assumption that the personality is composed of needs and traits that predispose the individual to respond in predetermined ways. With this assumption, that behavior is independent of the situation, the emphasis is on "fixing" the individual rather than restructuring the setting in which the behavior occurs. Bersoff and Grieger have proposed that rather than viewing behavior as resulting from basic needs or traits, one should regard it as the individual's inability to respond in certain ways in certain situations. In their model, behavior is seen as a function of prior learning and the stimulus situation.

By means of the psychosituational assessment interview, it may be possible to determine to what extent the learner's behavior is reinforced and maintained by the environment and to what extent it may be modified by the manipulation of environmental stimuli. Thus, the primary aspects of the setting in which the behavior occurs are analyzed in the interview. These aspects are (1) the child's behavior, (2) the environmental variables surrounding the behavior, and (3) the attitudes and expectations of the parents.

Behavior refers to the actual behaviors for which the child was referred, including the antecedents and consequences of that behavior, that is, teacher, parental, and peer responses. *Environments and situations* refer to the specific places and circumstances in which the behavior occurs, including the presence of significant others. *Attitudes and emotions* refer to the beliefs and feelings of the referring agent, that is, the parent or parents.

A parent's concern about a child's behavior may be based on irrational ideas and attitudes that lead to unwarranted expectations, demands, and feelings, all of which result in inappropriate actions toward the child following emission of the target behavior. *Expectation* has a dual meaning: it refers to the specific performance that the adult would like the child to achieve (short-term goals) and to the long-range aspirations that the adult has for the child.

The four major tasks to be accomplished during the interview are (1) defining the target behavior(s), (2) explicating specific situations in which the behavior occurs, (3) uncovering the contingencies that seemingly sustain the behavior, and (4) detecting any irrational ideas that make it difficult for the parent or parents to objectively understand, accept, and modify the behavior.

Defining the target behavior involves analyzing the following: (1) its *frequency rate*, the number of times the behavior occurs within a particular time period; (2) its *intensity*, the strength or force of the behavior; and (3) its *duration*, the length of time that the behavior is maintained. A careful analysis of the problem within a behavioral framework helps delineate and define it so that it becomes remediable. This process helps the parents check their perceptions and focus on the relevant problem.

Obtaining information about the specific situations in which the behavior occurs is important because behavior is considered a function of interaction between the learned response of the child and the situation in which the behavior occurs. This information helps the interviewer plan the intervention.

Exploring the contingencies and consequences (results) of the behavior is the next interviewer task. The parents must be aware that *they are part of the problem* and may have a role in sustaining the behavior.

Finally, the interviewer must be aware of the parent or parent's irrational and unrealistic ideas about the child. The following irrational ideas of parents are frequently apparent:

1. The notion that the child is infallible and has wide-ranging competence. When the parents' expectation is that the child is competent in all respects, inefficiency in one or two areas of school functioning is regarded as general failure.

2. The maintenance of absolutistic, unsupportable, and unreasonable expectations of the child. These ideas are usually expressed in "ought" and "should" terms. A parent may say, "He should be able to sit longer" or "He ought to know better."

3. The feeling that it is helpful to become angry over the child's misbehavior. This feeling may lead to guilt and anxiety on the part of the parents that may further interfere with parent-child interactions.

4. The belief that the child is blameworthy and needs to be punished for misdeeds. The failure to accept things as they exist inhibits rational problem solving.

It is recommended that both parents be present at the interview. A joint interview is desirable because differing perceptions and inconsistencies in parental behavior management strategies can be uncovered. It also allows the interviewer to gauge the amount and frequency of mutual support that the parents provide to each other.

The psychosituational assessment interview may be a single session or a series of sessions. If the interviewer is only concerned with obtaining data in an effort to design an intervention that includes parental participation, two or three sessions may be sufficient.

However, frequently the strategy can be applied to an ongoing intervention program.

During the initial interview the interviewer may suggest that the parents gather behavioral data, such as frequency counts. Sometimes parents find it difficult to estimate the number of times during a specified period of time that the misbehavior occurs.

The following are specific interviewer tasks:

1. Establish rapport with the parent or parents.
2. Have the parents specify the target behavior(s), that is, the specific behavior(s) that are disturbing. Explore the frequency, intensity, and duration of the behavior.

   EXAMPLE QUESTIONS
   What exactly does the child do that you find unacceptable or annoying?
   What exactly does he do that makes you say he is hyperactive, nonresponsive, or disobedient?
   What else does he do that makes you say he is hyperactive, nonresponsive, or disobedient?
   In the course of an hour how often is he hyperactive, nonresponsive, or disobedient?

3. Have the parents delineate the specific situations and environments in which the behavior occurs. Establish where the behavior takes place and who is present when the behavior occurs.

   EXAMPLE QUESTIONS
   Where does this behavior occur? In the house? In the yard? On the playground? In a store?
   Does it occur when the child is working on a particular project? With a particular group? While watching TV? When getting ready to go to bed? When getting up in the morning?
   Who is present when the behavior occurs? The mother? The father? Brothers? Sisters? Playmates? Visitors?

4. Explore the contingencies that may stimulate and sustain the behavior.

Determine what happens immediately before and after the behavior occurs, that is, the antecedents and consequences of the behavior.

   EXAMPLE QUESTIONS
   What happens just before the behavior occurs?
   What happens just after the behavior occurs?
   What do you usually do when the child engages in this behavior?
   How do other people indicate to the child that the behavior is unacceptable?

5. Attempt to determine the ratio of positive-to-negative interactions between the child and the parents.

   EXAMPLE QUESTIONS
   Is your relationship with the child usually pleasant or unpleasant?
   Do you usually praise his accomplishments?
   Do you reprimand his failures and ignore his success?

6. Explore the methods the parents use for behavior control. Explore the type of punishment and the conditions for application.

   EXAMPLE QUESTIONS
   Do you punish the behavior?
   How do you punish inappropriate behavior?
   Who is responsible for administering the punishment?
   Do you always use this method of punishment?
   What other methods do you use?

7. Determine to what degree the parents are aware of how praise or punishment is communicated and its effect on the child's behavior.

   EXAMPLE QUESTIONS
   Can the child tell when you are angry? How?
   Can he tell when you want him to stop doing something?

8. Explore the manner in which expectations and consequences are communicated to the child by the parents.

EXAMPLE QUESTIONS

Are the rules you expect the child to follow clearly spelled out?

Does the child know what you expect him to do?

9. Detect irrational and unrealistic ideas that make it difficult for the parents to understand, accept, or modify the behavior. Be alert for and explore irrational ideas that may be expressed. Restate irrational ideas but avoid reinforcing or exploring them.

10. Conclude the session by restating the unacceptable behavior and presenting the desirable behavior. You may suggest that the parents keep a log of the child's behavior. (An example of a simple log is presented on the following page; additional copies are provided in tear-off form at the back of the text.) Explain fully how the log should be used. You may suggest one or two techniques for changing the behavior. (This is generally done if additional sessions are prohibited.) Make arrangements for a future meeting.

A careful reading of the parent-teacher psychosituational assessment interview presented below will clarify the use of this technique.

PARENT-TEACHER INTERVIEW

T: Good afternoon, Mr. _____.

P: Hello, Mrs. _____, how are you?

T: Fine, thank you. Glad to meet you. Sit down, please. I'm Mark's special education teacher this year, and I'd like to ask you some questions about Mark. Let's see. He's 9 years old, and he's presently in Mrs. Lee's class—that's third grade.

P: Yes.

T: Mrs. Lee has told me that Mark does rather well in some of his subjects. He's particularly good in math. He enjoys that very much. He has a little bit of difficulty with reading and writing, however. And behaviorally, she finds some problems with him leaving his seat fre-

quently. He's rather active in the classroom.

P: Yeah, she's not the only one who has problems with him.

T: I see.

P: He's a bad boy. We have trouble with him at home all the time.

T: Oh, you do?

P: Yeah, I'm, well, I know Mrs. Lee does, too, because my wife tells me that Mrs. Lee calls, and the principal calls about him and about sending him home from school all the time. My wife should be here today—she really spends most of the time with Mark; but she didn't want to come, because she wasn't feeling very good. I drive a truck, and I'm on the road most of the time. I don't see much of him.

T: It was very nice of you to come today.

P: Well . . . thank you.

T: I'd like to ask you some more questions about Mark's behavior at home. You said that he seems to . . . you have some trouble with him, too. Would you explain that to me a little?

P: He fights all the time. He's just always getting in fights. Like I said, I'm gone a lot, but my wife tells me that she has trouble with him all the time. Fights with his brothers, and every once in a while he fights with the neighbors—he just always getting into trouble. That seems to be about it.

T: Fighting seems to be the biggest problem.

P: Oh, yeah, he fights all the time. Always in trouble.

T: Could you give me an example of how one of these fights occurs?

P: Well, my wife was telling me last night that he and the older boy were playing Chinese checkers, and he lost. Mark lost, and Bill picked up a handful of—not Bill, but Mark—picked up a handful of marbles and threw them at Bill and went at him with his fists.

T: He became so agitated by losing that he started a fight.

P: He can't lose . . . he just goes . . . losing . . . he fights. That's just automatic—one, two. He just can't stand to lose. As long as he's winning, he gets along fine.

T: Are there any cases you can tell me about when he wins—how he acts?

Behavior Log Form

Target behavior _____

Child _____

Observer _____

Date	Time		Antecedents	Consequences	Applied interventions	Comments
	Begins	Ends				

P: Well, I take the boys fishing in the spring and in the summer.

T: That's nice.

P: Oh, yeah, I like to fish. Actually it's comforting, and it's lot of fun. We enjoy it—being out—and usually Mark, when he goes with us, he catches most of the fish.

T: Oh, really.

P: Oh, yeah. And, yeah, he has a good time then, bragging around and measuring, comparing the size of his fish and the other boys' fish and boasting about it. Yeah, he likes that.

T: He doesn't seem to fight much when you go fishing, does he?

P: Well, it all depends. Now, if one of the other boys catches a bigger fish or more fish, then he'll fight. He'll go at them, hit them, holler at them. Yeah, he can't stand to lose.

T: But if he's winning, and especially when he's fishing, he must enjoy that—going with you.

P: Yeah, he likes to go fishing. We have a good time.

T: Do you ever go with him by yourself?

P: We all go fishing. I tried to get my wife to go, but she doesn't care much for fishing. She doesn't like to bait the hook. You know how women are.

T: Oh, yes. So fishing is one thing that Mark really enjoys, especially when he's winning. And he's pretty good at it, from what you say.

P: That's right.

T: He must have had some good training. Let's talk about the fighting that goes on at home. Could you tell me a little bit more about it? You said that if losing is involved, then he seems to fight.

P: Yeah, that's right.

T: One example was with the Chinese checkers and his older brother. Could you give me any other examples?

P: Yeah, if he thinks one of the other kids gets more ice cream—like his younger brother—he'll poke him and start a fight. You know. It's really bad. My wife says that he's on the younger boy all the time at home, and she has to spank him or send him out of the house or send him up to bed, and it keeps going on. He's really a bad boy at home.

T: And you say he fights all the time. It probably seems like it's all the time because it's rather upsetting.

P: She's always complaining about it.

T: Do you have any idea of how often exactly this happens? Once a night, twice a night, once a week?

P: Well, it may be two or three times a week.

T: Two or three times a week?

P: Yeah, about two or three times a week—mainly because he wins the other two or three days.

T: Oh, I see.

P: Yeah, he's pretty good.

T: On the winning days he's really not that much of a problem?

P: No problem. As long as he's winning, he gets along with everyone really well.

T: Let's talk about these fights a little. You mentioned that he gets into almost real fisticuffs. Do you mean that he actually punches?

P: Not *almost.* He really does. Punches. And he keeps punching until the other kid gives up.

T: That's how the fight usually is settled?

P: That's how it's settled, unless one of the adults steps in and stops it.

T: By one of the adults, I assume you mean yourself or your wife.

P: My wife is home most of the time—she does this. When I'm home, I'm watching television; and if he starts a ruckus, I get in there and grab him and shake him. I stop it right away. I don't let anything go on. I stop it unless it's a tight inning, and then I may wait until the action's over and then I stop it. But it doesn't stop until I stop it.

T: You mentioned shaking him to stop it.

P: Yeah, I shake him.

T: Does that seem to work?

P: Well, you know, shake them till their teeth rattle—that straightens them out. That's what my daddy always said.

T: Do you use any other forms of punishment besides shaking?

P: Well, if that doesn't work, yeah, sure. I spank them when I feel that I should, and sometimes I just send them out of the house.

T: How long do these fights last? Just until . . . someone gives up? Maybe a minute? Two, 5 minutes?

P: If an adult's not there, sometimes they'll go on sometimes 5 or 10 minutes, 15 minutes. If an adult's there, of course, the adult stops it. Or an older kid can stop it, but they usually like to watch the fight.

T: Do you think what you're doing—this shaking and spanking—has changed his behavior any? Has it stopped the fighting?

P: It stops it then.

T: It stops it for that time?

P: Yeah.

T: When he loses, he fights; and when he fights, it's physical. It's dangerous to the other person.

P: Sometimes he yells and just hollers and screams at the other kids. One time, he hit his older brother with a chair because he was losing the fight. And I mean, he really gets violent. He really wants to win.

T: These fights, even though they are violent, last sometimes less than 5 minutes? Sometimes up to 15 minutes?

P: Yeah, that's about right.

T: And they seem to happen two or three times a week?

P: Yeah, that's about right.

T: But it seems like, otherwise, the rest of the time he's really pretty agreeable and easy to get along with. Things seem to go all right as long as he's winning.

P: As long as things are going his way and nobody steps on him or steps on his toes, he's all right.

T: Fine. Most of the time when you're dealing with Mark, is it a pleasant interaction or are there problems? Let's say for the most part.

P: See, I'm not home very much, and when I'm home I like to do what I like to do. I like to watch television and sports and so forth. And you know, of course, we do go fishing in the spring and summer, and then we get along fine—unless, of course, someone catches more fish than he does. But when I'm home, I like to watch television. I really don't pay that much attention to the kids. But my wife says that, you know, some days he can be very nice. But most of the time he's a bad, rotten kid.

T: Well, I think maybe we should start to work on this fighting behavior. I could help you with some suggestions.

P: Well, I'll tell you, we'd appreciate anything you could suggest.

T: Well, one thing I think would be a good idea is if you and your wife could keep what we call a log. We train our teachers to keep this. All it is, is that you would write down every day whether or not there was a fight. Then, what time the fight occurred, what the behavior was just before the fight happened, and how it was resolved. So, an example of this, which was done by another parent, would show that, like, Monday there was a fight, Tuesday nothing, Wednesday nothing—but Thursday there were two fights. Then, if you and your wife together would keep this kind of log . . .

P: Well, I know what a log is. That's what I do, because I'm a truck driver. We keep a log, and I can show my wife how to do it. I can't guarantee she'll do it, but I can show her how, and . . .

T: That would be very helpful.

P: Yeah, fine.

T: I think that you can probably explain it better than I could.

P: Probably so, right.

T: Then maybe in 3 weeks' time, we'll make another appointment for an interview and you and your wife can come together.

P: Well, I'm not sure that I'll be able to make it, because I'm on the road. But I think if my wife has something to talk about and hold onto, why, she'll probably be willing to come and chat with you.

T: Let's see if we can't arrange it for the three of us.

P: All right.

T: I'll do it at your convenience.

P: OK, right.

T: And if you will bring in the log for the next three weeks of behavior—how many times the fights—we won't worry about anything else, just the fighting behavior. Until that time, I'd also like you maybe to take some time with Mark alone and let me know how it works out with you just dealing with him individually, apart from his brothers. Just once in a while. I realize that you're very busy, but that may give us some insights.

P: Kind of father-son talks.

T: That kind of thing; that might work out well.

P: I'll try that.

Other assessment aids

Several of the behavior checklists and inventories discussed in this section can be helpful in the effort to assist parents in the objectification of their perception of the child's problem areas. In addition, these techniques are of assistance to the parent and teacher wishing to select a target behavior. These instruments are most effectively and appropriately used as part of a battery of diagnostic assessment instruments. They may be applied in the effort to focus the initial psychosituational assessment interview sessions on specific areas of conflict and behavior.

Among the checklists and inventories found helpful in work with parents are:

Behavior Problem Checklist (Quay and Peterson, 1967)

Devereux Child Behavior Rating Scale (Spivack and Spotts, 1966)

Devereux Adolescent Behavior Rating Scale (Spivack, Spotts, and Haimes, 1967)

Bristol Social Adjustment Guides (Stott and Marston, 1970)

Vineland Social Maturity Scale (Doll, 1965)

Child Behavior Rating Scale (Cassel, 1962)

Walker Problem Behavior Identification Checklist (Walker, 1976)

Burks' Behavior Rating Scales (Burks, 1977)

In general, the statistical reliability and validity of these inventories, checklists, and scales is questionable. However, if properly applied in conjunction with an interview, they can facilitate efforts to focus the parent or parents' attention on the child's specific behavior problem.

Another instrument that can be applied to assist parents in the selection of a target behavior is the Target Behavior kit (Kroth, 1972). The kit applies the Q-sort technique, developed by Stephenson (1953). It can be applied to facilitate the psychosituational assessment interview, that is, to assist the parent or parents in the selection and ranking of the child's behaviors.

The Target Behavior kit contains:

A 9-column target behavior board that is divided into 25 squares. The columns vary in length from 1 to 5 squares. The 5-square column is in the center of the board; the 1-square columns are located on the extreme left and right of the board. The column designations range from "most like me" to "most unlike me," with the "undecided" category in the center of the board. For work with parents, the column designations can be changed to "most like my child," "least like my child," and so on.

Two sets of cards listing 25 observable and measurable behaviors. One set lists home behaviors; the other lists classroom behaviors.

Several blank cards on which additional observable and measurable behaviors may be written.

A manual.

Record sheets.

In completing the behavior-sorting task, the parents are instructed to arrange the cards on the board from the perspective of the child's real or actual behaviors. In a second ranking, they are instructed to arrange the cards from the perspective of the ideal behaviors, that is, "how I would like my child to be." As the parents complete the two sortings, the interviewer notes the discrepancies between their perceptions of the child's real and ideal behaviors. These discrepancies then become material for interview sessions.

HOME REINFORCERS

In this section a list of potentially effective home reinforcers is presented. These have been found useful to parents needing suggestions on rewards they may apply at home. Additional suggestions can be gotten from the extensive list of reinforcers in Chapter Three.

Consumable food reinforcers
  Fruits
  Candies
  Snack foods
  Gum
  Ice cream
  Cookies
  Cake
  Crackers
  Milk
  Soda
  Juice

Reinforcing activities in relation to food reinforcers
  Baking cookies or a cake with a parent
  Preparing dinner with a parent
  Operating the toaster, mixer, or another appliance
  Adding spices, flour, or the like
  Washing dishes or operating the dishwasher
  Setting the table for snack time
  Serving snacks
  Cleaning the table after snack time

Tangible reinforcers
  Pencils or pens
  Magic markers
  Erasers
  Money to purchase desired items
  Records
  Surprise gifts
  Toys
  Games
  Coloring books
  Pads of paper
  Books
  Jewelry
  Clothing
  Pets
  Pet supplies

Token reinforcers
  Points
  Stars
  Chips
  Play money
  Check marks

Game activity reinforcers
  Playing outdoors alone with friends or a parent
  Participating in organized sports
  Flying a kite
  Participating in table games: checkers, backgammon, cards, etc.

Social reinforcers
  Smiles
  Hugs
  Pats
  Kisses
  Attention from parents
  Compliments about activities, efforts, appearance

Reinforcing activities
  Reading or looking at books, magazines, catalogs
  Watching television
  Getting additional playtime
  Going to the zoo
  Fishing
  Obtaining and caring for a pet
  Spending the night with a friend or relative
  Shopping with a parent
  Having a friend spend the night
  Going to the movies
  Using the stereo
  Getting telephone privileges
  Receiving help from a parent on a homework assignment or chore
  Attending a recreational activity or sporting event

Attending or having a party

Staying out later than usual

Accompanying parents instead of remaining with a sitter

Driving the family car

Going for ice cream, hamburgers, french fries

Working on a project with a parent

Visiting a parent's place of work

Joining and participating in a club or team

Taking lessons (music, dance, swimming)

Using the family typewriter

Listening to a story as a parent reads

PARENT TRAINING PROGRAM

The parent training program presented in this section has two objectives: (1) to train parents in the theory and application of behavior modification principles and practices and (2) to assist parents' efforts to systematically modify selected target behaviors manifested by their children. Although not a primary objective of the program, a benefit derived by many participants is mutual support and understanding of their child management problems from other members of the group and the parent educator.

Preparation phase

Before beginning the instructional phase of the training program, the parent educator should conduct one or more psychosituational assessment interviews with each parent or couple. The objective of these interviews is (1) to determine the parent or parents' needs, interests, and readiness to participate in a formal training program and (2) to clarify at least one child behavior they wish to modify.

The individual interview sessions are an excellent time for the educator to discuss the program objectives, organization, and requirements and to invite the parent or parents' participation.

Instructional phase

The instructional phase of the parent training program includes eight weekly sessions, excluding the preparation phase and follow-up phase. The 1½-hour sessions are divided into two 40-minute segments and a 10-minute break.

The first 40-minute segment is devoted to brief formal presentations by the parent educator on the principles and practices of behavior modification. The remainder of this segment is devoted to a question-and-answer session, group discussion, and practice exercises and activities.

The 10-minute break is devoted to informal discussion. Coffee, tea, milk, and soft drinks as well as snacks can be served. These items may be furnished by the parent educator or by the parents.

The second 40-minute segment of the weekly session is devoted to planning, implementing, and evaluating the parents' behavioral intervention programs. These programs are concerned with the behaviors selected during the preparation phase. During this second segment, considerable time is devoted to participants' reports on their interventions. All members of the group are expected and encouraged to question, discuss, and make suggestions for improving the interventions. A positive and helpful attitude must be maintained by all participants throughout this segment. Maintaining a positive tone is a primary function of the parent educator.

Meetings are conducted in a mutually agreed-on location. The parent educator's and participants' homes are *not* recommended, in large part to avoid potential embarrassment, competition, or inconvenience to the participants. A school, YMCA, YWCA, or community center is an excellent location for meeting. The facility must be accessible to the participants. If necessary, car pools can be arranged among the participants. In some cases child care services will be needed. In addition, the meeting room should ensure the group's privacy. Appropriate adult furnishings are necessary. A worktable should be available.

Group membership is limited to 12 or 14 persons, excluding the parent educator. Teachers of the parent-members' children can become group members. Groups are open to both women and men. Participation by both parents is desirable.

Attendance should be regular because of the cumulative nature of the material. If parents are unable to attend a particular session, the parent educator must update them in an individual session. However, absences should be discouraged for the sake of group cohesion and the parent educator's time.

The parent educator functions as an instructor and group facilitator during weekly sessions. Although the parent educator's function as an instructor remains relatively constant throughout the program, parents should be permitted and encouraged to make instructional presentations. The parent educator's function as group facilitator should diminish as the instructional phase of the program progresses and the participants begin to assert leadership.

Occasionally a team of two parent educators may present the training program. This is an excellent idea, particularly if one assumes the functions of instructor and the other the functions of facilitator. Of course, success in team teaching assumes personal-professional compatibility as well as fundamental agreement on the subject matter and instructional methods.

Any person who is knowledgeable of the principles and practices of behavior modification, child behavior, and group facilitation can serve as a parent educator. This includes both regular and special education teachers, college instructors, counselors, psychologists, nurses, social workers, and others.

The instructional materials needed during the parent training program are this text, especially the work sheets at the back. Each participant should have a copy of the text. Additional instructional aides are suggested in the lesson plans.

Follow-up phase

All contact with the participants should not be terminated at the end of the 8-week training program. It is suggested that the parent educator develop a follow-up plan, maintaining periodic contact with the group and with individual members to reinforce their efforts and assist in the planning and implementation of additional interventions. Contact can be maintained by individual interviews, telephone conversations, and monthly meetings of the training group.

The periodic reinforcement offered the participants during the follow-up phase will increase the probability that the skills learned during the training program will not fall into disuse.

PARENT TRAINING LESSONS
Lesson 1. An introduction to behavior modification*

GOALS

1. To familiarize participants with the models of causation of human behavior and with the behavior change process
2. To enable participants to exemplify each of the principles of behavior modification
3. To enable participants to complete two

---

*Time constraints may necessitate making this lesson into two sessions.

or more target behavior selection checklists correctly

4. To enable participants to accurately observe and record a target behavior

CONTENT

1. Models of causation of human behavior
2. Principles of behavior modification
3. Overview of the behavior change process
4. Selecting a target behavior
5. Observing and recording a target behavior

INSTRUCTIONAL METHODS

1. Lecture
2. Discussion
3. Demonstration
4. Completion of a target behavior selection checklist
5. Recording the target behavior rate or frequency

ACTIVITIES

1. Segment A (40 minutes)
   a. Introduction of the parent educator and individual participants
   b. Overview of the course organization and content
   c. Brief lecture on contemporary theories of causation of human behavior
   d. Brief lecture or overview of the behavior change process
   e. Lecture on the principles of behavior modification; each participant requested to cite a personal example of each principle (may be written)
   f. Examples of target behaviors presented and explanation of the target behavior selection process: demonstration of how to complete a target behavior selection checklist; Each participant requested to select a target behavior and complete a target behavior selection checklist
   g. Procedures for observing and re-

cording target behaviors presented, exemplified, and discussed

2. Break (10 minutes)
3. Segment B (40 minutes)
   a. Target Behavior 1 (home behavior)
      (1) Each participant (or mother and father) presents to the group the target behavior selected during the psychosituational assessment interview of the course preparation phase. Participants also present and discuss the data that they recorded on the behavior log form.
      (2) Each participant completes a target behavior selection checklist on Target Behavior 1.
      (3) Each participant transfers the data on the behavior log form to an appropriate tally form (see Table 5, p. 41).

RESOURCES*

1. Segment A
   a. Parent educator and individual participants
   b. Chapter Six: Preparation phase of program and lesson titles
   c. Chapter One: Models of human behavior
   d. Chapter Three: Entire chapter
   e. Chapter Two: Principles of reinforcement
   f. Chapter Three: Selecting a target behavior
      Target behavior selection checklist (back of text)
   g. Chapter Three: Collecting and recording baseline data
2. Break

---

*Where appropriate, the numbers and letters in this section are in agreement with those in the activities section.

3. Segment B
   a. Target behavior 1
      (1) Behavior log form (back of text)
      (2) Target behavior selection check-list (back of text)
      (3) Chapter Three: Collecting and recording baseline data

EVALUATION

1. Quiz on or written examples of the principles of reinforcement
2. Completed behavior log form, target behavior selection checklist, and tally form

HOME ASSIGNMENT

1. Observe and record baseline data on Target Behavior 1.
2. Read:
   a. Chapter Two: Consequences of behavior; Schedules of reinforcement
   b. Chapter Three: Collecting and recording baseline data

Lesson 2. Consequences of behavior

GOALS

1. To familiarize participants with the consequences of human behavior and the common reinforcement schedules
2. To enable participants to accurately chart baseline data on Target Behavior 1

CONTENT

1. Review of Lesson 1
2. Consequences of behavior
3. Schedules of reinforcement
4. Collecting and recording baseline data
5. Charting baseline data

INSTRUCTIONAL METHODS

1. Lecture
2. Demonstration
3. Discussion
4. Completion of a behavior chart

ACTIVITIES

1. Segment A (40 minutes)
   a. Review
   b. Lecture/demonstration on the consequences of human behavior, the common reinforcement schedules, and the procedure of charting baseline data
   c. Discussion of (b)
   d. Examples of baseline data presented; each participant requested to chart example baseline data on a behavior chart
2. Break (10 minute)
3. Segment B (40 minutes)
   a. Target behavior 1 (home behavior)
      (1) Each participant charts baseline data collected between Lessons 1 and 2 (Baseline 1 data).
      (2) Participants present their raw data to the group for discussion, clarification, and practice charting

RESOURCES

1. Segment A
   a. Lesson 1 resources
   b. Chapter Two: Consequences of behavior; Schedules of reinforcement Chapter Three: Collecting and recording baseline data
   c. Parent educator and participants
   d. Chapter Three: Collecting and recording baseline data Behavior chart (back of text)
2. Break
3. Segment B
   a. Target Behavior 1
      (1) Behavior chart (back of text)
      (2) Behavior tally form used during Week 1

EVALUATION

1. Quiz on or written examples of the consequences of behavior and the common schedules of reinforcement
2. Completed tally form and behavior chart

HOME ASSIGNMENT

1. Continue observing and recording Baseline 1 data on Target Behavior 1.
2. Observe and note those things and ac-

tivities the child likes to do during free time.

3. Read:
   a. Chapter Three: Identifying appropriate reinforcers
   b. Chapter Six: Home reinforcers

Lesson 3. Selecting potentially effective reinforcers

GOALS

1. To familiarize participants with the behavior modification intervention strategies for increasing, maintaining, and decreasing behavior
2. To enable participants to compile a list of potentially effective home-based reinforcers
3. To enable participants to accurately chart Baseline 1 data on Target Behavior 1
4. To facilitate the participants' selection of reinforcers, a reinforcement schedule, and an intervention strategy for Target Behavior 1

CONTENT

1. Review of Lesson 2
2. Selecting potentially effective reinforcers
3. Overview of behavior modification intervention strategies
4. Charting or graphing baseline data
5. Selecting an appropriate reinforcement schedule and intervention strategy

INSTRUCTIONAL METHODS

1. Lecture
2. Discussion
3. Completion of behavior chart
4. Individual/group project

ACTIVITIES

1. Segment A (40 minutes)
   a. Review
   b. Lecture on selecting potentially effective reinforcers and on behavior modification intervention strategies
   c. Discussion of (b)

d. Individual/group development of a list of children's rewards observed as home assignment

2. Break (10 minutes)
3. Segment B (40 minutes)
   a. Target Behavior 1 (home behavior)
      (1) Each participant charts Baseline 1 data collected between Lessons 2 and 3.
      (2) Each participant (with parent educator's assistance) selects reinforcers, a reinforcement schedule, and an intervention strategy to modify Target Behavior 1.

RESOURCES

1. Segment A
   a. Lesson 2 resources
   b. Chapter Three: Identifying appropriate reinforcers
      Chapter Four: Entire chapter
      Chapter Five: Entire chapter
      Chapter Six: Home reinforcers
   c. Parent educator and participants
   d. Chapter Three: Identifying appropriate reinforcers
2. Break
3. Segment B
   a. Target Behavior 1
      (1) Behavior chart (back of text)
      (2) Participant with assistance of parent educator and other participants

EVALUATION

1. Quiz on methods of selecting appropriate reinforcers
2. Results of individual/group list of children's rewards
3. Behavior chart on Target Behavior 1

HOME ASSIGNMENT

1. Implement intervention strategy for Target Behavior 1 and continue observing and recording data.
2. Read Chapter 4: Shaping; Modeling; Contingency contracting.

Lesson 4. Strategies to increase behavior

GOALS

1. To familiarize participants with modeling, shaping, and contingency contracting intervention strategies
2. To enable participants to accurately chart intervention data on Target Behavior 1
3. To enable participants to accurately complete a target behavior selection checklist on Target Behavior 2 (home or home-school behavior)

CONTENT

1. Review of Lesson 3
2. Intervention strategies: shaping, modeling, and contingency contracting
3. Charting intervention data
4. Selecting a target behavior

INSTRUCTIONAL METHODS

1. Lecture
2. Discussion
3. Completion of contingency contract form
4. Completion of target behavior selection checklist
5. Completion of behavior chart

ACTIVITIES

1. Segment A (40 minutes)
   a. Review
   b. Lecture/demonstration on shaping, modeling, and contingency contracting
   c. Discussion of (b)
   d. Participants requested to present examples of shaping and modeling from home setting (may be written)
   e. Completion of one or more contingency contracts
2. Break (10 minutes)
3. Segment B (40 minutes)
   a. Target Behavior 1 (home behavior)
      (1) Each participant charts or graphs intervention data collected between Lessons 3 and 4 (Intervention 1 data).

      (2) Participants discuss charts.
   b. Target Behavior 2 (home or home-school behavior)
      (1) Each participant completes a target behavior selection checklist.
      (2) Participants discuss checklists.

RESOURCES

1. Segment A
   a. Lesson 3 resources
   b. Chapter Four: Shaping; Modeling; Contingency contracting
   c. Parent educator and participants
   d. Same as (c)
   e. Contingency contract form (back of text)
2. Break
3. Segment B
   a. Target Behavior 1
      (1) Behavior chart (back of text)
      (2) Parent educator and participants
   b. Target Behavior 2
      (1) Target behavior selection checklist (back of text)
      (2) Parent educator and participants

EVALUATION

1. Quiz on or written examples of shaping and modeling
2. Completed contingency contract forms
3. Behavior chart on Target Behavior 1
4. Target behavior selection checklist on Target Behavior 2

HOME ASSIGNMENT

1. Observe and record Intervention 1 data on Target Behavior 1.
2. Observe and record Baseline 1 data on Target Behavior 2.
3. Read Chapter 4: Token economy.

Lesson 5. Strategies to increase behavior—cont'd

GOALS

1. To familiarize participants with the token economy intervention strategy
2. To enable participants to accurately

chart Intervention 1 data on Target Behavior 1

3. To enable participants to assess the effectiveness of the behavior change program for Target Behavior 1
4. To enable participants to plan an evaluation of Target Behavior 1 by means of observing and recording new baseline data following the intervention (Baseline 2 data)
5. To enable participants to chart Baseline 1 data on Target Behavior 2

CONTENT

1. Review of Lesson 4
2. Token economy intervention strategy
3. Charting data
4. Assessing intervention effectiveness
5. Planning evaluation phase (charting Baseline 2 data)

INSTRUCTIONAL METHODS

1. Lecture
2. Discussion
3. Completion of behavior charts

ACTIVITIES

1. Segment A (40 minutes)
   a. Review
   b. Lecture/demonstration on token economy
   c. Discussion of (b)
   d. Participants requested to present an example of a home token economy including target behavior(s), reinforcement schedule, reward menu, and proposed point card or tally form (may be written)
2. Break (10 minutes)
3. Segment B (40 minutes)
   a. Target Behavior 1 (home behavior)
      (1) Each participant charts or graphs Intervention 1 data collected between Lessons 4 and 5.
      (2) Each participant assesses the effectiveness of the intervention by analyzing the behavior chart.
      (3) Each participant plans an evaluation phase based on Baseline 2 data.
   b. Target Behavior 2 (home or home-school behavior)
      (1) Each participant charts or graphs Baseline 1 data collected between Lessons 4 and 5.

RESOURCES

1. Segment A
   a. Lesson 4 resources
   b. Chapter Four: Token economy
   c. Parent educator and participants
   d. Participants
2. Break
3. Segment B
   a. Target Behavior 1
      (1) Behavior chart (back of text)
      (2) Participant with assistance of parent educator and other participants
      (3) Same as (2)
   b. Target Behavior 2
      (1) Behavior chart (back of text)

EVALUATION

1. Quiz on or written examples of token economy
2. Behavior chart on Target Behavior 1
3. Behavior chart on Target Behavior 2

HOME ASSIGNMENT

1. Observe and record evaluation (Baseline 2) data on Target Behavior 1.
2. Observe and record Baseline 1 data on Target Behavior 2.
3. Read:
   a. Chapter Five: Extinction; Time-out; Reinforcement of incompatible behaviors
   b. Chapter Six: Aids to communication

Lesson 6. Strategies to decrease behavior

GOALS

1. To familiarize participants with extinction, time-out, and reinforcement of incompatible behaviors intervention strategies

2. To familiarize participants with the aids to communication between home and school
3. To enable participants to chart evaluation (Baseline 2) data and plan the re-imposition of the intervention (Intervention 2) for Target Behavior 1
4. To enable participants to chart Baseline 1 data and plan the specific reinforcers, reinforcement schedule, and intervention strategy to modify Target Behavior 2

CONTENT
1. Review of Lesson 5
2. Extinction, time-out, and reinforcement of incompatible behaviors intervention strategies
3. Aids to communication
4. Charting or graphing data
5. Planning the reimposed intervention (Intervention 2) phase for Target Behavior 1
6. Planning the initial intervention (Intervention 1) phase for Target Behavior 2

INSTRUCTIONAL METHODS
1. Lecture
2. Discussion
3. Completion of behavior charts

ACTIVITIES
1. Segment A (40 minutes)
   a. Review
   b. Lecture/demonstration on extinction, time-out, and reinforcement of incompatible behaviors
   c. Lecture/demonstration on aids to communication
   d. Discussion of (b) and (c)
   e. Participants requested to present examples of extinction, time-out, and reinforcers (may be written)
2. Break
3. Segment B (40 minutes)
   a. Target Behavior 1 (home behavior)
      (1) Each participant charts Baseline 2 data collected between Lessons 5 and 6.

(2) Each participant compares Baseline 2 data with baseline 1 and Intervention 1 data.
(3) Each participant plans the reimposition of the intervention strategy.
   b. Target Behavior 2 (home or home-school behavior)
      (1) Each participant charts Baseline 1 data collected between Lessons 5 and 6.
      (2) Each participant selects a reinforcement schedule, reinforcers, and an intervention strategy to modify Target Behavior 2.

RESOURCES
1. Segment A
   a. Lesson 5 resources
   b. Chapter Five: Extinction; Time-out; Reinforcement of incompatible behaviors
   c. Chapter Six: Aids to communication
   d. Parent educator and participants
   e. Participants
2. Break
3. Segment B
   a. Target Behavior 1
      (1) Behavior chart (back of text)
      (2) Participants
      (3) Participant with assistance of parent educator and other participants
   b. Target Behavior 2
      (1) Behavior chart (back of text)
      (2) Participants

EVALUATION
1. Quiz on or written examples of extinction, time-out, reinforcement of incompatible behaviors, and aids to communication
2. Behavior chart on Target Behavior 1
3. Behavior chart on Target Behavior 2

HOME ASSIGNMENT
1. Observe and record behavior data on

the reimposed intervention (Intervention 2) for Target Behavior 1.
2. Observe and record behavior data on the initial intervention (Intervention 1) for Target Behavior 2.
3. Read Chapter Five: Punishment; Desensitization.

Lesson 7. Strategies to decrease behavior—cont'd

GOALS

1. To familiarize participants with punishment and desensitization intervention strategies
2. To enable participants to chart Intervention 2 data on Target Behavior 1
3. To enable participants to chart Intervention 1 data on Target Behavior 2

CONTENT

1. Review of Lesson 6
2. Punishment and desensitization intervention strategies
3. Charting data

INSTRUCTIONAL METHODS

1. Lecture/demonstration
2. Discussion
3. Completion of behavior charts

ACTIVITIES

1. Segment A (40 minutes)
   a. Review
   b. Lecture/demonstration on punishment and desensitization
   c. Discussion of (b)
   d. Participants requested to present examples of punishment and desensitization (may be written)
2. Break (10 minutes)
3. Segment B (40 minutes)
   a. Target Behavior 1 (home behavior)
      (1) Each participant charts Intervention 2 data collected between Lessons 6 and 7.
      (2) Each participant compares Intervention 2 data with previously collected data: Baseline 1,

Intervention 1 and Baseline 2 data.
   b. Target Behavior 2 (home or home-school behavior)
      (1) Each participant charts Intervention 1 data collected between Lessons 6 and 7.

RESOURCES

1. Segment A
   a. Lesson 6 resources
   b. Chapter Five: Punishment; Desensitization
   c. Parent educator and participants
   d. Participants
2. Break
3. Segment B
   a. Target Behavior 1
      (1) Behavior chart (back of text)
      (2) Participants
   b. Target Behavior 2
      (1) Behavior chart (back of text)

EVALUATION

1. Quiz on or written examples of punishment and desensitization
2. Behavior chart on Target Behavior 1
3. Behavior chart on Target Behavior 2

HOME ASSIGNMENT

1. Observe and record behavior data on Intervention 2 for Target Behavior 1.
2. Observe and record behavior data on Intervention 1 for Target Behavior 2.
3. Read Chapter Eight: Some guidelines for application; Some principles concerning individual rights of children.

Lesson 8. Ethical and effective application

GOALS

1. To familiarize participants with the guidelines for the application of behavior modification strategies and with the principles concerning the individual rights of children
2. To enable participants to chart Intervention 2 data for Target Behavior 1
3. To enable participants to plan the phas-

ing out of the intervention imposed on Target Behavior 1

4. To enable participants to chart Intervention 1 data for Target Behavior 2 and assess the effectiveness of the intervention

5. To enable participants to plan the remainder of the behavior change program for Target Behavior 2, which may include Baseline 2 data, Intervention 2, and phasing out

6. To establish procedures for follow-up of course participation

CONTENT

1. Review of Lessons 1 through 7

2. Guidelines for application, and principles concerning the individual rights of children

3. Charting data

4. Planning intervention phases and phasing out

INSTRUCTIONAL METHODS

1. Lecture/demonstration

2. Discussion

3. Completion of behavior charts

ACTIVITIES

1. Segment A (40 minutes)
   a. Review
   b. Lecture/demonstration on the guidelines for application and the principles concerning the individual rights of children
   c. Discussion of (b)
   d. Participants requested to present examples of the application of the guidelines and principles (may be written)
   e. Plans agreed on for course follow-up activities

2. Break (10 minutes)

3. Segment B (40 minutes)
   a. Target Behavior 1 (home behavior)
      (1) Each participant charts Intervention 2 data.
      (2) Each participant plans the phasing out of the intervention.

   b. Target Behavior 2 (home or home-school behavior)
      (1) Each participant plans the remainder of the behavior change program, which may include Baseline 2 data, Intervention 2, and phasing out.
      (2) Discussion of (1).

RESOURCES

1. Segment A
   a. Lessons 1 through 7 resources
   b. Chapter Eight: Some guidelines for application; Some principles concerning individual rights of children
   c. Parent educator and participants
   d. Participants
   e. Parent educator and participants

2. Break

3. Segment B
   a. Target Behavior 1
      (1) Behavior chart (back of text)
      (2) Participant with assistance of parent educator and other participants
   b. Target Behavior 2
      (1) Participant with assistance of parent educator and other participants
      (2) Parent educator and participants

EVALUATION

1. Quiz on or written examples of application of the guidelines and principles

2. Behavior chart on Target Behavior 1 and phasing out plan

3. Behavior chart on Target Behavior 2 and plan for remainder of intervention

HOME ASSIGNMENT

1. Continue application of course content and learned skills.

2. Attend follow-up session.

AIDS TO COMMUNICATION

During the implementation phase of a home-school behavior change intervention, the parents and teacher need to communicate precisely and frequently to ensure the integrity of the program. Although it is possible to use telephone conversations and handwritten notes to communicate, the parents and teacher may find these methods imprecise and inordinately demanding of time.

In this section several aids to parent-teacher communication that appear to minimize time and inconvenience for both parties are presented. In addition, these methods increase the precision and clarity of communication.

The passport

The "passport" (Runge and others, 1975) is an effective technique for increasing and maintaining parent-teacher communication and cooperation.

The passport is an ordinary spiral notebook that the child carries daily, to and from home, and to and from the classrooms in which the child is instructed. The passport is a medium for communications among parents, special teachers, regular teachers, aides, bus drivers, and others concerned with the child's behavior change or academic remediation program. All concerned adults are encouraged to make notations in the notebook.

Prior to the actual initiation of a behavior change program, the passport procedures are explained to the child, who is told that he or she will be rewarded for carrying the notebook and presenting it to the appropriate adults.

The child is rewarded with points for carrying the passport and for appropriate efforts, accomplishments, and behavior in the home, in the classroom, on the bus, in the gym, and so on. Points may be awarded at home for appropriate behavior and home-study activities. If the child forgets or refuses to carry the "passport," he or she cannot earn points. At the appropriate time, the accumulated points are exchanged for tangible as well as social rewards.

Most elementary school students respond enthusiastically to carrying the passport, receiving points and awards, and reading the comments written about their behavior and achievement by adults.

Parents are introduced to the passport concept and procedures at an evening meeting. At this meeting the method is explained and discussed. Parents' questions and concerns must be appropriately responded to by the teacher. At this session instruction for making notations in the passport are given. Similar meetings or informal discussions should be held with other adults who will be using the passport, such as classroom teachers, special teachers, administrators, bus drivers, and so on.

The guidelines for writing comments in the passport are:

1. Be brief. (Parents are busy, too.)
2. Be positive. (Parents know their child has problems. They don't need to be reinforced.)
3. Be honest. (Don't say a child is doing fine if he is not. However, rather than writing negative notes, write neutral ones or request a parent visit.)
4. Be responsive. (If a parent asks for help, respond immediately.)
5. Be informal. (You are a professional but parents are still your equal.)
6. Be consistent. (If you use the passport, do so consistently and expect the same from the parent.)
7. Avoid jargon. (Parents don't understand educators' jargon. For that matter, do we?)
8. Be careful. (If you are having a bad day, personally, do not project your feelings onto the child or his parents.) (p. 92)*

Points are awarded to the child on the basis of a mutually agreed-on reinforcement schedule and rate. The procedures applied

*Reprinted from A passport to positive parent-teacher communications by A. Runge, J. Walker, and T. M. Shea, *Teaching Exceptional Children*, 1975, 7(3), 91-92, by permission of The Council for Exceptional Children; 1920 Association Drive, Reston, Va. 22091.

10/25/79

9:00 AM

To: Ms. Dolores

Good day on the bus. Tom sat in his assigned seat and waited his turn to leave the bus. I praised his behavior and gave him two points.

Mr. Parker, Bus Driver

10/25/79

10:30 AM

To: Ms. Dolores

During PE today the group played kickball. Tom was well behaved but had difficulty participating effectively. I awarded him six points. He was praised for his behavior. Can we meet to discuss some means of increasing his participation?

Ms. Minton, PE

10/25/79

2:30 PM

To: Mr. and Mrs. Hogerty

As you can see from the notes above, Tom had a good day at school.

He received 89% on his reading test this morning. That's real progress. Please praise him for this accomplishment.

This evening, Tom is to read pp. 1-5 in his new reading book.

Even better news! Tom remembered to walk in the hallways today. He is very proud of himself.

I shall talk to Ms. Minton today about increasing Tom's participation at PE. I'll let you know what we decide at parent meeting tomorrow night.

Ms. Dolores

10/25/79

9:00 PM

To: Ms. Dolores

We praised and rewarded Tom for his hard work on the reading test, the bus, and the hallways. You're right; he feels good about himself today.

Tom read pp. 1-5 in the new book with his father. The words he had trouble with are underlined.

We will be at parent meeting tomorrow night.

Mary Hogerty

---

in the passport are similar to those presented in the section on the token economy in Chapter Four. Points are recorded on a point card similar to those presented in that section. The card is usually affixed to the inside of the front or back cover of the notebook.

An example of the types of notations to be made in the passport is presented above. The example involves an exchange of information among an elementary school teacher, a bus driver, a physical education teacher, and the child's parents.

Daily report cards

Edlund (1969) reported a home-school behavior management program in which children were reinforced at home for school performance. A token economy procedure of this nature is based on the use of a daily report card. Points may be awarded for acceptable social-emotional behavior and for acceptable academic performance.

The teacher completes the daily report by awarding (or not awarding) the child points at various periods during the day. The card is taken home by the child, who must present the card to the parents. (If the card is lost or forgotten, the child cannot be rewarded.) Rewards are given by the parents during the afternoon and evening hours. Special rewards are given for exceptional behavior and achievement.

Dickerson and associates (1973) developed a daily reporting system similar to Edlund's approach. Their system was used with considerable success with more than 1,000 children, 5 to 15 years of age, over a 4-year period. In this system, which is applicable in both regular and special education settings, a daily report card is given to the child, who is rewarded at home for acceptable behavior and achievement in school. (Cards have been designed for children in grades K to 3 and 4 to 6.) Dickerson and associates emphasize this as a positive approach to behavior change and suggest that negative comments be avoided.

Readers seeking suggestions on the format of daily report cards, awards, certificates, passes, and the like, are referred to an excellent book by Kaplan and associates (1974). This book contains scores of formats for daily reports, awards, passes, and so on.

SUMMARY

In this chapter a method that may be applied by the educator interested in training parents in behavior modification procedures and principles is presented. The program is designed primarily to increase parental knowledge and skill in the application of behavior modification techniques. The training program also has the potential to increase parent-teacher cooperation. Although not a primary objective of the program, parents are provided a setting in which they may receive emotional support as they struggle with their child's problem.

EXERCISES FOR CHAPTER SIX
Quiz

1. According to Clements and Alexander (1975), "Extensive research demonstrates unequivocally that children _____ more, _____ better, and _____ _____ faster when _____ training is effected" (p. 7).

2. List six defense mechanisms parents may apply in response to their recognition of a problem with a child.

   a. _____

   b. _____

   c. _____

   d. _____

   e. _____

   f. _____

3. McDowell (1976) has classified parent programs under three categories:

   a. _____

   b. _____

   c. _____

4. The objectives of the parent training program presented in this chapter are:

   a. _____

   _____

   b. _____

   _____

   c. _____

   _____

5. The psychosituational assessment interview is primarily an _____

   _____ technique.

6. The four major tasks to be accomplished in the psychosituational assessment interview are:

   a. _____

   b. _____

   c. _____

   d. _____

7. The phases of the parent training program presented in this chapter are:

   a. _____   c. _____

   b. _____

8. List five of the eight guidelines for writing comments in the "passport."

   a. _____   d. _____

   b. _____   e. _____

   c. _____

Projects

1. Write a 300-word essay on the topic "Parent Education and Training: A Significant Component of the School Service Program."
2. List 25 home reinforcers not presented in this chapter. Classify these as social or tangible.
3. Conduct a psychosituational assessment interview in which a classmate plays the role of a parent. Record and analyze the interview.
4. Obtain, study, and write a report for verbal presentation to your class on one of the checklists and inventories listed on p. 113. As part of the verbal presentation, demonstrate to the group the administration of the instrument.
5. Using one of the lesson plans in the chapter, prepare, present, and evaluate a parent training session. Your classmates can role play as parents.

REFERENCES

Auerbach, A. B. *Parents learn through discussion: Principles and practices of parent group education.* New York: John Wiley & Sons, Inc., 1968.

Barsch, R. H. *The parent teacher partnership.* Reston, Va: The Council for Exceptional Children, 1969.

Bersoff, D. N., and Grieger, R. M. II. An interview model for the psychosituational assessment of children's behavior. *American Journal of Orthopsychiatry,* 1971, *41*(3), 483-493.

Blackham, G. J., and Silberman, A. *Modification of child and adolescent behavior,* (2nd ed.). Belmont, Calif.: Wadsworth Publishing Co., Inc., 1975.

Brockway, B. S. *Training in child management: A family approach.* Dubuque, Iowa: Kendall/Hunt Publishing Co., 1974.

Burks, H. F. *Burks' Behavior Rating Scales: Manual.* Los Angeles: Western Psychological Services, 1977.

Buscaglia, L. (Ed.): *The disabled and their parents: A counseling challenge.* Thorofare, N.J.: Charles B. Slack, Inc., 1975.

Cassel, R. N. *The Child Behavior Rating Scale: Manual.* Los Angeles: Western Psychological Services, 1962.

Clements, J. E., and Alexander, R. N. Parent training: Bringing it all back home. *Focus on Exceptional Children,* 1975, *7*(5), 1-12.

Cooper, J. O., and Edge, D. *Parenting: Strategies and educational methods.* Columbus, Ohio: Charles E. Merrill Publishing Co., 1978.

Denhoff, E. The impact of parents on the growth of exceptional children. *Exceptional Children,* 1960, *26*(5), 271-274.

Dickerson, D., Spellman, C. R., Larsen, S., and Tyler, L. Let the cards do the talking—A teacher-parent communication program. *Teaching Exceptional Children,* 1973, *4*(4), 170-178.

Dinkmeyer, D., and McKay, G. D. *Raising a responsible child: Practical steps to successful family relationships.* New York: Simon & Schuster, Inc., 1973.

Doll, E. A. *The Vineland Social Maturity Scale* Circle Pines, Minn.: American Guidance Service, Inc., 1965.

Dreikurs, R. *The challenge of parenthood.* New York: Hawthorn Books, Inc., 1958.

Edlund, C. V. Rewards at home to promote desirable school behavior. *Teaching Exceptional Children,* 1969, *1*(4), 121-127.

Galloway, C., and Galloway, K. C. Parent classes in precise behavior management. *Teaching Exceptional Children* 1971, *3*(3), 120-128.

Gardner, W. I. *Children with learning and behavior problems: A behavior management approach.* Boston: Allyn & Bacon, Inc., 1974.

Gordon, S. A parent's concerns. *The Exceptional Parent,* 1976, *6*(3), 19-22.

Gordon, T. *Parent effectiveness training.* New York: Wyden Books, 1970.

Homan, W. E. *Child sense: A guide to loving, level-headed parenthood.* New York: Basic Books, Inc., Publishers, 1977

Jogis, J. L. To be spoken sadly. In L. Buscaglia (Ed.), *The disabled and their parents: A counseling challenge.* Thorofare, N.J.: Charles B. Stack, Inc., 1975.

Kahn, R. L., and Cannell, C. F. *The dynamics of interviewing: Theory, technique, and cases.* New York: John Wiley & Sons, Inc., 1957.

Kaplan, P., Kohfeldt, J., and Sturla, K. *It's positively fun: Techniques for managing learning environments.* Denver: Love Publishing Co., 1974.

Karnes, M. B., and Zehrbach, R. R. *Flexibility in getting parents involved in the school.* Teaching Exceptional Children, Fall 1972, 5, 6-19.

Kratoville, B. L. What parents feel. In L. Buscaglia (Ed.), *The disabled and their parents: A counseling challenge.* Thorofare, N.J.: Charles B. Stack, Inc., 1975. (a)

Kratoville, B. L. What parents need to hear. In L. Buscaglia (Ed.), *The disabled and their parents: A counseling challenge.* Thorofare, N.J.: Charles B. Stack, Inc., 1975. (b)

Kroth, R. *Target behavior.* Olathe, Kansas: Select-Ed, Inc., 1972.

Lichter, P. Communicating with parents: It begins with listening. *Teaching Exceptional Children,* 1976, *8*(2), 66-71.

McDowell, R. L. Parent counseling: The state of the art. *Journal of Learning Disabilities,* 1976, *9*(10), 614-619.

Quay, H. C., and Peterson, D. R. *Manual for the Behavior Problem Checklist.* Champaign, Ill: Children's Research Center, University of Illinois, 1967.

Ross, A. O. *The exceptional child in the family: Helping parents of exceptional children.* New York: Grune & Stratton, Inc., 1964.

Runge, A., Walker, J., and Shea, T. M. A passport to positive parent-teacher communications. *Teaching Exceptional Children,* 1975, *7*(3), 91-92.

Shea, T. M. *Teaching children and youth with behavior disorders.* St. Louis: The C. V. Mosby Co., 1978.

Shea, T. M., Whiteside, W. R., Beetner, E. G., and Lindsey, D. L. *Microteaching module: Psychosituational interview.* Edwardsville: Southern Illinois University, 1974.

Spivack, G., and Spotts, J. *Devereux Child Behavior (DCB) Rating Scale.* Devon, Pa.: The Devereux Foundation, 1966.

Spivack, G., Spotts, J., and Haimes, P. E. *Devereux*

Adolescent Behavior (DAB) Rating Scale. Devon, Pa.: The Devereux Foundation, 1967.

Stephenson, W. *The study of behavior: q-technique and its methodology.* Chicago: University of Chicago Press, 1953.

Stigen, G. *Heartaches and handicaps: An irreverent survival manual for parents.* Palo Alto, Calif.: Science & Behavior Books, 1976.

Stott, D. H., and Marston, N. C. *Bristol Social Adjustment Guides: The child in the school.* San Diego: Educational and Industrial Testing Service, 1970.

Susser, P. Parents and partners. *The Exceptional Parent,* 4(3), 1974, 41-47.

Walker, H. M. *Walker Problem Behavior Identification Checklist: Manual.* Los Angeles: Western Psychological Services, 1976.

Webster, E. J. *Counseling with parents of handicapped children: Guidelines for improving communications.* New York: Grune & Stratton, Inc., 1977.

Wood, M. M. Services to parents. In M. M. Wood (Ed.), *Developmental therapy: A textbook for teachers as therapists for emotionally disturbed young children.* Baltimore: University Park Press, 1975.

CHAPTER SEVEN

Alternative behavior management interventions

PSYCHOANALYTIC-PSYCHODYNAMIC, BIOPHYSICAL, AND ENVIRONMENTAL

In this chapter several behavior management interventions associated with the psychoanalytic-psychodynamic, biophysical, and environmental models of behavior (briefly discussed in Chapter One) are reviewed. Many of these interventions can be directly implemented by the teacher with appropriate training and experience. This is particularly true of the psychoanalytic-psychodynamic and environmental interventions. The educator serves in an important supportive role to other professional personnel in relation to the biophysical interventions.

It is not feasible in a single chapter to explore in detail all of the interventions developed from these three theoretical perspectives that have potential applicability to the management of children. Consequently, the review is selective; some interventions are discussed in some detail whereas others are merely mentioned. The reader is encouraged to use the chapter references to study in depth any intervention of interest

Portions of this chapter are adapted from Shea, T. M. *Teaching children and youth with behavior disorders*. St. Louis: The C. V. Mosby Co., 1978, Chapters 9 and 10.

before attempting to implement with a specific child in a particular educational setting.

IDEAS, ACTIONS, OUTCOMES

In an intervention, ideas, actions, and outcomes are all tied together and greatly affect each other. Ideas, in and of themselves, are inert unless active energy is added to their influence. Active energy, in and of itself, is meaningless and chaotic unless it is directed. In an intervention, the conceptual framework directs and channels the action, by providing an analysis of the nature of the problem which dictates the intervention, and by suggesting the outcome toward which the intervention is directed.

One form of intervention, carried out within two different conceptual frameworks can have radically different meanings and lead to radically different experiences and outcomes for the participants. (Rhodes, 1972, pp. 23-24)

Educators' perceptions of children, if Rhodes is correct, are in large part determiners of the behavior management interventions selected and imposed. For example, the teacher who perceives the child as primarily determined by the environment approaches the problems of behavior management from a radically different point of view from the teacher who perceives a child as controlled primarily by intrapsychic or biophysical factors.

DEFINITION OF BEHAVIOR MANAGEMENT

The majority of school staff meeting and discussion time is often devoted to considerations of behavior management. The same few, but important, questions are asked repeatedly:

How can this child's behavior be changed?

How can this classroom group's behavior be changed?

Should I punish this behavior?

Should I discuss this behavior with the individual?

Should I ignore this behavior?

Will this intervention work?

Is it ethical to use this intervention technique?

Will it harm or hurt the child?

Hour after hour is devoted to discussions of these and similar questions and concerns about the management of children's behavior in the classroom and school.

In this text behavior management interventions are defined as *all those actions (and conscious inactions) teachers engage in to enhance the probability that children, individually and in groups, will develop effective behaviors that are personally self-fulfilling, productive, and socially acceptable.*

Behavior management is a complex problem that cannot be approached from a simplistic point of view. It is a teacher function that must be studied, planned, and objectively utilized and evaluated, with equal emphasis given to all relevant variables: the individual or group whose behavior is to be managed, the behavior under consideration, the setting in which the behavior occurs, the individual applying the intervention, and the purpose of the intervention. A specific technique that is an effective intervention for one specific behavior of one specific child in a particular setting may be ineffective under another set of circumstances when applied by a different individual to change a different behavior of a different individual or group.

PSYCHOANALYTIC-PSYCHODYNAMIC INTERVENTIONS

The psychoanalytic-psychodynamic interventions presented in this section are, in part, directly applicable by the educator. Several important psychodynamic interventions employed by trained professionals in the allied mental health disciplines are not reviewed. These include individual and group psychotherapy, transactional analysis, directive and nondirective counseling, and family therapy. In addition, the psychoeducational teaching methodology is not reviewed. Readers interested in this educational approach are referred to Long and others (1976) and Shea (1978).

Two basic categories of interventions for application with children are counseling techniques and the expressive arts. The counseling techniques discussed here are the life-space interview, reality therapy, and the psychosituational assessment interview. The expressive arts discussed include free play, puppetry, role playing and psychodrama, creative movement and dance, music, the written word, the spoken word, two-dimensional arts, and three-dimensional arts.

Before beginning study of these interventions, the reader is encouraged to review the theoretical framework underlying the psychoanalytic-psychodynamic perspective.

Counseling techniques

Life-space interview. Redl (1959) recommended the application of the life-space interview as an integral part of milieu therapy. Milieu therapy is discussed in this chapter as an environmental intervention.

The life-space interview is a here-and-now

intervention built around a child's direct life experience. It is applied by a teacher perceived by the child to be an important part of the child's life-space. The interviewer has a definite role and power influence in the child's daily life (Redl, 1959; Reinert, 1976). The life-space interview technique is imposed to structure an incident in the child's life to enable the child to solve the problems confronting him or her. The interviewer's role is primarily facilitative.

According to Redl, the life-space interview technique may be applied by an educator for either of two purposes: clinical exploitation of life events or emotional first aid on the spot.

In the first situation, *clinical exploitation of life events*, the interviewer uses an actual incident to explore with the child habitual behavioral characteristics. This is primarily an effort by the interviewer to use the incident to attain a long-range therapeutic goal previously established for the child by a clinical and/or interdisciplinary team.

When the life-space interview technique is employed for the exploitation of life events, the interviewer assists the child in increasing conscious awareness of distorted perceptions of existing realities, pathological behavioral characteristics, hidden social and moral values and standards, or reactions to the behaviors and pressures of the group. In addition, the interviewer uses the technique to discuss with the child more personally productive and socially acceptable means of solving personal problems. This particular application of the life-space interview is not recommended for use by the teacher lacking appropriate training and experience.

The life-space interview technique is also use to give a child *emotional first aid on the spot* at times of unusual stress. When the technique is applied for this purpose, minimal training and experience is required.

The purpose of the life-space interview

technique in on-the-spot first aid is to assist the child over a rough spot in the road in order to continue an activity. The interview is imposed to (1) reduce the child's frustration level, (2) support the child in emotionally charged situations, (3) restore strained child-teacher and child-child communications, (4) reinforce existing behavioral and social limits and realities, or (5) assist the child in efforts to find solutions to everyday problems of living and emotionally charged incidents, such as fights and arguments.

As in any counseling situation, the application of the life-space interview is dependent on a variety of variables: the purpose and goal, the specific environment, the training and experience of the teacher, and especially the child and the particular problem or difficulty.

The application of the life-space interview technique in the clinic or school is a clinical decision involving all members of the team. When the technique is adopted for use, it should be used with consistency by all staff personnel under the supervision of trained and experienced professionals.

Morse (1971) has outlined a series of steps that occur during the life-space interview. This is not a rigid series of steps; on occasion during an interview, some steps are omitted and others reordered.

Generally, the interview begins as a result of a specific incident in the individual's (or group's) actual life-space. The interviewer encourages those involved in the incident to state their personal perceptions of the occurrence. At this time the interviewer must determine if this is an isolated happening or a significant part of a recurring central issue.

The interviewer *listens* to those involved in the incident as they reconstruct it, accepting their feelings and perceptions without moralizing or attacking. Although these individual perceptions of the incident are accepted, the interviewer may suggest alternative perceptions for consideration by those involved.

The interview process then moves into a resolution phase. This phase should be non-judgmental in tone. Many conflicts and confrontations are resolved at this point, and the interview is terminated.

However, if the problems are not resolved, the interviewer may offer his or her view of the happening as it is related to the situation in which the individual or individuals find themselves. Finally, the individual or individuals involved and the interviewer attempt to develop an acceptable plan to deal with the present problem and similar problems in the future.

Several guidelines for interviewer behavior have been offered by Brenner (1969):

1. Be polite to the individual. If you do not have control of your emotions, do not begin the interview.

2. Sit, kneel, or stand to establish eye contact. Talk with, never at, the individual being interviewed.

3. When you are unsure of the history of the incident, investigate. Do not conduct an interview on the basis of second- or third-hand information or rumors.

4. Ask appropriate questions to obtain a knowledgeable grasp of the incident. However, do not probe areas of unconscious motivation; limit the use of "why" questions.

5. Listen to the individual and attempt to comprehend his or her perception of the incident.

6. Encourage the individual to ask questions and respond to these questions appropriately.

7. When the individual is suffering from apparent shame and/or guilt as a result of the incident, attempt to reduce and minimize these feelings.

8. Facilitate the individual's efforts to communicate what he or she wishes to say. If the individual is having difficulty in this area, provide help.

9. Work carefully and patiently with the individual to develop a mutually acceptable plan of action for immediate or future implementation.

Reality therapy. In his 1965 and 1969 publications, Glasser offers a unique perspective on mental health and the treatment of mental illness. His thesis is a distinct departure from traditional Freudian and Neo-Freudian theoretical frameworks that mental health is a state of contentment and mental ill health, a state of discontent. From Glasser's reality therapy point of view, mental health is the ability to function competently in the environment, whereas mental illness is incompetence.

An individual in need of psychiatric assistance is unable to fulfill essential psychological needs. The objective of reality therapy is to lead the individual toward competent functioning in the environment. This technique is designed to help the individual grapple successfully with the tangible and intangible aspects of the real world and as a result be able to fulfill personal needs.

According to Glasser (1965), human beings have two basic psychological needs: (1) to love and be loved and (2) to feel worthwhile to self and others.

To feel worthwhile to self and others, an individual must maintain a satisfactory standard of behavior. The individual who fails to maintain an acceptable standard of behavior suffers pain or discomfort. This discomfort is *mental illness,* that is, lack of responsible involvement with significant others in the environment. A mentally ill person desiring to return to the state of mental health, that is, responsible and competent functioning in reality, must have somebody whom he or she genuinely cares about; and the person must believe that the feeling is mutual.

In reality therapy the process of therapy and the process of teaching are identical. The therapist or teacher's primary objective is to teach the mentally ill person responsible behavior. Responsibility is the ability to fulfill one's personal needs in a manner that does not deprive other individuals of their ability to fulfill their personal needs.

According to Glasser's thesis, learning to be a responsible person is not a natural developmental process. Individuals are taught to be responsible through involvement with responsible and significant others. This involvement with others includes love and discipline. The majority of individuals learn to be responsible from loving and disciplining parents or guardians and others, such as teachers.

In summary, reality therapy is the process of teaching an irresponsible individual to face existing reality, to function responsibly, and, as a result, to fulfill personal needs.

For the mentally ill individual, the therapeutic process includes:

Involvement with an acceptable person who is perceived by the mentally ill person as caring about him or her. The quality of the involvement must be sufficient to permit the mentally ill individual to face existing reality and begin to view personal behavior as irresponsible.

A therapist who is accepting of the individual and maintains involvement with the individual while rejecting irresponsible behavior.

The learning of responsible means of fulfilling personal needs in reality. This learning process is a cooperative activity that may include direct instructions, discussions, conversations, and planning sessions relative to any element of the individual's present life-style.

Reality therapy processes assume that the therapist is an acceptable and accepting person. The therapist, who may be a teacher, is also assumed to be appropriately trained and experienced in reality therapy techniques.

In an educational program reality therapy's goal is to guide individuals and groups toward a more responsible behavior. This goal is attained by means of the reality therapy interview.

Guidelines for teachers engaged in the interview are:

1. Be personal. Demonstrate to the individual that you are a friend who cares about the individual and who is interested in his or her welfare.

2. Focus the therapeutic process on the individual's present behavior, not on past behavior. Accept the individual's expressed feelings but do not probe into unconscious motivation. Ask "what," "how," and "who" questions. Limit the asking of "why" questions.

3. Do not preach, moralize, or make value judgments about the individual's behavior.

4. Help the individual formulate a practical plan to increase responsible behavior. Plannning is a cooperative effort.

5. Encourage the individual to overtly make a commitment to the mutually agreed-on plan.

6. Do not accept the individual's excuses for irresponsible behavior. When a plan fails or cannot be implemented, develop another.

7. Do not punish the individual for irresponsible behavior. As a general principle, allow the individual to realize the logical consequences of irresponsible behavior unless the consequences are unreasonably harmful.

8. Provide the individual with emotional support and security throughout the therapeutic process.

Psychosituational assessment interview.[*]
The objectives of the psychosituational assessment interview technique are to (1) identify and clarify an inappropriate behavior; (2) uncover and analyze the antecedents and consequences of the behavior; and (3) plan, implement, and evaluate a behavior change intervention (Bersoff and Grieger, 1971).

The model of behavior applied in this technique is a distinct departure from the predominant assumptions among psychodynamic theorists: that personality is composed of needs and traits that predispose an individual to respond in predetermined ways to the environment.

Bersoff and Grieger have suggested that, rather than viewing inappropriate behavior as resulting from personality needs and traits, one should perceive it as an individual's inability to respond in certain ways in certain situations. Simply stated, the individual has not learned the responses required for appropriate functioning in the environment.

Through the interview it is possible to determine to what extent the individual's behavior is reinforced and maintained by the environment and to what extent it may be possible to change the behavior by environmental manipulation.

In the interview the primary elements of the environment in which the inappropriate behavior is exhibited are analyzed. These elements are (1) the individual's behavior, (2) the environmental variables impinging on the behavior, and (3) the attitudes and expectations of the individual, the parents, and the teacher.

As indicated in Chapter Six, *behavior* refers to the actual behavior for which the individual is referred, including its antecedents and consequences. *Environmental variables* refer to the specific places and circumstances in which the behavior occurs. *Attitudes and expectations* refer to the beliefs and feelings of the individual and significant others about the behavior. *Expectation* has a double meaning in the interview process; it refers to the specific performance desired as a result of therapy and to the long-range aspirations of the individual.

The four major tasks to be accomplished with this technique are (1) defining the behavior, including its frequency, intensity, and duration; (2) explicating a specific situation in which the behavior is exhibited; (3) uncovering the contingencies that appear to maintain the behavior; and (4) detecting any irrational and unrealistic ideas about the behavior and the individual exhibiting it.

The interview process itself is a direct question-and-answer format focusing on these four major tasks. It is assumed that the interviewer is an acceptable and accepting person who has developed rapport with the individual being interviewed.

This technique has been primarily applied with parents and teachers about children. However, it appears to have definite potential for direct application with older children and adolescents.

Expressive arts

The expressive arts refers to activities that encourage and permit children to express personal feelings and emotions in creative activities with minimal constraints.

All human beings, especially children, according to psychodynamic theory, have feelings and emotions that must be expressed in some manner if mental health is to be maintained or developed. A child's feelings and emotions, positive and negative, can be expressed verbally and physically. Frequently children (and adults) unconsciously express

---

[*]This presentation on the psychosituational assessment interview technique could have been placed under the heading "Behavioral Interventions" or "Environmental Interventions." It is presented here for reader convenience. The intervention is discussed in detail in Chapter Six.

their feelings and emotions in socially unacceptable ways. This can result in conflicts with parents, teachers, and peers and may have a negative impact on the individual's self-concept.

The expressive arts, used in an appropriate environment and under competent guidance, can be an acceptable and legitimate means for expressing positive and negative feelings and emotions. Adults frequently reduce personal stresses and frustrations in verbal exchanges with trusted friends and relatives or by means of avocations, hobbies, games, projects, trips, sports, vacations, and so on. For children, who are generally less capable in verbal communications and less in control of their personal life-style, the expressive arts are an opportunity to reduce stresses and frustrations without danger of conflict with significant others.

The expressive arts can provide many benefits for children. Not only are they beneficial in the affective domain but because of their nature, they provide a variety of cognitive and psychomotor learning benefits.

If the arts are to be used as a behavior management technique, the child must be provided with opportunities to find a personally satisfying media of expression. The individual must be provided with consistent, repeated opportunities to express feelings and emotions by means of the chosen media.

Cheney and Morse (1972) have summarized the value of the expressive arts for behavior-disordered children as follows:

This group of interventions supports and develops the child's expressive abilities. Such techniques serve to mobilize the child's internal resources in a number of ways: they facilitate involvement through activity rather than retreat and withdrawal; they provide acceptable channels for cathartic release; they serve as means of both externalizing the child's conflicts and communicating his feelings about them to others (though both the signal and response may be nonverbal,

and nonconscious and not discussed); many of the expressive media seem to embody inherent "therapeutic" qualities. For children with verbal inhibitions the whole "language" may be nonverbal. (p. 352)

Axline (1947) presented eight basic principles for therapeutic play. These principles appear to be applicable to all interventions discussed in this section:

1. The therapist must develop a warm, friendly relationship with the child, in which good rapport is established as soon as possible.
2. The therapist accepts the child exactly as he is.
3. The therapist establishes a feeling of permissiveness in the relationship so that the child feels free to express his feelings completely.
4. The therapist is alert to recognize the *feelings* the child is expressing and reflects these feelings back to him in such a manner that he gains insight into this behavior.
5. The therapist maintains a deep respect for the child's ability to solve his own problems if given an opportunity to do so. The responsibility to make choices and to institute change is the child's.
6. The therapist does not attempt to direct the child's actions or conversation in any manner. The child leads the way; the therapist follows.
7. The therapist does not attempt to hurry the therapy along. It is a gradual process and is recognized as such by the therapist.
8. The therapist establishes only those limitations that are necessary to anchor the therapy to the world of reality and to make the child aware of his responsibility in the relationship. (pp. 75-76)

Although the eight principles were proposed for play therapists, they are applicable by teachers with one possible exception. This exception is related to Principle 4, where it states, "reflects those feelings back to him." Skill in the art of reflecting feelings back to an individual in nondirective therapy requires training and experience under supervision. Most teachers lack training in nondirective therapy.

Although some limitations and structure in the therapeutic application of expressive arts relative to time, place, media, and behavior are desirable, the child's activities should not be prescribed. The child is encouraged to express self as he or she desires, not as the teacher wishes the child to express self.

Minimal limits include (1) a time limit on the play period; (2) a limit on the use (and abuse) of materials and equipment; (3) a limit on the location of equipment and materials; (4) limits to prevent the destruction of facilities, equipment, and materials, and (5) limits to ensure the safety of the child and the teacher. Limits must be established and communicated to the child either verbally or by demonstration (Ginott, 1959).

Free play. Play therapy as described by Axline (1947), Baruch (1952), Moustakas (1953), and Solomon (1951) is difficult, if not impossible, to initiate in the classroom because of (1) the restrictions inherent with the classroom setting, (2) the traditional role of the teacher, and (3) the teacher's lack of training in psychotherapy, especially play therapy.

Free-play sessions can be provided for either individuals or groups. If a free-play program is instituted, sessions should be scheduled with regularity. Play materials and equipment, located in the designated free-play area, should be "primitive" materials that the child or group can use to create an environment and express feelings and emotions. Complicated toys and games, although entertaining, restrict the child's creative activities. These complex items require the child to be passive rather than active during the sessions.

In a free-play session the child is invited to play with any of the materials in the play area and is encouraged to select materials of interest. Activity is only restricted by the limits previously discussed. The teacher's role is that of nonparticipant-observer and facilitator.

Puppetry. Frequently puppets are the media that help children freely express feelings and emotions to parents, teachers, and peers. Many children who cannot or will not communicate with others directly will do so through a puppet.

Many contemporary language development and affective education programs have successfully implemented puppetry into their program. Perhaps the child feels safe and secure in the world of puppets, which can be manipulated and managed to express personal needs and moods.

Children enjoy not only playing spontaneously with the puppets but also creating and producing puppet shows for teachers, parents, and peers. Children who are not involved directly in the puppet show can profit from this activity. They respond and converse with the puppet being manipulated by a teacher or peer.

Role playing and psychodrama. Role playing and psychodrama are potential valuable therapeutic interventions for use with children. Psychodrama was originally developed for therapeutic purposes by Moreno (1946).

According to Raths and others (1966), role playing can assist an individual in the clarification of feelings and emotions as they relate to existing reality in three ways:

1. It can focus on real occurrences. An incident may be reenacted and the participants told to attend to the feelings aroused, or an incident may be reenacted with the participants changing roles and attending to the feelings aroused by these new roles. An individual may be directed to deliver a soliloquy to re-create an emotionally loaded event (Moreno, 1946). Emphasis here is on expressing feelings that were hidden or held back when the event first occurred.

2. It can focus on significant others. The individual may portray a significant

person in his or her life about whom a great amount of conflict is felt.

3. It can focus on processes and feelings occurring in new situations. Directions for this type of role playing may be very specific, with the participants provided with special characters and actions; or directions may be vague, allowing the participants to form their own characters.

Role playing and psychodrama techniques have been incorporated into several affective education programs concerned specifically with the learning of values and standards.

Creative movement and dance. As therapeutic interventions, creative movement and dance have the capacity to assist children in expressing their feelings and emotions in an acceptable manner (Chace, 1958). This can be accomplished in a variety of ways, such as by imitating nature or animals or by expressing feelings of others or personal feelings, under various circumstances. During creative movement sessions the child can express past, present, and even future feelings and emotions. These activities encourage the child to externalize personal feelings and begin to deal with them.

Movement activities can be conducted with or without music. On occasion, voices, hand clapping, feet stamping, recorded environmental sounds, and rhythm instruments are used to facilitate sessions.

Music. It is an accepted fact in contemporary society that human beings are affected by music. We are exposed to mood-modifying music in restaurants, factories, supermarkets, department stores, banks, and so on. Presumably this music has some effect on our behavior and moods.

Music is applied as a therapeutic intervention for children in several ways:

1. Children enjoy listening to recordings.
2. Music is an effective tool for reducing excitement and activity levels after high-interest, strenuous activities.

3. Young people enjoy producing music. Although every child cannot successfully learn to play a piano or guitar, most children can learn to enjoy singing and participating in a rhythm band.

Through music, children can express feelings and emotions in an acceptable way.

The written word. Few studies have been conducted on the therapeutic benefit of writing as an intervention for children, although writing has been repeatedly demonstrated to be a useful therapeutic intervention for adults. It seems logical that children can express personal feelings and emotions through written communications. By writing and at times sharing with others that which is written, it is possible to externalize personal conflicts and frustrations.

Writing for therapeutic benefit is not concerned with any particular format. Concern is focused entirely on content. The written forms may include poetry, stories, essays, articles, books, diary entries, and so on.

The spoken word. Although many children are not developmentally or emotionally prepared to enter formal verbal psychotherapy, they frequently enjoy and profit from communicating verbally. Communications may take the form of group story-telling sessions or informal conversations and discussions with teachers. In each of these the child is encouraged to express feelings and emotions.

Two-dimensional arts. All two-dimensional productions, from the young child's scribbling to the young adult's realistic drawings and paintings, are expressions of self.

All children should be afforded opportunities to express their feelings and emotions through the two-dimensional arts. These productions may be finger paintings, pencil drawings, water colors, oil, tempera, and so on. Teachers should remember that their personal perceptions of the form and content of a child's art production is secondary. The important element is the child's perceptions and feelings.

Two excellent volumes on art as a therapeutic intervention for use by teachers are by Kellogg and O'Dell (1967) and Kramer (1971). In their text Kellogg and O'Dell review the development of artistic skills. Their work is useful to teachers wishing to place a child's art skill into the normal developmental sequence. In Kramer's text an extensive overview and in-depth discussion of art, art therapy, and several therapeutic techniques is provided.

Three-dimensional arts. The three-dimensional arts are more limited than the two-dimensional arts for classroom use because of the nature of the materials and equipment. They are, nevertheless, valuable therapeutic tools.

In three-dimensional art forms the child can externalize feelings and emotions through the manipulation of clay, plaster, sand, wood, plastic, and a variety of other materials. Arts and crafts projects are included in this group of therapeutic interventions.

BIOPHYSICAL INTERVENTIONS

In this section several biophysical interventions about which educators should have knowledge are discussed. These include several preventive and curative techniques, such as genetic counseling, proper nutrition, general and specialized physical examinations, and medication.

In the majority of these interventions the educator plays an important supportive role to that of the physician and other medical personnel. This section includes an analysis of the educator's functions in referral, collaboration and reporting, the modification of classroom structure and curriculum content, the obtaining of permission to administer medication, and the safeguarding and administering of medication.

In addition to the educator's "need to know," the biophysical techniques are reviewed because the probability exists that some of the behavior problems of children are a direct result of heredity or heredity-environment interactions. In addition, the social-emotional (secondary) effects of many biophysical handicaps on the individual's lifestyle are of direct concern to educators.

Prenatal considerations

According to the National Foundation–March of Dimes (1975a), there are 200,000 children born annually with birth defects (blind, deaf, retarded, anemic, diabetic, and so on). The daily lives of some 15,000,000 Americans alone are affected by birth defects.

Many of the children having birth defects are students enrolled in regular elementary and secondary classrooms. Only a minority of this group attend special education programs. Thus, it is important that the regular class teacher be familiar with the characteristics and symptoms of these defects and the interventions applied to lessen their impact on the child.

There are two known causes of birth defects in unborn and newborn children: environment and heredity. Environmental factors of special importance to the health of the child are maternal factors (metabolic disorders, maternal age, and number and frequency of pregnancies) and factors that affect the mother during pregnancy (viral diseases and infections, veneral disease, drugs, alcohol, tobacco, diet, and injuries). The larger environment may have an effect on the child as a consequence of pollution, radiation, and the like.

Heredity, or the transmission of the characteristics or traits of the parents to the child is a factor in many birth defects. Hereditary characteristics are transmitted from parents to child by means of the chromosomes. Chromosomes are present in every human cell, including the ovum and sperm. The chromosomes are composed of genes, the units of heredity (Redding and Hirschhorn, 1968). The inherited characteristics of a child are determined by the composition and manner in which the gene-carrying chromosomes from the parents combine at the time of conception.

It is generally agreed that birth defects are best reduced or controlled by preventive, rather than curative, techniques. Among the curative interventions available are chemical regulation, corrective surgery, and rehabilitation through training.

Chemical regulation includes such familiar interventions as medication and diet. Corrective surgery is frequently effective in reducing the debilitating effects of clubfoot, cleft lip and palate, and some vision, hearing, and speech problems, among others. Cosmetic surgery is a valuable aid in reducing the effects of observable deformities on the individual. Rehabilitation and training services have a significant positive impact on the life of the mentally retarded, blind, deaf, mute, physically handicapped, learning-disabled, or behavior-disordered individual.

Preventive interventions include prenatal care and genetic counseling, among others.

Prenatal care involves a variety of examinations and interventions designed to ensure that the unborn child develops normally in a healthy environment. By means of prenatal care, the parents and physician cannot only determine the growth and development patterns of the unborn child but are in a position to immediately intervene if there are indications of an abnormal pregnancy. Prenatal care includes consideration of the mother's diet, exercise, and personal hygiene as well as the emotional status of both parents, especially the mother.

Genetic counseling involves providing an estimate of the probability of occurrence (or recurrence) of a disease or defect for a particular individual (Kameya, 1972). The major goal of genetic counseling is the prevention of birth defects. The genetic counselor cannot predict with exactitude the occurrence of a defective child but can predict the probability of occurrence of some abnormalities in the offspring of specific parents and parents-to-be.

As a consequence of its capacity to predict the probability of birth defects, genetic counseling has raised some important ethical issues in contemporary society:

Should a defective child be aborted?

Do parents have an inalienable right to knowingly produce a defective child?

It should be remembered that the genetic counselor provides the parents with medical information on the *probabilities* that a defective child will be born. The counselor is *not* the ultimate decision maker. The parents must make the final decision concerning the unborn child (Shaw, M. W. 1974).

Postnatal care

Postnatal health care is essential for the continued health and well-being of every child. There is in our society a high risk of injury, illness, and infection during childhood and adolescence. Children should be examined by a physician annually. Conscientious health care permits the family physician and parents to guide the child through the developmental years and to recognize and intervene if abnormalities develop. Postnatal care includes vision, hearing, and dental care.

Nutrition

Nutrition (or malnutrition) is defined as the relationship of nutrient intake to bodily needs (Kameya, 1972). In general, exact scientific relationships have not been demonstrated to exist between specific nutrients and specific behavior problems in children. However, a logical relationship between these factors in all probability does exist. Research has amply demonstrated the relationships between several nutrients and specific disorders of a physical nature.

It is hardly disputable that children suffering from malnutrition are neither happy nor productive. The malnourished child manifests signs of fatigue, sleepiness, and irritability and appears to lack motivation. Such a child is prone to infections, diseases, and injuries.

The importance of proper nutrition for children cannot be overemphasized. When parents are unable to provide for their children in the home, the school—using local, state, and federal funds—must provide needy children with lunch and breakfast. However, malnourishment is not confined to a specific socioeconomic group.

Medical examination

Differential diagnoses among children with behavior disorders, minimal brain damage, hyperkinesis, a specific learning disability, and similar syndromes require a thorough medical examination. And, because there is no single test or combination of tests that conclusively rules out organic disease (Schulman, 1967), the full physical evaluation includes a variety of tests.

The ideal evaluation for a suspected hyperactive and/or hyperanxious child is a collaborative effort by the parents, teachers, school psychologist, and physician (Renshaw, 1974). Parental evaluation includes a family history and the child's medical, developmental, and behavioral histories. The teacher reports on the child's learning capacity and style, and behavioral and perceptual difficulties. The school psychologist contributes the results of a psychological evaluation. The physician's evaluation includes information on the pregnancy, a family history, and a history of the child's birth, neonatal years, development, and behavior.

A full physical examination includes laboratory tests (blood and urine), a skull x-ray, and a neurological examination, including an electroencephalogram (EEG), if needed. The physician may prescribe medication on a trial basis as part of the diagnostic process.

A general physical examination is performed to *exclude* the possibility of diseases involving bodily systems that could account for the child's difficulties (Millichap, 1975). The neurological examination is performed to determine the probability of neurological malfunction and includes an evaluation of the individual's gait, coordination, deep tendon reflexes, muscular power and tone, handedness, sensory perception, speech, vision, and hearing. The EEG may be included in this examination.

The EEG, or brain wave recording, consists of simultaneous records of electrical discharges from several parts of the brain. Occasionally the results of the EEG are used by educators to determine an exceptional child's educational placement. This is an unwise procedure (Bakwin and Bakwin, 1960; Renshaw, 1974). The EEG retains its experimental status.

Medication

Several articles have been written in both the professional and popular literature concerning the use and abuse of various medications prescribed for children (Dupree, 1971; Ladd, 1970; Laufer, 1970; Witter, 1971). In these articles problems surrounding the prescribing, administration, and effects of drugs on children are discussed, topics include the increasing use of drugs with children, referral procedures, evaluation procedures, toxicity, addiction, and the effects of drugs on learning and maturation.

As a consequence of these articles and other factors, society has become concerned with the use of drugs with children. Public hearings were conducted by Congress, and a national conference of experts was convened by the U.S. Department of Health, Education, and Welfare to study the problem in 1971. These efforts have been useful in bringing the problem into the public view, but they have also confused many parents and professionals.

Although behavior-modifying or symptom-controlling medications have been prescribed for children for several decades, the treatment-evaluation process is complicated by many factors (Baldwin, 1973). The physician must not be concerned only with the individual child's personal status but must also evaluate (1) the environments in which the child functions in the home and in the school; (2) the potentially biased evaluations of those associated with the child, such as parents, peers, and teachers; and (3) the actual and potential efforts of ancillary interventions, such as counseling and instructional methods, on the child.

Millichap (1975) has provided an excellent summary of the drugs prescribed in the treatment of hyperkinetic behavior in children. Similar reviews have been offered by Baldwin (1973) and Renshaw (1974). Their efforts are summarized in the following paragraphs.

Central nervous system (CNS) stimulants. The CNS stimulants are prescribed for their calming effect on prepubertal children of both sexes. This is called a paradoxical effect. Although at this time the reason for this paradox is unknown, stimulant drugs have an effect on children that differs significantly from their effect on adults. A prepubertal child is calmed and quieted by a stimulant, whereas an adult is stimulated.

Trade names of the stimulants include Ritalin, Dexedrine, Cyclert, and Deaner, among others. Caffeine as a stimulant is discussed under the heading "Other Biophysical Interventions."

The sought-for positive effects of the stimulants are (1) increased controlled physical activity; (2) increased goal-directedness; (3) decreased impulsivity and disruption; (4) decreased distractibility; (5) increased attending behavior; (6) improved voice modulation; (7) improved performance, cognition, and perception; (8) improved motor coordination; (9) improved cooperativeness with family and peers and consequent improved self-concept; (10) improved personal neatness; (11) decreased negative and increased positive behavior; (12) improved sleep habits (infrequent); and (13) decreased enuresis (infrequent).

The possible negative effects of the stimulant drugs are (1) stomach distress, loss of appetite, and consequent weight loss; (2) insomnia; (3) nervousness, including nail biting and finger picking; (4) depression and crying; (5) infrequent drowsiness; (6) infrequent blood circulation problems in hands and feet; (7) severe shaking and fear when the stimulant is initially introduced; (8) delayed growth; and (9) skin rash.

Antianxiety and antipsychotic drugs. The antianxiety and antipsychotic tranquilizers are prescribed for their calming effects; some individuals may return to a more acceptable mode of functioning as a result of these medications.

Trade names of the tranquilizers include Mellaril, Thorazine, Librium, Atarax, Sparine, Prolixin, Permitil, Miltown, and Equanil, among others. Mellaril and Thorazine are the most frequently prescribed tranquilizers for children.

The desired positive effects of the tranquilizers are increased calmness and improved functioning.

The possible negative effects are (1) nausea, (2) daytime drowsiness, (3) dry mouth and nasal congestion, (4) nervousness and/or tremors, (5) skin rash, (6) more of an increase in behavioral and social functioning than in cognitive learning, (7) increased appetite and consequent weight gain, and (8) lowered blood count—an indication to stop medication (infrequent).

Anticonvulsants and antihistamines. Anticonvulsants are used to treat children whose behavior problems are complicated by convulsive seizures. Trade names for the anticonvulsant medications include Dilatin, Mysoline, Mesatoin, and Diamox, among others.

Antihistamines are used to counteract the effects of various allergies. Trade names for the antihistamines include Benadryl, Vistaril, and Phenergan, among others. According to Renshaw (1974), these medications are exceptionally safe. They are often prescribed for their sedative effects on children in pain and as a nighttime sedative.

• • •

In summary, teachers should remember that although properly prescribed and monitored medication can have a beneficial effect on the child, it cannot (1) compensate for "lost" years of learning, (2) provide the discipline needed to develop acceptable functioning, (3) improve the self-esteem needed for self-acceptance, (4) provide the love the child needs for normal development, or (5) reverse essential deficits, such as mental retardation and cerebral palsy (Renshaw, 1974).

Other biophysical interventions

In his 1975 publication Millichap includes several unofficial interventions in the biophysical area for which little or no controlled research evidence is available to substantiate their effectiveness. Several of these techniques are included here because they have gained some popularity in contemporary society.

Coffee and caffeine. The administering of coffee in lieu of amphetamines has come to the attention of regular and special education teachers. This technique has, in some cases, been used without parental permission and medical supervision. There is little research evidence to substantiate the claims of therapists using this intervention (Schnackenberg, 1973). Although a child's behavior may improve as a result of the ingestion of caffeine, there is no evidence that academic achievement and perceptual skills are improved (Millichap, 1975; Renshaw, 1974).

Of concern to physicians are the side effects of caffeine (stomach and bladder irritation) and the standardization of dosage, which is extremely difficult.

Diet. Included in the interventions using specialized diets are hypoallergenic diets, hypoglycemic diets, and diets concerned with chemical food additives and preservatives. Millichap's comments on each of these specialized diets are essentially the same: few diets have been demonstrated to be effective in experimental research studies.

Visual training. Visual training has gained considerable popularity in recent years as a technique to overcome visual perceptual disorders and their concomitant learning disabilities. According to Millichap, however, there is no known scientific evidence to support improvement in visual perception as a result of eye muscle exercises and laterality training.

Educator's role in biophysical interventions

The educator plays an important supportive role to medical personnel in the application of biophysical interventions. This supportive role includes (1) referral, (2) the collaboration with and reporting of observations to the physician, (3) the modification of classroom structure and curriculum content to meet the needs of the child, (4) the obtaining of permission to administer medication, and (5) the safeguarding and administering of medication to the child in school.

Referral. The educator is not in a position by experience, training, or function to refer a child directly to a physician. Neither is the educator in a position to suggest the prescribing of medication to a physician for a specific child. In addition, the educator should not attempt to coerce parents to accept any particular treatment.

It is proper for teachers to inform parents of a child's problems. The school initiates contact with medical personnel in behalf of a particular child only with parental consent. It is suggested that an educator not directly involved with the child in school serve as a contact person and intermediary between the teacher and parents during the referral process (Report of the Conference on the Use of Stimulant Drugs, 1971).

Collaboration with and reporting of observations to the physician. A primary role of the teacher in biophysical interventions is the provision of current and objective feedback to the physician on the observable effects of the medication on the child's behavior and learning. As previously suggested, the majority of the present-day medications are experimental substances whose effects on a particular child cannot be predicted with exactitude. Thus, meaningful feedback to the prescribing physician will assist the physician in maximizing the positive effects of medication on the child. The teacher, a trained observer who is with the child throughout the day, is in an excellent position to observe the effects of the medication and report, through proper channels, to the physician.

Modification of classroom structure and curriculum content. During the biophysical treatment process, especially during the beginning weeks, the child's behavior and learning styles may change radically. Consequently, it will be necessary for the teacher to modify, on occasion, both classroom structure and curriculum content to respond to the child's needs. Classroom structure may have to be increased or decreased to permit the child to adjust to his or her "new" behavior and interest. The curriculum may

have to be changed to allow the child to learn the knowledge and skills neglected during the "lost" years.

Obtaining of permission to dispense medication. The teacher must obtain permission to dispense medication in the school when medical personnel (a physician and/or nurse) are not available. A child should not be dismissed from school because medical personnel are not immediately available. Teachers may dispense medication with proper permission. A permission form suggested by Renshaw (1974) is shown in Fig. 21.

Safeguarding and administration of medication. When medication is dispensed in the school, the following guidelines should be adhered to:

1. Proper permission forms, completed by parents and physicians, should be obtained and filed in the child's record folder.

2. All medication should be stored in a central location. This facility should be clean, ventilated, and lighted and should contain a locked cabinet. A water tap is needed. A refrigerator is necessary for some medications.

3. All medication must be properly labeled with the child's name and the physician's name. The label should include directions for use.

4. All medication, including new prescriptions and refills, received from and returned home should be logged in and out of the school. Medication should be inventoried frequently. One individual from the school's faculty or staff should be appointed to inventory the medication and function as a contact person in all communications with parents, physicians, and other medical personnel in relation to medication.

5. A responsible adult must be present when a child takes a medication.

6. A log, to be filled in each time a child takes a medication, should be affixed

School Medication Consent and Directions

Parent permission: Date _____

Child _____Birthdate _____

Address _____Phone _____

School _____Grade _____ Teacher _____

_____

I hereby consent for the above-named school to supervise the medication prescribed below by my physician for my child.

_____

Physician's direction: Date _____

Child _____

Medication and instruction _____

_____

Doctor requests teacher's comments:

Please observe the following _____

Phone _____ Best time to call _____

_____

Physician's signature
Physician/Clinic name

Address _____

Fig. 21. School medication consent form and directions. (From Renshaw, D. C. *The hyperactive child.* Chicago: Nelson-Hall Publishers, 1974.)

to the wall in the medication center. This form is presented in Fig. 22. The completed forms should be retained in a file.

ENVIRONMENTAL INTERVENTIONS

In varying degrees, the interventions discussed in this section focus attention on the child's environment as the locus of the problem. There are three groups of environ-

mental interventions; these are distinguished from one another by the degree of emphasis placed on the individual's environment as the determiner of behavior.

According to Wagner (1972), these groups are:

1. Excitor-centered (child-centered) interventions, which focus the change-effects almost exclusively on the child
2. Respondent-centered (environment-

Medication Log

Child's name	Date	Time	Medication	Person dispensing medication	Notes

Fig. 22. Medication log. (From Shea, T. M. *Teaching children and youth with behavior disorders.* St. Louis: The C. V. Mosby Co., 1978.)

centered) interventions, which focus almost exclusively on the responding environment

3. Exchange-centered (child-environment—centered) interventions, which focus on the exchange patterns between the child and the environment

The distinctions between these classifications are blurred; the degree of emphasis focused on the child, the environment, and the relationship between these two variables is not clear-cut. Wagner made an attempt to place the environmental interventions on a continuum ranging from primary emphasis on the child to primary emphasis on the environment. It is impractical to discuss all of these environmental interventions in this chapter; rather, a few are presented for informational purposes.

Child-centered interventions

Among the child-centered interventions, which are primarily concerned with accommodating the child to the environment, are:

Remedial programs aimed at psychomotor, cognitive, and affective learning: These interventions include programs in gross and fine motor coordination, perceptual training, academic education, and affective education, among others.

Natural community interventions: Although few, if any, opportunities exist for this type of intervention in this century, the general thrust of the intervention is the placement of an individual in a natural community setting where behavior is changed by naturally occurring processes inherent in community living (Byrne, 1869; cited in Wagner, 1972).

School community interventions: Primarily aimed at the child, these interventions involve the manipulation of the school environment for the child's therapeutic benefit (Stickney, 1968).

Artificial community interventions: Aimed at the child, these interventions involve the development and systematic manipulation of an artificial community (commune, collective, or residential center) to modify the child's behavior (Makarenko, 1951).

Artificial group interventions: These interventions involve attempts to change the child in the home community by means of an artificial group. This approach is used frequently in delinquency rehabilitation programs. Groups are organized to maintain and change the individual in the community. The group provides the individual with social and psychological support as well as guidance and direction.

Environment-centered interventions

Among the environment-centered interventions, which are primarily focused on changing the child's environment, are:

Architectural interventions: These interventions are primarily concerned with the designing of physical environments to modify behavior. The architect's focus is on designing a physical setting that has the capacity to modify the disturbed child's behavior (Bayes, 1967).

Family environment interventions: Aimed at the child's family unit, these interventions are accomplished primarily by training and education in child rearing, behavior management, and family living. Family counseling and therapy are often included in this intervention (Vogel and Bell, 1960).

School environment interventions: Aimed at modifying the school environment and thus increasing the child's probability of success and acceptance, these interventions are accomplished through in-service teacher training, consultation, and the like (Newman, 1967).

Child-environment–centered interventions

Child-environment–centered interventions, which focus on both the child and the environment, include:

Natural group in the urban environment interventions: These interventions involve the manipulation and redirection of existing natural groups, such as street gangs. The gang is redirected from primarily destructive or deviant effects on the community to constructive effects (Leissner, 1965).

Child-school–environment interventions: In these interventions, the focus is on the remediation of the child's behavior and learning and on the environment's responsiveness to the child (Lewis, 1967; Weinstein, 1968).

Interface interventions: These interventions are aimed at modifying the reciprocal relationship between the child and the environment, including persons in the environment. The focus is on changing the quality of individual-environment transactions (Rhodes, 1967).

Group composition and group processes

A number of potent behavior management interventions are closely associated with classroom and activity groups. Some specific management techniques employed as a part of these environmental interventions are discussed in this chapter as counseling techniques (under that heading) and in the remainder of the text as behavior modification interventions. However, when the group is a significant part of a child's overall behavior management program, two important topics must be considered in the selection and imposition of these management techniques: group composition and group processes.

Grouping children on the basis of school records and admission data is an important but difficult task (Morse and Wineman, 1957). It is a process that of necessity involves the cooperation of all persons familiar with the children.

Among the variables to be given consideration during the grouping process are (1) age; (2) sex; (3) interests; (4) handicapping conditions, if any; (5) personality traits; (6) the degree, intensity, and kind of behavior problems, if any; and (7) group experiences and skills. When grouping children, one should make an effort to avoid extremes in group composition and at the same time attempt to form a "balanced" group. In the organization of groups the teacher and aide are considered group members.

Extremes in group (and subgroup) composition are avoided when:

1. Children of greatly different ages are not placed in the same group.
2. Children without common interests are not placed in the same group.
3. An individual is not placed in a group that lacks a like-sex peer.
4. A child with a severe handicap is not placed in a group of nonhandicapped children if the placement prohibits either from participating in important curricular activities. However, if adequately trained personnel (aides or teaching assistants) are available to assist, the curriculum can be modified and this potential limitation circumvented.
5. Children with potentially conflicting personality traits and behavior problems are not placed in the same group.
6. An unskilled child is not placed in a group composed of individuals who are highly skilled and experienced in group processes. This placement is only permissible if the group members, including the adults, are aware of the child's lack of skill and experience in

groups and agree to facilitate the child's integration.

7. An individual who is neither ready nor willing to participate in group activities is not placed in a group environment. Reference here is to children with severe behavior and learning problems who lack skills needed 'for meaningful group participation. Frequently, these individuals remain in the group but do not become "functioning" members.

Grouping is a difficult process because the staff must deal with a variety of intangible variables that defy precise measurement.

The group process itself can be of therapeutic benefit to some children. Loughmiller (1965) used self-governing, problem-solving groups in the camp setting. Also applicable in the school setting, these groups are set up to expose students to a wide range of successful interpersonal experiences and as a result of these experiences encourage participation, responsibility, and cooperation in activities (Rickard and others, 1971).

In this intervention children and teachers are responsible for their daily activities within predetermined limits established by the administration. The members find themselves in a situation where majority rule prevails. Each individual is responsible for personal behavior and for the behavior of the group (Rickard and Lattal, 1969; Shea, 1977).

Some limits on the group's behavior and activities are imposed by an administrator or other nongroup authority figure rather than by the teacher who is a member of the group. However, the group members may impose, by means of majority rule, additional limits on behavior and activities. The limits imposed by the administrator are few in number and are concerned with dining and work schedules, attendance at assemblies, transportation, health, safety, and the like. These limits must be imposed by the admin-

istration if it is to meet its responsibilities to the members of the group.

Any social cosmos requires certain routines (Morse, and Wineman, 1957). Without routines, limits, and prescribed ways of behaving, anarchy would result and the group would disintegrate. Thus, the group, as a group, decides (1) the limits to be set on social interaction, (2) how extreme behaviors are to be managed if they occur, (3) how activities and schedules of events are to be developed and executed, (4) who is to be responsible for various phases of daily living, and (5) how problems and conflicts are to be resolved.

The problem-solving process becomes a part of the group's daily life. When conflicts or unfamiliar problems occur that prohibit the group from attaining its immediate goals, problem solving begins immediately. During the problem-solving process, the group attempts to develop alternative solutions to the circumstances confronting them. The members have two major tasks: (1) identifying and clarifying their problem and (2) discussing (evaluating) and agreeing on one or more solutions to the problem. The agreed-on solution can be imposed either immediately or in similar situations in the future (Rickard, and others, 1971). In addition to the above tasks, the members of the group must deal with the positive and negative social-emotional behaviors that naturally occur during the problem-solving process (Hare, 1962; Hare, and others, 1965; and Redl, 1942).

Morse and Wineman (1957) recommended the application of life-space interview techniques in the group on a regular and emergency basis. Discussed earlier in this chapter as a counseling technique, the life-space interview may focus on a variety of critical group-process issues:

Existing social realities that prohibit group desires

Existing defense or coping mechanisms that the group and its members unconsciously apply for protection against those who are not members of the group

Techniques for application by the members to admit mistakes, misdeeds, and asocial behaviors

Ways to use the group as a setting in which emotions and frustrations may be expressed, and the limits on such expression

Ways to strengthen the group's and the individual member's self-concept, especially after conflicts, frustrations, and failures

Procedures for identifying, clarifying, and agreeing to mutually acceptable solutions to common problems

As a group member, the teacher's role is important if group behavior management interventions are to be effectively applied in the classroom and school. The teacher must be a model of "give and take" democratic leadership and must be willing to permit the members of the group to make meaningful decisions, implement programs, and realize the consequences of their actions.

The teacher allows the logical consequences of the group's decisions and actions to occur. At the same time, however, the teacher protects the group from constant or excessive failure and individual members from physical and psychological harm.

Classroom environment

The classroom environment can have a significant impact on behavior management. A classroom should be designed to assist in the implementation of the behavior management interventions and instructional methods (Hewett, 1968; Valett, 1969; and Wagner, 1972).

Some variables to be considered in the planning of the classroom environment are:

Comfort: The classroom should be a comfortable environment in which the children feel free to function. It should be a place in which they enjoy working and playing. This may require the placing of couches, bean bag chairs, pillows, area rugs, and the like, in the room. It may also require the elimination of distracting sights and sounds.

Organization: The room should be organized to facilitate large- and small-group lessons as well as individual study. This requires the designer to organize the environment to facilitate activities with a minimum of physical movement of furnishings and persons. Areas of the room should be designated for specific activities: small-group, large-group, and individual activities.

Child-teacher, teacher-child and child-child communications: Communications among group members should be maximized by the elimination of unnecessary physical barriers. With the exception of the time devoted to individual study, the student should be within the teacher's field of vision so that the teacher can provide assistance when it is needed. During individual work periods the student should be able to signal the teacher, either personally or mechanically, if help is needed.

Movement: Learning centers should be arranged about the room to minimize unnecessary movement. The centers should be located to facilitate the daily schedule. Noise levels are considered in the location of the various centers. Centers for potentially distracting activities should not be located near centers for quiet activities and individual study. The teacher's and teaching assistant's work stations should be located in the interior of the classroom to minimize their physical movements and maximize supervision.

Privacy: All children (and adults) need privacy. Each student should be provided with an area of the room that belongs to that student alone. The student's desk and locker are "private property," where treasures and work materials can be stored. One area of the classroom should be provided for students who are frustrated or who have lost control of their behavior. This area should be available to others who wish to be alone for a short period of time. The classroom itself should be private. Unexpected visitors should be minimized.

Size and shape: A standard-size classroom is recommended. It is easier to divide a large room into working areas than to attempt to organize a small room into several working areas or learning centers. A square or rectangular room is preferable to a circular or odd-shapped, angular room. The square or rectangular room provides structure and definite boundaries for group activities.

Scale: All furnishings except those of the teacher and teaching assistant should be scaled to the appropriate size for the children using them. Oversized furnishings are difficult for children to manipulate. Undersized chairs and desks are equally frustrating and uncomfortable for larger students.

Interest: A child should find the environment interesting. Areas of the classroom should be designated for exploring and constructing activities. These areas should contain high-interest materials and equipment, including games, pets, science experiments, audiovisual materials, reading material, puzzles, and the like.

Color: A room and its furnishings should be decorated with warm colors, which tend to relax the individual, rather than with harsh, cold colors, which tend to generate excitement and activity.

Accessibility: The materials and equipment in a classroom are primarily for student use. Although cabinets are recommended for storage of materials and equipment, they should be readily accessible to the students.

Usability: The materials and equipment should be usable. All materials should be evaluated for ease of operation, safety in the hands of children, and durability.

Clutter: The classroom environment should be devoid of clutter (piles of books, papers, magazines, and records; distracting bulletin boards; and other odds and ends). Sufficient cabinets, bookcases, and desks should be available for storage.

There is little available definitive research evidence on the effects of these environmental variables on children (Bednar and Haviland, 1969). However, at a minimum, the teacher should give the above variables consideration in the design of the classroom.

Class meetings

A democratic class meeting intervention can be instituted by the teacher as a part of the normal classroom procedure. Class meetings can be called to deal with the common problems of living and learning in a group setting. Over a period of time the members of the class learn, with guidance, to seek solutions to problems through verbal transactions with peers and the teacher rather than by means of physical and/or verbal confrontation or withdrawal. During properly conducted class meetings, the members grow in understanding of themselves and others. They learn to conceptualize problems from another person's point of view.

Three kinds of meetings for classroom application have been suggested by Vogel and Smith (1974):

1. *Open meeting:* This meeting is called to permit an individual to express covert feelings. The individual is given an op-

portunity to state to the group the frustrations and feelings that the individual believes are the result of another member's actions. This other member, or antagonist, may be a peer or the teacher. Any member of the group may request an open meeting. The session is generally conducted by a peer.

2. *Problem-solving meeting:* This meeting is focused primarily on potential problems. It may be called by any member of the class. Topics include such items as tardiness, disorganization, lack of follow-through on previous commitments, group responsibilities, distractions in the classroom, lack of time to complete assignments, and the like. During the meeting a solution to the problem is sought by the group. The agreed-on-solution is implemented.

3. *Decision-making meeting:* This meeting focuses primarily on programs and curriculum decisions. It gives the program direction: What is to be done? How is it to be accomplished? Where? When? Who is responsible? Why? The decision-making meeting is an excellent medium for involving all members of a class in the curriculum-planning process.

These class meetings are designed to find practical solutions to real problems. In addition, the class meeting intervention has significant potential as a preventive technique if consistently and appropriately applied.

Milieu therapy

Milieu therapy is a clinical concept; although it varies in ease of application, it can be applied in any setting in which children function. In varying degrees this intervention can be applied in residential settings, day schools, special classrooms, regular classrooms, and camp settings.

According to Long and associates (1976),

"Milieu implies the total environment a child lives in, the whole culture that surrounds him, in other words, everything that is done to, with, for, or by an individual in the place where he finds himself" (p. 243).

According to Redl (1959), a specific milieu is not "good" or "bad" for an individual in itself; its effects on the person or group are dependent on their needs in interaction with the milieu. Redl further indicated that no single aspect of the environment is more important than any other aspect. The importance of the various discrete aspects of the environment is dependent on the needs of the individual or group living in that particular setting.

Since it is not possible, a priori, to design with certitude a therapeutic milieu for an individual, milieu therapy is a continuous process throughout the child's placement in a particular setting. The staff must be constantly alert to the impact of the milieu on the individual and adjust it when necessary. Although these adjustments may appear simple when presented in a written statement, such environmental manipulations are difficult tasks requiring personnel who are observant and sensitive to the needs of the individual and the group.

Redl (1959) identified several critical elements in the milieu; these elements are presented here as questions that persons responsible for a particular milieu must ask themselves:

Social structures: What are the roles and functions of various individuals and groups in the milieu? What is the role of the therapist? Of the teacher? Of the administrator? Of the housekeeping personnel? Of the children? Are staff members parent surrogates? Are they like brothers and sisters? Are they confidants? Are they friends? Are they authority figures? Are they servants? Who is in charge here? Staff? The children? Administrators? No one? Are there open or closed communications channels between staff and the children? Between the children and staff? Among staff personnel? Among the children?

Value systems: What values and standards are consciously and unconsciously being communicated among and between the children and staff? Sympathy? Empathy? High expectations? Low expectations? Like? Dislike? Acceptance? Rejection? Trust? Mistrust?

Routines, rituals, and regulations: Are routines, rituals, and behavioral regulations and limits facilitating or frustrating the goals of the program for the individual?

Impact of group processes: What is the impact of the natural group processes on individuals and subgroups within the milieu? On the total group? Are individual group members cast in the role of a leader? In the role of a follower? In the role of an antagonist? In the role of a scapegoat? In the role of an isolate? In the role of a mascot or pet? In the role of a clown? Can the individual at his or her present stage of development function effectively in a group setting such as this milieu provides?

Impact of the individual's psychopathological characteristics: What are the effects of abnormal behaviors on the individuals themselves and on others in the milieu? Are these effects positive? Are they negative? Do they result in aggression? In withdrawal? In respect? In pity? In fear?

Personal attitudes and feelings: What are the staff's attitudes and feelings toward each other and the children? What is the impact of these attitudes and feelings on their behavior and on the behavior of others (staff and children)? Is the impact positive? Is it negative? Is it neutral? Is it productive? Is it destructive?

Overt behavior: Regardless of the individual's intentions, what are group members really doing to each other? What is their overt behavior? Is their relationship helpful? Is it harmful? Is it supportive? Is it personal? Is it vindictive?

Activities and performance: Is the activity program, including its structure, designed to facilitate the developmental process? Is it productive? Is it constructive? Is it busywork? Is it tedious? Is it frustrating? Is it boring? Is it wasteful? Is it negative? Is it destructive?

Space, equipment, time, and props: Are space, equipment, time, and props available in the environment to adequately conduct the activities in the program?

Effects of the outside milieu: What is the effect of information, visits, news, telephone calls, and the like, from persons on the outside on the individual or group?

Effects of the nonimmediate milieu: What are the effects of administrators, nurses, physicians, housekeepers, cooks, and others on the individual or group?

Limits and enforcement: Are the behavioral limits within which the individual and group must function established? Are these limits reasonable? Are they enforced? Are they enforced consistently and fairly? How are extremes of behavior handled?

Program responsiveness: Is the total milieu adequately and objectively monitored to ensure recognition of nontherapeutic elements? Is the structure of the milieu sufficiently flexible and responsive to allow and encourage modification to reduce or neutralize nontherapeutic elements?

The therapeutic milieu in any setting, residential or day, must be continuously monitored, discussed, evaluated, and manipulated for the benefit of the child.

SUMMARY

In this chapter several psychoanalytic-psychodynamic, biophysical, and environmental interventions of relevance to the teacher interested in a broad understanding of behavior management are briefly reviewed. The careful reader will note that significant overlapping exists between the three groups of interventions. The educator should seek to synthesize the various conceptual frameworks (theories) and their interventions into a personal prespective of behavior management.

EXERCISES FOR CHAPTER SEVEN
Quiz

1. Define behavior management as applied in this text. _____

   _____

   _____

2. The basic categories of psychoanalytic-psychodynamic interventions are:

   a. _____

   b. _____

3. According to Redl (1959), the life-space interview may be applied for either of two purposes:

   a. _____

   b. _____

4. List five expressive arts that may be used as behavior management interventions.

   a. _____

   b. _____

   c. _____

   d. _____

   e. _____

5. The educator plays an important supportive role to medical personnel in the biophysical interventions. The educator's functions in this supportive role are:

   a. _____

   b. _____

   c. _____

   d. _____

   e. _____

6. According to Wagner (1972), the three groups of environmental interventions are:

   a. _____

b. _____

c. _____

7. Among the variables to be considered during the process of grouping are:

a. _____

b. _____

c. _____

d. _____

8. List eight variables to be considered in planning the classroom environment.

a. _____

b. _____

c. _____

d. _____

e. _____

f. _____

g. _____

h. _____

9. The three kinds of classroom meetings suggested by Vogel and Smith (1974) are:

a. _____

b. _____

c. _____

Projects

1. Write a brief essay (300 words) on the following topics:
   a. The advantages and disadvantages of the psychoanalytic-psychodynamic interventions
   b. The advantages and disadvantages of environmental interventions
2. Discuss the role of the educator in biophysical interventions.
3. Conduct a life-space interview with a classmate. Evaluate your performance.
4. Conduct a library research study of one of the expressive arts as a behavior management intervention.
5. Invite a physician to discuss biophysical interventions with your class.

REFERENCES

Axline, V. M. *Play therapy.* Boston: Houghton Mifflin Co., 1947.

Bakwin, H., and Bakwin, R. M. *Clinical management of behavior disorders in children.* Philadelphia: W. B. Saunders Co., 1960.

Baldwin, R. W. The treatment of behavior disorders with medication. In S. G. Sapir and A. C. Nitzberg (Eds.), *Children with learning problems.* New York: Brunner/Mazel, Inc., 1973.

Baruch, D. W. *One little boy.* New York: Dell Publishing Co., Inc., 1952.

Bayes, K. *The therapeutic effect of environment on emo-*

tionally disturbed and mentally subnormal children. Surrey, England: Union Brothers Ltd., 1967.

Bednar, M. J., and Haviland, D. S. *The role of the physical environment in the education of children with learning disabilities.* Troy, N.Y.: Center for Architectural Research, Rensselaer Polytechnic Institute, 1969.

Bersoff, D. N., and Grieger, R. M. II. *An interview model for the psychosituational assessment of children's behavior.* American Journal of Orthopsychiatry, 1971 *41*(3), 483-493.

Brenner, M. B. Life space interviewing in the school setting. In H. Dupont (Ed.), *Educating emotionally disturbed children.* New York: Holt, Rinehart & Winston, 1969.

Chace, M. Dance in growth or treatment settings. *Music Therapy,* 1958, *1*, 119-112.

Cheney, C., and Morse, W. C. Psychodynamic interventions in emotional disturbance. In W. C. Rhodes and M. L. Tracy (Eds.), *A study of child variance.* Vol. 2. *Interventions.* Ann Arbor: The University of Michigan Press, 1972.

Dupree, D. Pills for learning. *Wall Street Journal,* January 28, 1971, p. 74.

Ginott, H. G. The theory and practice of therapeutic interventions in child treatment. *Journal of Consulting Psychology,* 1959, *23*, 160-166.

Glasser, W. *Reality therapy: A new approach to psychiatry.* New York: Harper & Row, Publishers, Inc., 1965.

Glasser, W. *Schools without failure.* New York: Harper & Row, Publishers, Inc., 1969.

Haas, R. B., and Moreno, J. L. Psychodrama as a projective technique. In H. H. Anderson and G. L. Anderson (Eds.), *An introduction to projective techniques.* Englewood Cliffs, N.J.: Prentice-Hall, Inc., 1951.

Hare, A. P. *Handbook of small group research.* New York: The Free Press, 1962.

Hare, A. P., Borgatta, E. F., and Bales, R. F. *Small groups: Studies in social interaction.* New York: Alfred A. Knopf, Inc., 1965.

Hewett, F. M. *The emotionally disturbed child in the classroom.* Boston: Allyn & Bacon, Inc., 1968.

Kameya, L. I. Biophysical interventions in emotional disturbance. In W. C. Rhodes and M. L. Tracy (Eds.), *A study of child variance.* Vol. 2. *Interventions.* Ann Arbor: The University of Michigan Press, 1972.

Kellogg, R., and O'Dell, S. *The psychology of children's art.* New York: CRM-Random House Publication, CRM, Inc., 1967.

Kramer, E. *Art as therapy with children.* New York: Schocken Books, Inc., 1971.

Ladd, E. T. Pills for classroom peace? *Saturday Review,* November 21, 1970, pp. 66-68.

Laufer, M. W. Medications, learning and behavior. *Phi Delta Kappan,* November 1970, pp. 169-170.

Leissner, A. *Street-club work in New York and Tel-Aviv.* Action-Research Project on Delinquent Street Corner Groups in Tel-Aviv, Israel, February 1965.

Lewis, W. W. Project Re-Ed: Educational intervention in discordant child-rearing systems. In E. L. Cowne, E. A. Gardner, and M. Zax (Eds.), *Emergent approaches to mental health problems.* New York: Appleton-Century-Crofts, 1967.

Long, N. J., Morse, W. C., and Newman, R. G. Milieu therapy. In N. J. Long, W. C. Morse, and R. G. Newman (Eds.), *Conflict in the classroom: The education of emotionally disturbed children* (3rd ed). Belmont, Calif.: Wadsworth Publishing Co., Inc. 1976.

Loughmiller, C. *Wilderness road.* Austin: University of Texas, The Hogg Foundation for Mental Health, 1965.

Lucas, A. R. Psychopharmacologic treatment. In C. R. Shaw (Ed.), *The psychiatric disorders of childhood.* New York: Appleton-Century-Crofts, 1966.

Makarenko, A. S. *The road to life: An epic of education* (Vols. 2 and 3). Moscow: Foreign Languages Publishing House, 1951.

Millichap, J. G. *The hyperactive child with minimal brain dysfunction.* Chicago: Year Book Medical Publishers, Inc., 1975.

Moreno, J. L. *Psychodrama.* Beacon, N.Y.: Beacon House, 1946.

Morse, W. C. Worksheet on life space interviewing for teachers. In N. J. Long, W. C. Morse, and R. G. Newman, (Eds.), *Conflict in the classroom: The education of emotionally disturbed children* (2nd ed). Belmont, Calif.: Wadsworth Publishing Co., Inc., 1971.

Morse, W. C., and Wineman, D. Group interviewing in a camp for disturbed boys. *Journal of Social Issues,* 1957, *13*(1), 23-31.

Moustakas, C. E. *Children in play therapy.* New York: McGraw-Hill Book Co., 1953.

National Foundation–March of Dimes. *Birth defects: The tragedy and the hope.* White Plains, N.Y.: The Foundation, 1975. (a)

National Foundation–March of Dimes. *Genetic Counseling.* White Plains, N.Y.: The Foundation, 1975. (b)

Newman, R. G. *Psychological consultation in the schools: A catalyst for learning.* New York: Basic Books, Inc., Publishers, 1967.

Raths, L. E., Harmin, M., and Simon, S. B. *Values and teaching.* Columbus, Ohio: Charles E. Merrill Publishing Co., 1966.

Redding, A., and Hirschhorn, K. Guide to human chromosome defects. *Birth Defects Original Article Series,* 1968, *4*(1), 1-16.

Redl, F. Group emotion and leadership. *Psychiatry,* 1942, *5,* 573-596.

Redl, F. The concept of the life space interview. *American Journal of Orthopsychiatry,* 1959, *29,* 1-18.

Reinert, H. R. *Children in conflict.* St. Louis: The C. V. Mosby Co., 1976.

Renshaw, D. C. *The hyperactive child.* Chicago: Nelson-Hall Publishers, 1974.

Report of the Conference on the Use of Stimulant Drugs in the Treatment of Behaviorally Disturbed Young School Children. *Journal of Learning Disabilities,* 1971, *4,* 523-530.

Rhodes, W. C. Psychosocial learning. In E. M. Bower and W. G. Hollister (Eds.), *Behavioral science frontiers in education.* New York: John Wiley & Sons, Inc., 1967.

Rhodes, W. C. The disturbing child: A problem of ecological management. In P. S. Graubard (Ed.), *Children against schools.* Chicago: Follett Publishing Co., 1968.

Rhodes, W. C. Overview of interventions. In W. C. Rhodes and M. L. Tracy (Eds.), *A study of child variance.* Vol. 2. *Interventions.* Ann Arbor: The University of Michigan Press, 1972.

Rhodes, W. C., and Gibbins, S. Community programming for the behaviorally deviant child. In H. C. Quay and J. F. Werry (Eds.), *Psychopathological disorders of childhood.* New York: John Wiley & Sons, Inc., 1972.

Rhodes, W. C., and Tracy, M. L. *A study of child variance.* Vol 1. *Theories.* Ann Arbor: The University of Michigan Press, 1972. (a)

Rhodes, W. C., and Tracy, M. L. *A study of child variance.* Vol. 2. *Interventions.* Ann Arbor: The University of Michigan Press, 1972. (b)

Rickard, H. C., and Lattal, K. A. Group problem-solving in a therapeutic summer camp: An illustration. *Adolescence,* 1969, *4*(15), 319-332.

Rickard, H. C., Serum, C. S., and Wilson, W. Developing problem-solving attitudes in emotionally disturbed children. *Adolescence,* 1971, *5*(24), 451-456.

Schnackenberg, R. C. Caffeine as a substitute for Schedule II stimulants in hyperkinetic children. *American Journal of Psychiatry,* 1973, *130*(7), 796-798.

Schulman, J. L. *Management of emotional disorders in pediatric practice.* Chicago: Year Book Medical Publishers, Inc., 1967.

Shaw, C. R. *The psychiatric disorders of childhood.* New York: Appleton-Century-Crofts, 1966.

Shaw, M. W. Genetic counseling. *Science,* 1974, *184,* 751.

Shea, T. M. *Camping for special children.* St. Louis: The C. V. Mosby Co., 1977.

Shea, T. M. *Teaching children and youth with behavior disorders.* St. Louis: The C. V. Mosby Co., 1978.

Shea, T. M., Whiteside, W. R., Beetner, E. G., and Lindsey, D. L. *Microteaching module: Psychosituational interview.* Edwardsville: Southern Illinois University, 1974.

Solomon, J. C. Therapeutic use of play. In H. H. Anderson and G. L. Anderson, (Eds.), *An introduction to projective techniques.* Englewood Cliffs, N.J.: Prentice-Hall, Inc., 1951.

Stickney, S. B. Schools are our community mental health centers. *American Journal of Psychiatry,* 1968, *124,* 1407-1414.

Valett, R. E. *Programming learning disabilities.* Belmont, Calif.: Fearon Publishers, Inc., 1969.

Vogel, E. E., and Bell, N. W. The emotionally disturbed child as the family scapegoat. In N. W. Bell and E. E. Vogel, (Eds.), *A modern introduction to the family.* New York: The Free Press, 1960.

Vogel, J., and Smith, A. R_x for change: The classroom meeting. *Learning,* 1974, *2*(7), 69-72.

Wagner, M. Environmental interventions in emotional disturbance. In W. C. Rhodes and M. L. Tracy (Eds.), *A study of child variance.* Vol. 2. *Interventions.* Ann Arbor: The University of Michigan Press, 1972.

Weinstein, L. Project Re-Ed: Schools for emotionally disturbed children—Effectiveness as viewed by referring agencies, parents, and teachers. *Exceptional Children,* 1968, *35,* 703-711.

Witter, C. Drugging and schooling. *Transaction,* 1971, *8*(9/10), 31-34.

Woltmann, A. G. The use of puppetry as a projective method in therapy. In H. H. Anderson and G. L. Anderson (Eds.), *An introduction to projective techniques.* Englewood Cliffs, N.J.: Prentice-Hall, Inc. 1951.

CHAPTER EIGHT

Ethical issues

Before beginning the behavior management interventions suggested in this text, the reader is encouraged to consider several ethical issues concerning the use of behavior modification with children. In this chapter the following issues are discussed: (1) some questions of ethics concerning the principles of behavior modification, (2) humane behavior management, (3) some guidelines for application, and (4) some principles concerning individual rights. The chapter is concluded with a brief discussion of behavior modification as a preventive technique.

SOME QUESTIONS OF ETHICS

Scientific inquiry has led to the development of the principles of learning and their resultant interventions for the modification of human behavior. It is difficult to refute the findings of experimental studies: the principles of learning presented in this text are in operation, and the results of controlled research studies are, in the main, positive. Learning theory research has contributed immeasurably to our knowledge of human behavior.

However, we cannot sweep aside the ethical issues created by the application of scientific principles to the processes of human learning. Both the principles of learning and the findings of research have caused confusion, concern, and in some cases, anxiety, among those individuals holding a more tra-

ditional view of human behavior and human freedom. Many scholars have discussed these issues in a depth that is not possible in this text. The reader is referred to the works by Bandura (1969), Bellack and Hersen (1977), Fargo and others (1970), Skinner (1953 and 1971), and Ulrich and others (1966) for an in-depth study of these important issues.

The following are some basic metaphysical questions:

What is a human being?

Are human beings free; that is, do we have freedom of choice?

Do we behave in accordance with specific principles of behavior that are observable, measurable, and repetitive?

Can our behavior be changed by external forces?

Who can modify whose behavior?

The reader who admits that external control of human behavior is possible must consider the following ethical issues:

Who shall decide who will be the modifier?

Who shall decide who will be modified?

How can modifiers be controlled?

What type of interventions shall be applied?

Who will determine the type of interventions to be legitimized?

To what ends will the interventions be applied?

These basic questions have vast implications for our future (as individuals and as members of the human species) and for the future of society. They must be considered and responded to by the professional behavior modification practitioner as well as by the general public.

When these questions are applied to the training of children, they have profound implications for educational practice. The queries are rephrased to point out these implications, which are not only philosophical issues but pragmatic issues of immediate importance:

What is a child?

Is a child free to make choices?

Should a child be free to make choices?

Does a child act in accordance with specific principles of behavior that are observable, measurable, and repetitive?

Can a child's behavior be changed by external forces?

Can a teacher modify a child's behavior?

Can another child or a parent modify behavior?

Who shall determine whose behavior is to be modified?

What types of interventions shall be applied in the classroom and school to change children's behavior?

Who will legitimize and monitor the interventions being utilized to modify behavior?

To what ends will the interventions be applied?

We are not convinced that the issue posed by the questions "What is a human being?" and "Do we have freedom of choice?" is the central concern of those individuals holding a more traditional view of human behavior. That we can and do exert some control over our behavior would not be denied by the majority of behaviorists.

The central issue appears to focus on the relative influences of our nature and environment on our behavior. The behaviorist emphasizes the importance of our external environment in the determination of our behavior. The behaviorist maintains that the influence of the environment on us is systematic, constant, and the prime determinant of our behavior. This systematic, constant influence is observable and measurable. As a result, our actions can be explained by means of the principles of behavior (or learning). The principles are derived by applying the scientific methods of discovery to the modification of overt human behavior.

Few would deny that, in general, the majority of us respond in a predictable manner under specified conditions. For example, if we go to a sports event, we cheer; to a funeral, we cry or sigh; to a college class, we sit passively, praying for the end; and so on.

In addition to the issues of whether and how human beings can be controlled, professionals in psychology, the social sciences, and education have focused attention on the issue of the *means* of control. Many professionals suggest that the overt controls applied to human behavior by means of behavior modification interventions are unacceptable and can lead to unethical practices. These individuals fail to recognize or acknowledge that other, more traditional, forms of interventions, such as those reviewed in Chapter Seven, may exert equally potent, although less obvious, control over human behavior. For example, traditional nondirect and direct psychotherapeutic interventions, such as client-centered counseling, individual and group psychotherapy, psychoanalysis, transactional analysis and life-space interviewing, have as their objective a change in the client's behavior or encourage the client to change his or her own behavior with the therapist's assistance. The silent, evasive therapist and the permissive teacher influence the child's behavior, and this influence limits the child's freedom of choice. Such limiting (or controlling), rather than being denied, should be recognized, evaluated, and monitored for the child's benefit.

Behavior modification, unlike the more traditional forms of therapy, recognizes and capitalizes on its potency as a direct behavior change agent. This emphasis on changing overt or observable behavior should be nurtured and perfected.

Because behavior modification is primarily concerned with changing behaviors that are observable and quantifiable, it is amenable to strict control. Its effects are known, rather than unknown, quantities, as in the case of many other behavior change interventions.

HUMANE BEHAVIOR MANAGEMENT

In this section specific examples of behavioral interventions are examined in an effort to substantiate the position that the behavior modification techniques recommended in this text are humane.

Positive reinforcement

It would be difficult to comprehend how the traditionalist could object to the use of positive reinforcement with school age children. One of the basic goals of any humane society is to provide its individual members with a feeling of accomplishment and well-being. Positive reinforcement for acceptable behavior contributes to this basic need of the individual. Children who are positively reinforced for acceptable behavior tend to generalize this positive quality to other life situations. In addition, they tend to seek out, recognize, and foster positive qualities in others.

EXAMPLE

Mr. Michaels, a biology teacher, discovered that Tina, a student in his senior fourth-period class, appeared to have the necessary skills, knowledge, and interest to become, with proper training, a superior biologist. During the year Mr. Michaels provided Tina with appropriate praise and approval for her outstanding work.

This positive reinforcement influenced Tina to pursue the study of science and enroll as a biology major when she entered college.

Although certain positive attributes and interests of Tina's were recognized and reinforced by Mr. Michaels, the final decision to major in biology remained Tina's.

Extinction

Perhaps more than any of the other behavior modification interventions, extinction directly facilitates the humanization process. By means of extinction a child may be helped to decrease or eliminate unwanted or unacceptable behaviors and thus become free to pursue more productive modes of interacting and living with others.

In schools today, the alternative to extinction is generally punishment, which is a less humane intervention. It appears to be more productive to ignore unacceptable behavior (that is, extinguish it) rather than unwittingly reinforce it by means of punishment.

EXAMPLE

Butch and Sonny exhibited many behaviors that were inappropriate in the classroom. They were always throwing papers, erasers, clay, pencils, or other debris about the classroom. Many times, Butch and Sonny hit their classmates and even Ms. Reynolds, their teacher, during class.

Ms. Reynolds frequently sent the boys to the counselor, Mr. Marshall, for exhibiting these unacceptable behaviors. She was unaware that this was just what the boys wanted; thus, she was unwittingly reinforcing their unacceptable behavior.

When the behavior continued and increased in frequency, she became very frustrated. Mr. Marshall came to her aid. Together, they reevaluated the situation and designed a new approach to the problem.

Butch and Sonny were placed on a fixed interval (FI) schedule of reinforcement for remaining in their seats without throwing missiles about the classroom or striking others. When they successfully exhibited the appropriate behaviors for the established period of time, they were reinforced with free time in the classroom music center. In this area they would put on earphones and listen to their favorite records.

This disruptive behavior slowly decreased in frequency. After several weeks, Butch and Sonny were put on a variable interval (VI) schedule. Their behavior continued to improve.

Punishment

With the use of punishment to control behavior, the traditional educator abandons any humane philosophy of education. While continuing to condemn various behavior modification interventions as *too controlling*, the educator grabs the paddle and swings away at the child in an effort to control unacceptable behavior by means of anxiety, fear, and physical discomfort.

We have avoided *any* endorsement of either physical or psychological punishment. *Punishment should be used only after all other methods of changing behavior have been consistently applied and have failed.* If punishment is imposed, it should be implemented by applying the principles of application presented in Chapter Five. Punishment, in our opinion, is usually inhumane. It is generally applied because it is expedient; that is, it is simple to implement, and it relieves the punisher of frustration.

EXAMPLE

Mr. Paddy, the gym teacher, does not think twice before he applies the "board of education" to the posteriors of the boys and girls in his classes. In fact, he is so infamous within the local professional community that other, less hardy teachers send their unruly children to him for punishment.

There are a number of distasteful and unkind statements that could be made about Mr. Paddy and his colleagues; however, the most depressing fact is that Mr. Paddy appears to derive pleasure and attain status by punishing the children. He honestly believes it is the "best" thing for them.

The teachers who send their students to Mr. Paddy have no doubt lost their ability to control unacceptable behaviors of the children in their classrooms.

The children dislike both Mr. Paddy and the teachers who expose them to him. Such a punitive environment is frequently found to be counterproductive when a child's academic learning is evaluated.

Harsh and punitive interventions are far too common in today's schools. They tend to dehumanize educational institutions, whose purpose is to nurture and train children to live in a democratic society.

Shaping

Shaping involves the gradual improvement in an individual's skill until a level is reached that approximates what is assumed to be the individual's maximum potential. Encouraging and permitting a child to attain this maximum potential is in the best tradition of the humanist. With the development of skill, the child is appropriately rewarded, and his or her self-image as a person and learner usually assumes more positive characteristics.

EXAMPLE

Peter had difficulty learning the letters of the alphabet. By means of a shaping intervention, his parents successfully taught him to identify all the letters of the alphabet. During the shaping process they used positive reinforcement of appropriate behavior.

Modeling

Modeling is the presentation of an individual or a particular behavior of an individual that the child imitates. Children will model their behavior after some important individual in their environment; they will imitate both acceptable and unacceptable behavior. Consequently, exposing a child to models who manifest acceptable behaviors can be a powerful preventive technique, as well as a remedial intervention of great benefit to the child.

EXAMPLE

Mr. Caldwell, an expert in American geography, had tried for many years to get his students interested in the geography of the Americas, but he had not been successful. He decided to discuss his problem with the curriculum consultant, who suggested he use a modeling technique to increase student interest.

A few students with leadership qualities appeared to be interested in the subject matter. Mr. Caldwell reinforced their interest and efforts, whereas he ignored the apathetic behavior of the less interested students. After a few weeks of this intervention, he noted that many students not previously demonstrating interest in geography began to ask questions, participate in group discussions, and complete assignments.

Contingency contracting

Contingency contracting encourages children to commit themselves to specific behaviors and to accept responsibility for exhibiting or not exhibiting those behaviors. Contracting permits children to express their perception of assignments and determine the curriculum. The student, within realistic limits, is free to select material that is appealing and decides when and how to complete tasks. The student is encouraged to determine personal rewards for achievements.

EXAMPLE

Mr. Sherwood was preparing the Senior Debate Club for participation in the All-State Debate Contest in Capitol City. All the members of the club except John were practicing daily. Mr. Sherwood was concerned that John would not perfect this speaking style before the contest.

John and Mr. Sherwood negotiated and signed a contract. By the terms of the agreement, if John would practice public speaking for a half hour a day 5 days a week after school in Mr. Sherwood's classroom, then he (John) would be permitted to give the daily announcements over the school's public address system on the sixth day.

John selected both the reward and the day the reward was to be given.

Token economy

The token economy is a very versatile intervention designed to encourage personal freedom of choice and responsibility on the part of the child. Generally, the child chooses the rewards for personal achievements.

The token economy is comparable to the adult world of work that the child is preparing to enter. Table 12 shows the similarity between school rewards and rewards that the average adult worker strives to obtain.

What is more meaningful to a child or adult than systematically having an opportunity to contribute to decisions concerning present and future rewards?

Time-out

Time-out is primarily used to help children exert control over their personal behavior. This technique is far more humane than the negative actions that can, and often do, result when a child exhibits inappropriate behavior in school.

Time-out is a period during which the child is required to withdraw from negatively influencing situations. In time-out the child can make a decision concerning future behavior. This intervention is an effective means for teaching a child how to act, as well as how not to act, in relations with others.

EXAMPLE

Mr. Logar has a student by the name of Maggie in the morning business math class. Maggie always talked in class, seldom followed Mr. Logar's instructions, never completed assignments, and on occasion exhibited hostile verbal behavior toward her peers and teacher.

Mr. Logar tried several interventions to change Maggie's unacceptable behavior but did not have any positive results. As a last resort, he selected a time-out intervention.

Table 12. Comparison of student and adult work rewards

Student work rewards	Adult work rewards
Watch TV	Watch TV
Read a book or magazine	Read a book, magazine, or newspaper
Listen to records; view filmstrip	Attend a band concert or movie
Write to or visit a friend	Write to or visit a friend
Drink juice or soda	Drink a martini or beer
Be first in line	Be freed from work early
Receive recognition as student of the day	Receive recognition for safety or production
Enjoy free time and recess	Enjoy weekends, holidays, vacations, and coffee breaks

Maggie was given specific rules to follow during class. She was told that if she violated the rules, she would be sent to time-out for 3 minutes for each infraction. After several visits to the time-out area, Maggie realized Mr. Logar meant business. After approximately 1 week Maggie's unacceptable behavior began to decrease in frequency. Throughout the intervention phase the teacher reinforced Maggie's appropriate behavior with social rewards.

If Maggie's behavior had been allowed to continue, Mr. Logar might have had other students in the class imitate her inappropriate behavior. He could have lost control of the group. More important, he would have reinforced Maggie's inappropriate behavior, which was in conflict with the needs of others. Maggie would not have learned the academic lessons needed for success in school.

Satiation

Satiation is frequently used to eliminate "unauthorized borrowing." In our society we attempt to encourage individuals to develop respect for the property and time of others.

Stealing (time or property) is a behavior that is generally not accepted by society. With the use of satiation, certain types of stealing can be eliminated. The intervention is a far more humane approach to this problem behavior than paddling, detentions, or verbal reprimands that at best appear to be effective for only brief periods of time.

Children in school who steal money, supplies, or trinkets *not because they need them but because they want them* are the target of this intervention. Teachers must recognize that some children steal because they must steal to survive or to be accepted by their peers (these students are more highly motivated to continue stealing).

Satiation is also helpful to those children who dominate the personal time of others by repeatedly demanding attention.

EXAMPLE

Ms. Sharpe, the music teacher, had a problem with Kittie. Kittie was constantly "borrowing" other children's music sheets without their knowledge. It got to the point that the others began to blame Kittie for missing or misplaced music (and other items) even when she was not the culprit.

Ms. Sharpe introduced a satiation intervention to eliminate Kittie's "borrowing" behavior. The teacher duplicated enough extra copies of each music sheet so that Kittie could have several. Each day, Kittie, was given music sheets before, during, and as she departed from class.

After several weeks Kittie stopped "borrowing" music sheets from others and frequently showed her original sheet to Ms. Sharpe, indicating that she did not want additional copies.

Desensitization

Desensitization has been successfully used to eliminate or lessen fears in children. It is inhumane to permit a child to continue to be fearful of certain persons, objects, animals, or situations, especially when (1) the feared object is confronted daily, (2) the feared thing is not in itself fearsome, and (3) the fear prohibits the child from living a normal life.

Desensitization can be applied to help the child overcome the fear and thus more fully participate in life.

EXAMPLE

Katie, a high school senior, was extremely afraid of cats of all sizes and colors. She would not leave her home or school if a cat was in view. If she was walking down the street and saw a cat, she would be panic-striken; she would scream and run to the nearest safe place. This behavior made it very difficult for her to attend school or to socialize. She sought professional counsel to overcome the problem.

Katie's doctor initiated a desensitization program to help her overcome her fear. After 17 sessions, Katie can tolerate cats in her presence, although she continues to dislike them and won't touch one.

Follow-up in the third, sixth, and ninth months after treatment indicates that her fear of cats has not returned.

• • •

With these examples we have attempted to expand on our position that behavior modification interventions are humane. It is true that behavior modification interventions, *like any interventions*, can be abused by insensitive and unethical practitioners. However, it is possible that behavioral interventions are abused less often than other interventions because of their emphasis on the observability and measurability of the behavior change process.

SOME BEHAVIOR MANAGEMENT GUIDELINES*

The following are guidelines to be considered in the application of any behavior management intervention. They are presented here primarily to stimulate thought and discussion.

The teacher as model and leader

Outside of the family, the teacher is in all probability the most important element in the child's life-space. No other variable in the school appears to have a greater potential impact on a student than the interpersonal relationship developed between teacher and child.

Educational programs can be (and have been) operated successfully under extremely adverse conditions (without adequate facilities, materials, equipment, funds, personnel, transportation, and so on). However, no program has ever been successfully operated without teachers who can and do relate positively and productively with children.

Authentic teachers must be authentic people—real people. It is difficult to select for employment an authentic teacher by the traditional means of application and personal interview. However, there are several personal traits that successful teachers appear to have in common.

Self-insight: The teachers know why they wish to work with children. They have some understanding of why they engage in the activities that make up their lifestyle.

---

*Adapted from Shea, T. M. Camping for special children. St. Louis: The C. V. Mosby Co., 1977, Chapter 9.

Self-acceptance and realistic self-confidence: The teachers accept themselves as they are but seek to improve themselves. They are realistically confident in themselves and their capability to be effective but are not so overconfident of their abilities as to be considered naive; they do not have an "I can do anything" attitude. They can make honest and forthright statements concerning their strengths and weaknesses without excuses.

Love and acceptance of children: The teachers love and are able to demonstrate their love for children. They understand that love and compliance are not identical. Sometimes love is demonstrated through discipline. They accept children as worthwhile human beings even though they must at times reject a child's behavior. They are capable of accepting, without reservation, individuals who are different from themselves—whether these individuals are short or tall; male or female; black, white, brown, red, or yellow; rotund or slim; deformed or normal; intelligent or retarded; conforming, deviant, or radical.

An understanding of the behavior of children: The teachers not only understand human behavior at a cognitive level but are also able to empathize with children who manifest deviancy. They continually seek insight and understanding into such a child's behavior.

Curiosity and willingness to learn: The teachers have a bit of the child in their adult person. Like children, they are curious about their environment and enthusiastically explore it.

Patience with themselves and their students: The teachers realize that they are imperfect, that they make mistakes. They also recognize this quality in others. They realize that learning is a slow, complex, process for many individuals. However, they continually strive to attain learning goals for themselves and their students.

Flexibility: The teachers are flexible. They know when to change a lesson, intervention, or activity for the benefit of the students and when to change in order to attain a broader objective.

Humor: The teachers have a well-developed sense of humor. (Mistakes, accidents, and humorous happenings occur in the classroom daily. Teachers who cannot laugh will certainly cry.) The teachers are capable of laughing at themselves and with their students. They never laugh at their students.

Teachers become models for the children they instruct. For better or worse, children will probably model their behavior after a teacher, at least in part. It is of questionable value for children to have teachers who are highly skilled and knowledgeable in specific subject areas and activities but who lack the capacity to understand and accept themselves and their students.

In addition to the personal traits presented above, effective teachers need specific knowledge and skills to successfully lead children. The following are work characteristics of such individuals.

1. They establish routines in the daily lives of those in the classroom group.
2. They establish and enforce behavioral limits. They accomplish this difficult task without personal emotional involvement.
3. They do not permit emotionally charged situations to get out of control. They intrude themselves into conflicts and cause them to end in fairness to all involved.
4. They are consistent. All children are confused by teachers who condone a specific deviant behavior one day but do not condone the same deviation the next day.
5. They personally investigate an incident before acting rather than take action on the basis of second- or third-person information and rumors. They confer with all children and adults involved in the incident before acting.
6. They ignore certain behaviors. Many unacceptable behaviors manifested by children are normal, age-appropriate behaviors. Others are simply not of sufficient potential impact to require a response by the teacher. Effective teachers are selective in responding to and ignoring behaviors.
7. They communicate verbally and nonverbally with their students. They talk with students, not to them. They learn that many of the concepts they considered to be universal knowledge are mysteries to many students. They are tuned-in to the language and action of youth.
8. They learn to avoid personal confrontations with students when it is therapeutically appropriate. However, they confront an individual or group when necessary for the benefit of that person or group.
9. They learn to change activities and lessons for therapeutic purposes. Some teachers are so personally committed to "their thing" (lesson or subject) that they fail to recognize student disinterest, dislike, and resistance.
10. They work both independently and as team members by communicating with colleagues and supervisors. They hold themselves accountable for their actions or lack of action. They know they cannot succeed in isolation.
11. They make a direct appeal to students when the students' actions are confus-

ing and discomforting to them personally. Frequently, a direct appeal to a child's basic humanness and common sense will solve behavior problems as quickly and as effectively as sophisticated behavior management interventions.

12. They provide each child under their supervision with security. Effective teachers communicate to students that they will be provided needed security from physical and psychological harm while under teacher supervision.

The new teacher seldom arrives in the classroom with these specific behavior management skills in addition to instructional competence in all the need subject matter areas: reading, writing, mathematics, language, and so on. These skills are developed through experience and with the assistance of colleagues and supervisors.

Self-discipline

Self-discipline is the desired result of all behavior management interventions presented in this text. Self-discipline, or the process of attaining self-control over one's personal behavior in a variety of circumstances in association with a variety of individuals and groups, is not an instantaneous process. Self-control is developed by nearly all human beings over a long period of time (years) and includes a number of developmental phases. During the process of attaining self-control, children naturally progress and regress as they and their environment change. A child may appear perfectly self-controlled one day and not the following day. Progress—maturing and growing—is often measured by parents and teachers in slowly increasing lengths of time between occurrences of unacceptable behavior exhibited by the child.

The word *discipline* is derived from *disciple*, or follower of a master's teaching. This concept contains the idea of something

learned from a teacher whose example the learner personally desires to model. The best discipline is derived from the respect and understanding of one human being for another. Discipline should be cooperative and voluntary, not simply imposed from above by an authority figure (Chetkow, 1964).

In education, harsh, punitive, and negative disciplinary techniques are avoided. The majority of children, especially those with behavior problems, have a poor or distorted self-image as a result of repeated failure and negative discipline. Many of these children have psychologically isolated themselves from the effects of negative discipline. Benign and positive interventions leading ultimately to self-discipline are suggested to teachers of both regular and special classes.

Population and time

All children at one time or another during their school years exhibit some behavior problems. This simple fact is all too frequently forgotten by teachers.

It is not unusual to have a teacher become extremely frustrated with a child because the child's deviant behavior does not respond to intervention immediately. This same frustration among teachers is also exhibited relative to academic skill training. Perhaps we are too impatient and too easily frustrated as a result of living most of our adult lives in a society conditioned to instant change, instant solutions to problems, and little or no frustration. In education in the 1970s, the teacher must be patient and adjust to slow, time-consuming progress. Miracles and instant "cures" are few in number and difficult to observe when they do occur.

Children learn certain habitual ways of acting and reacting in their environment. These coping skills are developed over a span of years. Although unacceptable to others, they have been and continue to be more or less successful for the child. The child cannot (and should not be forced to) relinquish these coping mechanisms immediately and begin using "new" (and from our point of view more acceptable, more productive) ways of coping.

To change deviant behavior requires time and energy. Teachers must be patient and focus on the child's progress rather than on the desired end product.

Objectives and goals

Although teachers develop long-term goals for the children with whom they work, such goals are generally not a daily concern. Long-term goals are divided into a series of properly sequenced immediate objectives. The immediate objectives provide structure for the group's (teacher and students) daily, weekly, and/or monthly program of lessons and activities. The long-term goals provide the needed direction for the overall program for the individual child.

An important objective for each child enrolled in school is to have a pleasant and positive experience. The program must be enjoyable and rewarding for the child, or it will not meet the normal childhood needs of seeking out and exploring the new, the different, the unknown, and the exciting.

Even though the teacher has many academic remedial objectives for a particular child, these remedial tasks cannot be so demanding of the child's time and energy that school becomes drudgery. School must be a positive experience, offering the child a variety of opportunities to learn new skills and to participate in new activities of a nonacademic as well as of an academic nature.

Empathy, not sympathy

Behavior problem children do not need their teacher's sympathy. Ill-founded sympathy distorts the problems the teacher is attempting to help the child overcome. It places the teacher in an emotional condition that prohibits objective analysis of the child's behavior. A teacher who becomes deeply emotionally involved in a child's problem frequently functions in a biased, nonhelpful way. Such a teacher reacts to the child and others concerned with the child's welfare on a subjective rather than an objective level.

Although relationships based on sympathy are to be avoided in the educational setting, those based on empathy are necessary and should be encouraged. The teacher must be able to understand how the child feels and must be able to perceive the child's world from the child's point of view. This capacity is frequently referred to as "taking the position of the other" or "being in the other person's shoes."

The capacity to emphasize permits the teacher to provide the child or group with direction, guidance, and support when such assistance is needed.

Expectations

Many years ago we might have been told by our grandparents or parents, "As the twig is bent, so grows the tree." Some teachers ignore this simple truth. However, during the last decade, researchers have confirmed what our grandparents took for granted: our expectations for children have a significant effect on their performance (Beez, 1972; Rosenthal and Jacobsen, 1966; and Rubin and Balow, 1971, among others).

This self-fulfilling prophecy means that to a significant extent, if we believe a child is and will continue to be an incompetent, the probability is increased that the child will function as an incompetent. If we believe and communicate to a child that he or she will not learn to read, behave, compute, socialize, speak, and so on, the probability is significantly increased that the child will not accomplish these tasks. Conversely, if we believe and communicate to a child that he or

she will learn to behave, read, play, socialize, and speak, the probability is increased
that the child will respond to our expectations and learn these tasks.

As educators, we must maintain high but
realistic expectations for students. Classrooms should be environments developed
around a "can do" attitude. Children must
be told repeatedly throughout each day:
"You can do it." "You know and I know you
can do it." "You did it!" "Great!" "Super!"
"Beautiful!"

Obviously, such a "can do" attitude is
meaningless and perhaps harmful unless the
program is designed to ensure that the child
receives the needed support and skill training required to complete a task and fulfill
our expectations.

Freedom and independence to function

As a general policy, students should be
encouraged to grow and learn as much as
possible without teacher assistance. Within
realistic limits, anything that children can do
for themselves, they should do. The instructor's function is to facilitate, not dominate,
the child's activity program. The teacher is
available to instruct, demonstrate, assist,
counsel, and offer encouragement. All young
people need freedom to explore, investigate,
and implement new behaviors without adult
interference if they are to grow. Often they
will succeed in their efforts; occasionally they
will fail and require assistance.

Although constant failure is not recommended, failure is a part of every person's
life. The teacher cannot and should not
shelter children from all failure; at times,
they should be allowed to confront the logical
consequences—success and failure—of their
actions (Dreikurs and Grey, 1968). It is the
teacher's function to help the child learn to
cope appropriately with both success and
failure.

Complete freedom for many children becomes counterproductive. A child attends
school to learn productive skills and behaviors. The teacher is responsible for planning the curriculum for or, preferably, in
cooperation with the child. To do otherwise
would be irresponsible and a disservice to
the child. Behavior management and curriculum are partners; one is of little value
without the other.

Democracy without structure, discipline,
program, or predictability becomes anarchy.
Children are learners; they are not adults
skilled in the principles and practices of democracy. They must be encouraged to learn
and apply democratic principles in the classroom and school under teacher supervision
if they are to live by these principles as
adults.

SOME PRINCIPLES CONCERNING INDIVIDUAL RIGHTS OF CHILDREN

In 1969 Allen proposed three legal principles to be followed by individuals in the
helping professions in their actions toward
clients (children and adults). These principles
should serve as the foundation of all behavior
management decisions made by teachers of
both regular and special education classes.

They are (1) the principle of normalization,
(2) the principle of fairness, and (3) the principle of respect for the dignity and worth of
the individual.

Principle of normalization

To let the handicapped person obtain an existence
as close to the normal as is possible. (Nirje, 1967,
cited by Allen, 1969)

When applying this principle, the behavior modifier must use as a point of reference
the child's real environment (including the
behavior of the children and adults within it)
as well as the ideal democratic environment.
This principle demands understanding of the
similarities and differences between various

groups in society. The practitioner must base decisions on knowledge of the individual child's growth and development, needs, desires, strengths, and disabilities.

Before implementing and intervention, the practitioner must respond to the following query: Will the implementation of this specific behavioral intervention facilitate the child's movement toward the normally anticipated and observed behavior in this setting, or will it simply eliminate the child (and the behavior) as an inconvenience or annoyance to others in the environment, that is, the child's teacher, peers, administrators, and parents?

Many children who attend classes for retarded, disturbed, and learning-disabled children are in those classes simply because they are different; that is, they are black, Spanish-speaking, slow, nonreaders, poor, and so on. These children may be segregated primarily because they are an annoyance or inconvenience to others.

In this "special placement," their opportunity to obtain "an existence as normal as possible" is grossly inhibited, if not totally frustrated.

Principle of fairness

Fundamental fairness—due process of law—requires that in decision-making affecting one's life, liberty, or vital interests, the elements of due process will be observed, including the right to notice, to a fair hearing, to representation by counsel, to present evidence, and to appeal an adverse decision. (Allen, 1969)

Although this principle is phrased in legal terminology, it can be simply stated by the teacher: "Is the intervention I have selected to modify this child's behavior fair to the child as an individual?"

Many times interventions are arbitrarily applied on the whim of a practitioner without concrete evidence that the child is, in fact, exhibiting the target behavior. Fre-

quently interventions are applied that only serve to prohibit the child from finding *any* success in school. For example, a child who had difficulty learning French grammar is prohibited from going to recess, playing on the school athletic teams, and so on. This child may only be capable of meeting success in these prohibited activities. As do all humans, the child has a need for success. Interventions such as these appear to be unfair to the child.

Unfairness is evidenced frequently when a practitioner refuses to apply an intervention that is obviously needed if the child is to function in school. For example, frequently we are confronted with members of the teaching profession who will not use tangible rewards, simply because they do not "believe in them." Yet the child is found to respond only to tangible rewards.

Other examples of unfairness might include:

Refusal to try to modify a child's behavior systematically

Arbitrary placement of a child in a special therapy or instructional program without an attempt at classroom interventions

Unwillingness of teachers to provide needed service or request consultation because they believe that seeking help is a sign of incompetency

If the principle of fairness is to be implemented, we must begin all decisions from the point of view of the child's welfare: "What does this child need?"

Principle of respect for the dignity and worth of the individual

One's right to be treated as a human being, and not as an animal or a statistic. (Allen, 1969)

In our actions toward children, are we demonstrating respect for them as human beings? All interventions must be judged against this question. When the intervention is evaluated from this point of view, we find that many common "therapeutic" practices violate the principle of respect. The following are examples:

Physical punishment (spankings, slaps, paddlings)

Psychological punishment (sarcasm, embarrassment, name calling)

Deprivation (prohibiting a child the normal opportunities for success)

Segregation (arbitrary special-class placement)

Isolation (inconsistent, long-term use of time-out and restraint)

Medication (capricious use of symptom-control medications)

Extrahuman punishment (use of restraints, electric shockers)

All of these interventions have been used and remain in use in many of the institutions in our society. Generally, they are applied by individuals who justify the use of any means to attain their end. All of these interventions have been justified by some as the "only way" to accomplish an objective. These techniques are used (and justified) frequently, simply because they are convenient, efficient, and seemingly effective.

It cannot be denied that a beaten child will obey, that an electric cattle prod will get a disturbed child to pay attention, that enough medication will calm a hyperactive child, and that segregation and isolation will reduce conflict. However, we professional practitioners must establish limits on the interventions that can be applied with children. We must judge these interventions in the light of this third principle; that is, could or do the interventions inflict damage on the individual child or relegate the child to a less-than-human classification?

It is absolutely necessary that all behavior management practitioners develop a clear value system that incorporates the principles of normalization, fairness, and respect for the

dignity and the worth of the child. This value system must avoid the pitfall of justifying "any means to attain a desired end."

We should remember that any intervention can be misused and abused if the person using it lacks an ethical system of personal and professional values. Practitioners must never be allowed to forget that knowledge is power and that with power comes the responsibility to apply that power for the benefit of all persons.

• • •

For an in-depth discussion of the legal implications and restrictions on the application of behavior modification interventions, the student is referred to an excellent text by Martin (1975).

BEHAVIOR MODIFICATION AS A PREVENTIVE TECHNIQUE

Most of the behavior modification literature has been concerned with the remediation of academic and behavior problems in the home, school, institution, and clinic. Efforts have generally been directed toward the increase and decrease of acceptable and unacceptable behaviors. Very few research reports have focused on the maintenance of the acceptable behaviors of normally functioning children.

There are many opportunities in the regular classroom to prevent the development of inappropriate behavior by systematically maintaining the existing acceptable behavior. If teachers understand and apply the principles of behavior modification (presented in Chapter Two) as part of their normal teaching methodology, many potential problems and conflicts can be avoided.

Concerned teachers monitor and evaluate their personal teaching behaviors and the learning behaviors of their classroom groups. They do this by systematically evaluating the teaching-learning process. They recognize that children need positive reinforcement and rewards and that only the child being rewarded can indicate with certitude what is rewarding.

Experienced practitioners understand that as teachers, they can and do reinforce inappropriate behavior on occasion. Consequently, they attempt to reward only appropriate behaviors. They realize that the younger, less experienced child needs to be immediately reinforced for exhibiting appropriate behavior. They also recognize that delayed rewards are more desirable, from a societal point of view, than immediate rewards and that social rewards are more desirable than tangible rewards. They always give the child social reinforcement in conjunction with tangible rewards.

Prevention-minded teachers recognize that new behaviors must be rewarded more frequently and more consistently than established behaviors and that although continuous reinforcement is necessary when a new behavior is being established, intermittent reinforcement is ultimately desired and will effectively maintain established behaviors.

Prevention-conscious teachers systematically utilize high-frequency behaviors to facilitate the development of low-frequency behaviors.

By using the principles of behavior modification as a standard part of the teaching-learning process, teachers need not anxiously wait for problems to arise in the classroom but can prevent them and use the time saved to teach children those things they must know to live productively in society.

REFERENCES

Allen, R. C. *Legal rights of the disabled and disadvantaged.* Washington, D.C.: U.S. Department of Health, Education, and Welfare, National Citizens Conference on Rehabilitation of the Disabled and Disadvantaged, 1969.

Bandura, A. *Principles of behavior modification.* New York: Holt, Rinehart & Winston, Inc., 1969.

Beez, W. V. Influence of biased psychological reports on teacher behavior and pupil performances. In A. Morrison and D. McIntyre (Eds.), *The social psychology of teaching.* Baltimore: Penguin Books, 1972.

Bellack, A. S., and Hersen, M. *Behavior modification: An introductory textbook.* Baltimore: The Williams & Wilkins Co., 1977.

Chetkow, B. H. Discipline problems in camp. *Recreation,* 1964, *57*(3), 136-137.

Dreikurs, R., and Grey, L. *Logical consequences: A new approach to discipline.* New York: Hawthorn Books, Inc., 1968.

Fargo, G. A., Behrns, C., and Nolen, P. (Eds.). *Behavior modification in the classroom.* Belmont, Calif.: Wadsworth Publishing Co., Inc., 1970.

Hilts, P. J. *Behavior mod.* New York: Harper's Magazine Press, 1974.

Martin, R. *Legal challenges to behavior modification: Trends in schools, corrections, and mental health.* Champaign, Ill.: Research Press, 1975.

Nirje, B. The normalization principle and its human management implications. In R. Kugel and W. Wolfensberger, (Eds.), *Changing patterns in residential services for the mentally retarded.* Washington, D.C.: President's Committee on Mental Retardation, 1967.

Rosenthal, R., and Jacobson, L. Teachers' expectancies: Determinants of pupils' IQ gains. *Psychological Reports,* 1966, *19*, 115-118.

Rubin, R., and Balow, B. Learning and behavior disorders: A longitudinal study. *Exceptional Children,* 1971, *38*, 293-298.

Scottwood, W. (Ed.). *Issues in evaluating behavior modifications.* Champaign, Ill.: Research Press, 1975.

Skinner, B. F. *Science and human behavior.* New York: MacMillan Publishing Co., Inc., 1953.

Skinner, B. F. *Beyond freedom and dignity.* New York: Alfred A. Knopf, Inc., 1971.

Ulrich, R., Stachnik, T., and Mabry, J. (Eds.). *Control of human behavior,* Glenview, Ill.: Scott, Foresman & Co., 1966.

Additional readings

Ahr, A. E., and Simons, B. *Parent handbook: Developing your child's skills and abilities at home.* Skokie, Ill. Priority Innovations, 1968.

Arthur, A. Z. Behavior therapy versus psychotherapy and applied science. *Canadian Psychologist,* 1967, *8,* 105-113.

Benson, S. L. Systematic desensitization in the treatment of phobic reactions. *The Journal of General Education,* 1968, *20,* 119-130.

Brady, J. P. Psychotherapy, learning theory, and insight. *Archives of General Psychiatry,* 1967, *16,* 304-311.

Breger, L., and McGaugh, J. L. Critique and reformulation of "learning theory" approaches to psychotherapy and neurosis. *Psychological Bulletin,* 1965, *63,* 338-358.

Breyer, N. L. *Behavior modification in the classroom.* New York: MSS Educational Publishing Co., Inc., 1969.

Bugg, C. A. Systematic desensitization: A technique worth trying. *Personnel and Guidance Journal,* 1972, *50,* 823-828.

Cahoon, D. D. Symptom substitution and the behavior therapies: Reappraisal. *Psychological Bulletin,* 1968, *69,* 149-156.

Cruickshank, W. M., Paul, J. L., and Junkala, J. B. *Misfits in the public schools.* New York: Syracuse University Press, 1969.

Dupont, H. *Educating emotionally disturbed children.* New York: Holt, Rinehart & Winston, 1969.

Eysenck, H. J. Learning theory and behavior therapy. *Journal of Mental Science,* 1959, *105,* 61-75.

Holt, M. M., Hobbs, T. R., and Hankins, R. The effects of token reinforcement and delinquents' classroom behavior. *Psychology in the Schools,* 1976, *13*(3), 341-347.

James, M., and Jongeward, D. *Born to win: Transactional analysis with Gestalt experiments.* Reading, Mass.: Adidison-Wesley Publishing Co., Inc., 1971.

Johnson, J. L. Special education and the inner city: A challenge for the future or another means for cooling the mark out? *The Journal of Special Education,* 1970, *4,* 120-137.

Kelly, E. J. *Common sense in child raising.* Denver: Love Publishing Co., 1971.

LaBenne, W. D. *The cure is the cause—A humane approach to child discipline.* Ann Arbor, Mich.: Author, 1971.

O'Leary, K. D. Establishing token programs in schools: Issues and problems. In M. B. Harris (Ed.), *Classroom uses of behavior modification.* Columbus, Ohio: Charles E. Merrill Publishing Co., 1972.

Patterson, G. R., and Gullion, M. E. *Living with children.* Champaign, Ill.: Research Press, 1968.

Peter, L. J. *Prescriptive teaching.* New York: McGraw-Hill Book Co., 1965.

Poteet, J. A. *Behavior modification: A practical guide for teachers.* Minneapolis, Minn.: Burgess Publishing Co., 1973.

Shea, T. M., Whiteside, W. R., Beetner, E. G. and Lindsey, D. L. *Behavioral interventions.* Edwardsville: Southern Illinois University, 1974. (a)

Shea, T. M., Whiteside, W. R., Beetner, E. G., and Lindsey, D. L. *Ignoring and reinforcing.* Edwardsville: Southern Illinois University, 1974. (b).

Shea, T. M., Whiteside, W. R., Beetner, E. G., and Lindsey, D. L. *Selecting reinforcers.* Edwardsville: Southern Illinois Unviersity, 1974. (c)

Smith, J. M., and Smith, D. E. P. *Child management: A program for parents.* Ann Arbor, Mich.: Ann Arbor Publishers, 1966.

Thorndike, E. L. *The fundamentals of learning.* New York: Teacher's College Press, 1932.

Valett, R. E. *Effective teaching: A guide to diagnostic-prescriptive task analysis.* Belmont, Calif.: Fearon Publishers, Inc., 1970.

Woody, R. H. *Behavioral problem children in the schools: Recognition, diagnosis, and behavioral modification.* New York: Appleton-Century-Crofts, 1969.

Yates, A. J. *Behavior therapy.* New York: John Wiley & Sons, Inc., 1970.

Some journals publishing behavior modification articles and some basic reference texts on behavior modification are listed in Appendix B.

Answers to chapter quizzes

CHAPTER TWO

1. Immediately and/or consistently
2. Variable (or intermittent)
3. Extinction
4. Punishment
5. Differential reinforcement
6. Generalization
7. Negative reinforcement
8. Reinforcers
9. Ratio
10. Interval

CHAPTER THREE

1. a. Target
   b. Collecting; recording
   c. Appropriate
   d. Intervention
2. a. Frequency
   b. Duration
   c. Intensity
   d. Type
3. a. Increase
   b. Decrease
   c. Be maintained
4. Three of the following:
   a. Direct observation of the behavior with time sampling
   b. Analysis of anecdotal records
   c. Analysis of cumulative records
   d. Interview with the child
   e. Interview with an adult (parent or teacher) about the child
   f. Direct observation data collected by an aide, parent, supervisor, consultant, or the like

5. a. Frequency (number of times)
   b. Charting
6. Three of the following:
   a. Use of reinforcement preference scales
   b. Use of reinforcement lists
   c. Direct interview with the child
   d. Parent or teacher interview about the child
   e. Direct observation
7. Implementation (try it)
8. Intervention
9. Increase
10. Extinction

CHAPTER FOUR

1. Shaping; modeling; contracting; token economy
2. Modeling
3. Verbal; written
4. Shaping
5. Menu
6. Token economy
7. Verbal contract
8. Modeling
9. Model
10. Verbal contact

CHAPTER FIVE

1. a. Extinction
   b. Time-out
   c. Satiation
   d. Punishment
   e. Reinforcement of incompatible behaviors
   f. Desensitization
2. Extinction

3. a. Reinforcing (rewarding); nonreinforcing (nonrewarding)
4. Three of the following:
   a. Characteristics of the individual child
   b. Teacher's consistent application of the intervention
   c. Child's understanding of the rules of time-out
   d. Characteristics of the time-out area
   e. Duration of time-out
   f. Evaluation of the effectiveness of the intervention
5. Area should be:
   a. Out of the high traffic area
   b. Away from doors and windows
   c. Out of the other children's sight
   d. Within the view of the teacher or observer-supervisor (aide)
6. Satiation
7. Punishment
8. Reinforcing a behavior that is in opposition to or incompatible with the target behavior
9. Desensitization
10. a. Does not eliminate the behavior but merely suppresses it
    b. Does not provide a model for the acceptable behavior to be emitted
    c. May provide an undesirable model through the practitioner's aggression
    d. May cause emotional results of fear, tension, increased stress, or withdrawal
    e. May cause further behavior deviation as a product of the child's resulting frustration

CHAPTER SIX

1. Learn; adjust; progress; parent
2. Six of the following:
   a. Self-doubt
   b. Unhappiness and mourning
   c. Guilt
   d. Denial
   e. Projection
   f. Withdrawal
   g. Avoidance and rejection
   h. Embarrassment and social isolation
   i. Hostility
   j. Over-dependency and helplessness
   k. Confusion
   l. Frustration
3. a. Informational

b. Psychotherapeutic
c. Training
4. a. To increase the parents' knowledge of the techniques of behavior modification
   b. To increase the parents' skills in the application of behavior modification techniques in the management of their children's behavior
   c. To provide the parents and the teacher with a common perspective of child behavior management and to facilitate cooperative child behavior management efforts.
5. Information-gathering
6. a. Defining the target behavior(s)
   b. Explicating specific situations in which the behavior occurs
   c. Uncovering the contingencies that seemingly sustain the behavior
   d. Detecting any irrational ideas that make it difficult for the parent to objectively understand, accept, and modify the behavior
7. a. Preparation
   b. Instructional
   c. Follow-up
8. Five of the following:
   a. Be brief
   b. Be positive
   c. Be honest
   d. Be responsive
   e. Be informal
   f. Be consistent
   g. Avoid jargon
   h. Be careful

CHAPTER SEVEN

1. All those actions (and conscious inactions) teachers engage in to enhance the probability that children, individually and in groups, will develop effective behaviors that are personally self-fulfilling, productive, and socially acceptable
2. a. Counseling techniques
   b. The expressive arts
3. a. Clinical exploitation of life events
   b. Emotional first aid on the spot
4. Five of the following:
   a. Free play
   b. Puppetry
   c. Role playing and psychodrama
   d. Creative movement and dance

e. Music
f. The written word
g. The spoken word
h. Two-dimensional arts
i. Three-dimensional arts

5. a. Referral
    b. Collaboration with and reporting of observations to the physician
    c. Modification of classroom structure and curriculum content to meet the needs of the child
    d. Obtaining of permission to administer medication
    e. Safeguarding and administering of medication to the child in school

6. a. Excitor-centered (child-centered) interventions
    b. Respondent-centered (environment-centered) interventions
    c. Exchange-centered (child-environment–centered) interventions

7. Four of the following:
    a. Age
    b. Sex
    c. Interests
    d. Handicapping conditions, if any
    e. Personality traits
    f. Degree, intensity, and kind of behavior problems, if any
    g. Group experiences and skills

8. Eight of the following:
    a. Comfort
    b. Organization
    c. Child-teacher, teacher-child, and child-child communications
    d. Movement
    e. Privacy
    f. Size and shape
    g. Scale
    h. Interest
    i. Color
    j. Accessibility
    k. Usability
    l. Clutter

9. a. Open meeting
    b. Problem-solving meeting
    c. Decision-making meeting

APPENDIX B

Journals, reference texts, and instructional films

JOURNALS

Academic Therapy. San Rafael, Calif.: Academic Therapy Publications, published 6 times a year.

American Journal of Mental Deficiency. Albany, N.Y.: American Association on Mental Deficiency, published bimonthly.

American Journal of Psychology. Urbana: University of Illinois Press, published quarterly.

Behavior Modification. Beverly Hills, Calif.: Sage Publications, Inc., published quarterly.

Behavior Research and Therapy. Elmsford, N.Y.: Pergamon Press, Inc., published quarterly.

Behavior Therapy. New York: Academic Press, Inc., published 5 times a year.

Child Development. Chicago: The University of Chicago Press, published quarterly.

Childhood Education. Washington, D.C.: Association for Childhood Education International, published 6 times a year.

Developmental Psychology. Washington, D.C.: American Psychological Association, published bimonthly.

Education Horizons. Bloomington, Ind.: Pi Lambda Theta, published quarterly.

Education and Training of the Mentally Retarded. Montpelier, Vt.: Capital City Press, published quarterly.

Elementary School Journal. Chicago: The University of Chicago Press, published monthly (October through May).

Exceptional Children. Reston, Va.: The Council for Exceptional Children, published monthly.

Journal of Abnormal Psychology. Washington, D.C.: American Psychological Association, published bimonthly.

Journal of Applied Behavior Analysis. Lawrence, Kan.: Department of Human Development, University of Kansas, published quarterly.

Journal of Consulting and Clinical Psychology. Washington, D.C.: American Psychological Association, published bimonthly.

Journal of Counseling Psychology. Washington, D.C.: American Psychological Association, published bimonthly.

Journal of Educational Research. Madison, Wis.: Dembar Educational Research Services, Inc., published 10 times a year.

Journal of Experimental Child Psychology. New York: Academic Press Inc., published bimonthly.

Journal of Learning Disabilities. Chicago: The Professional Press, Inc., published monthly.

Journal of Personality and Social Psychology. Washington, D.C.: American Psychological Association, published monthly.

Journal of School Psychology. Provincetown, Mass.: The Journal Press, published quarterly.

Journal of Special Education. Philadelphia: Buttonwood Farms, Inc., published quarterly.

Mental Retardation. Albany, N.Y.: American Association on Mental Deficiency, published bimonthly.

Phi Delta Kappan. Bloomington, Ind.: Phi Delta Kappa, published monthly.

Psychology in the Schools. Brandon, Vt.: Clinical Psychology Publishing Co., Inc., published quarterly.

Review of Educational Research. Washington, D.C.: American Educational Research Association, published 5 times a year.

Sociology of Education. Washington, D.C.: American Sociological Association, published quarterly.

Teaching Exceptional Children. Reston, Va.: The Council for Exceptional Children, published quarterly.

REFERENCE TEXTS

Allyon, T., and Azrin, N. *The token economy.* New York: Appleton-Century-Crofts, 1968.

Bandura, A. *Principles of behavior modification.* New York: Holt, Rinehart & Winston, 1969.

Becker, W. *Parents and teachers.* Champaign, Ill.: Research Press, 1971.

Blackman, D. *Operant conditioning: An experimental analysis of behaviour.* Scranton, Pa.: Barnes & Noble Books, 1974.

Buckley, N. K., and Walker, H. M. *Modifying classroom behavior: A manual of procedures for classroom teachers.* Champaign, Ill.: Research Press, 1970.

Deibert, A., and Harmon, A. *New tools for changing behaviors.* Champaign, Ill.: Research Press, 1970.

Ferster, D., and Perrott, M. *Behavior principles.* New York: Appleton-Century-Crofts, 1968.

Gambrill, E. D. *Behavior modification: Handbook of assessment, intervention, and evaluation.* San Francisco: Jossey-Bass, Inc., Publishers, 1977.

Geiss, G., Stebbins, W., and Lundin, R. *Reflex and operant conditioning,* New York: Appleton-Century-Crofts, 1965.

Grambowski, J., and Thompson, T. *Behavior modification of the mentally retarded.* Fair Lawn, N.J.: Oxford University Press, Inc., 1977.

Greer, R. D., and Dorow, L. G. *Specializing education behaviorally.* Dubuque, Iowa: Kendall/Hunt Publishing Co., 1976.

Harris, M. B. (Ed.). *Classroom uses of behavior modification.* Columbus, Ohio: Charles E. Merrill Publishing Co., 1972.

Holland, J., and Skinner, G. *The analysis of behavior.* New York: McGraw-Hill Book Co., 1961.

Homme, L., Csanyi, A. P., Gonzales, M. A., and Rechs, J. R. *How to use contingency contracting in the classroom.* Champaign, Ill.: Research Press, 1969.

Johnson, K. R., Chase, P. N., and Maass, C. A. *Personalized system of instruction: Study guide for Sulzer-Azaroff/Mayer's Applying behavior-analysis procedures with children and youth.* New York: Holt, Rinehart & Winston, 1977.

Kanfer, F., and Phillips, J. *Learning foundations of behavior therapy.* New York: John Wiley & Sons, Inc., 1970.

Kazdin, A. *Behavior modification in applied settings.* Homewood, Ill.: Dorsey Press, 1975.

Krasner, L., and Ullman, L. (Eds.). *Research in behavior modification.* New York: Holt, Rinehart & Winston, 1965.

Lanyon, R., and Lanyon, B. *Behavior therapy: A clinical introduction.* Reading, Mass: Addison-Wesley Publishing Co., Inc., 1978.

Martin, G., and Pear, J. *Behavior modification: What is it and how to do it.* Englewood Cliffs, N.J.: Prentice-Hall, Inc., 1978.

Michael, J. *Laboratory studies in operant behavior.* New York: McGraw-Hill Book Co., 1963.

Mikulas, W. L. *Behavior modification.* New York: Harper & Row, Publishers, Inc., 1978.

Morris, R. *Behavior modification with children: A systematic guide.* Cambridge, Mass., Winthrop Publishers, Inc., 1976.

Neisworth, J., and Smith, R. *Modifying retarded behavior.* Boston: Houghton Mifflin Co., 1973.

O'Leary, K. D., and O'Leary, S. G. (Eds.). *Classroom management: The successful use of behavior modification.* New York: Pergamon Press, Inc., 1972.

Racklin, H. *Introduction to modern behaviorism.* San Francisco, Calif.: W. H. Freeman & Co., Publishers, 1976.

Reese, E. P. *Experiments in operant behavior.* New York: Appleton-Century-Crofts, 1964.

Reese, E. P. *The analysis of human operant behavior.* Dubuque, Iowa: Wm. C. Brown Co., Publishers, 1966.

Reynolds, G. S. *A primer of operant conditioning.* Glenview, Ill.: Scott, Foresman & Co., 1968.

Skinner, B. F. *Science and human behavior.* New York: Macmillan Publishing Co., Inc., 1953.

Skinner, B. F. *Cumulative record.* New York: Appleton-Century-Crofts, 1961.

Staats, A. (Ed.). *Human learning.* New York: Holt, Rinehart & Winston, 1964.

Sulzer-Azaroff, B., and Mayer, G. R. *Applying behavior-analysis procedures with children and youth.* New York: Holt, Rinehart & Winston, 1977.

Ullman, L., and Krasner, L. (Eds.). *Case studies in behavior modification.* New York: Holt, Rinehart & Winston, 1965.

Ullman, L., and Krasner, L. (Eds.). *A psychological approach to abnormal behavior.* Englewood Cliffs, N.J.: Prentice-Hall, Inc., 1969.

Ulrich, R., Stachnik, T., and Mabry, J. (Eds.). *Control of human behavior.* Glenview, Ill.: Scott Foresman & Co., 1966.

Valett, R. E. *Modifying children's behavior.* Belmont, Calif.: Fearon Publishers, Inc., 1969.

Verhave, T. (Ed.). *The experimental analysis of behavior: Suggested readings.* New York: Appleton-Century-Crofts, 1966.

Walker, H., and Buckley, N. *Token reinforcement techniques.* Eugene, Ore.: Englemen-Becker Press, 1974.

Watson, L. S. *Child behavior modification: A manual for teachers, nurses, and parents.* Elmsford, N.Y.: British Book Centre, 1973.

INSTRUCTIONAL FILMS

The ABC's of behavioral education. Baltimore: Halmark Films and Recordings.

Achievement place. Topeka: University of Kansas, 1970.

Behavior modification. New York: Appleton-Century-Crofts, 1971.

Behavior modification in the classroom. Berkeley: University of California, 1970.

Behavior theory in practice (4 parts). New York: Appleton-Century-Crofts, 1965.

Born to succeed. 1. The concept of number. New York: Appleton-Century-Crofts, 1971.

Born to succeed. 2. Arithmetic. New York: Appleton-Century-Crofts, 1971.

Changing Kip. Seattle: University of Washington, 1973.

Child behavior—You. Briarcliff Manor, N.Y.: Benchmark Films.

Childhood aggression: A social learning approach to family therapy. Solana Beach, Calif.: The Media Guild, 1972.

A conversation with B. F. Skinner. Delmar, Calif.: CRM Films, 1971.

Cynthia dresses herself. Monmouth, Ore.: Teaching Research, 1970.

Developing observational techniques. Madison: University of Wisconsin, 1972.

Disruptive behavior. Madison: University of Wisconsin, 1972.

Goofing off with objectives. Los Angeles: University of Southern California.

Help for Mark. Lexington: University of Kentucky.

Individualized instruction. Madison: University of Wisconsin, 1972.

Introduction to behavior counseling. Washington, D.C.: American Personnel Guidance and Counseling, 1969.

Jamie: A behavioral approach to family intervention. Solana Beach, Calif. The Media Guild, 1976.

Learning and behavior. Chicago: Carousel, Encyclopedia Britannica Educational Corp., 1960.

One hour a week. Washington, D.C.: U.S. Bureau of Education for the Handicapped, 1973.

One step at a time: An introduction to behavior modification. Ottawa: National Film Board, 1973.

Operation behavior modification. Parsons, Kan.: Parsons State Hospital, 1967.

Peer-conducted behavior modification. Solana Beach, Calif.: The Media Guild, 1976.

Poppe project. Berkeley: University of California: The Regents, 1967.

Rewards and reinforcement. Bloomington: Indiana University, 1968.

Reward procedures for behavior modification. Detroit, Mich.: Informatics, Dept. C., 1971.

Reward procedures for classroom management. Detroit, Mich.: Informatics, Dept. C., 1971.

Santa Monica project. Santa Monica, Calif.: Santa Monica School District (Aims Instructional Media Services, Inc.)

Siblings as behavior modifiers. Solana Beach, Calif. The Media Guild, 1976.

B. F. Skinner and behavior change: Research, practice, and promise, Delmar, Calif.: CRM Films, 1976.

B. F. Skinner on counseling. Washington, D.C.: American Personnel Guidance and Counseling, 1972.

That's what it's all about. Washington, D.C.: U.S. Bureau of Education for the Handicapped, 1973.

Time-out: A way to help children. Lemont, Pa.: Behavior Techniques, 1971.

Token economy: Behaviorism applied. Delmar, Calif.: CRM Films, 1972.

Treating the hospitalized mentally retarded through conditioning. Pomona, Calif.: Pacific State Hospital.

Try another way. Indianapolis: Film Productions of Indianapolis, 1975.

Which students get your attention? Albany: New York State Education Department, 1973.

Index

Work sheets and forms

In the following pages copies of the work sheets and forms used in this text are provided. They can be removed from the text for use by readers wishing to complete the projects suggested at the ends of Chapters Two through Seven.

Five copies of each work sheet and form are included.

Target Behavior Selection Checklist

1. What is the target behavior to be modified? _____

_____

_____

_____

_____

2. Each characteristic of the behavior that should be considered in the target behavior selective process is listed below. An X should be marked by each characteristic as it is considered. The pertinency of these characteristics varies with the specific target behavior under consideration.

(X)	Characteristic	Comment
( )	1. Frequency	
( )	2. Duration	
( )	3. Intensity	
( )	4. Type	
( )	5. Direction	
( )	6. Observability	
( )	7. Measurability	

3. Restate the target behavior in precise and specific terminology. _____

_____

_____

_____

_____

Target Behavior Selection Checklist

1. What is the target behavior to be modified? _____

_____

_____

_____

_____

2. Each characteristic of the behavior that should be considered in the target behavior selective process is listed below. An X should be marked by each characteristic as it is considered. The pertinency of these characteristics varies with the specific target behavior under consideration.

(X)	Characteristic	Comment
( )	1. Frequency	
( )	2. Duration	
( )	3. Intensity	
( )	4. Type	
( )	5. Direction	
( )	6. Observability	
( )	7. Measurability	

3. Restate the target behavior in precise and specific terminology. _____

_____

_____

_____

_____

Target Behavior Selection Checklist

1. What is the target behavior to be modified? _____

_____

_____

_____

2. Each characteristic of the behavior that should be considered in the target behavior selective process is listed below. An X should be marked by each characteristic as it is considered. The pertinency of these characteristics varies with the specific target behavior under consideration.

(X)	Characteristic	Comment
( )	1. Frequency	
( )	2. Duration	
( )	3. Intensity	
( )	4. Type	
( )	5. Direction	
( )	6. Observability	
( )	7. Measurability	

3. Restate the target behavior in precise and specific terminology. _____

_____

_____

_____

Target Behavior Selection Checklist

1. What is the target behavior to be modified? _____

_____

_____

_____

_____

2. Each characteristic of the behavior that should be considered in the target behavior selective process is listed below. An X should be marked by each characteristic as it is considered. The pertinency of these characteristics varies with the specific target behavior under consideration.

(X)	Characteristic	Comment
( )	1. Frequency	
( )	2. Duration	
( )	3. Intensity	
( )	4. Type	
( )	5. Direction	
( )	6. Observability	
( )	7. Measurability	

3. Restate the target behavior in precise and specific terminology. _____

_____

_____

_____

_____

Behavior Chart

Child _____

Observer _____ Date _____

Target behavior _____

DIRECTIONS: Indicate rate, frequency, etc., for vertical axis; hours, days, etc., for horizontal axis. Enter ordinate and abscissa points.

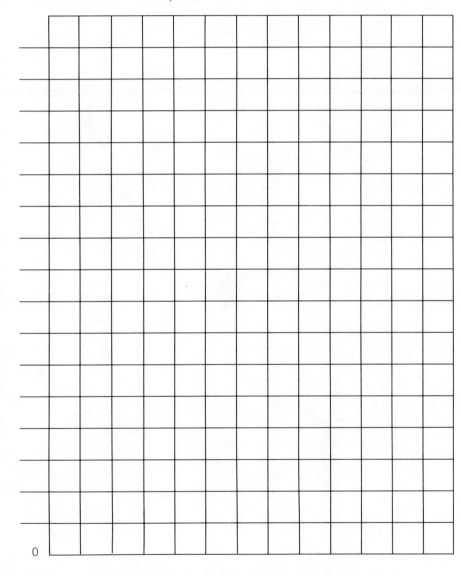

Ordinate points (rate, frequency, duration, percent, etc.)

0

Abscissa points (hours, days, sessions, treatment, etc.)

Behavior Chart

Child _____

Observer _____ Date _____

Target behavior _____

DIRECTIONS: Indicate rate, frequency, etc., for vertical axis; hours, days, etc., for horizontal axis. Enter ordinate and abscissa points.

Ordinate points (rate, frequency, duration, percent, etc.)

0

Abscissa points (hours, days, sessions, treatment, etc.)

Behavior Chart

Child _____

Observer _____ Date _____

Target behavior _____

DIRECTIONS: Indicate rate, frequency, etc., for vertical axis; hours, days, etc., for horizontal axis. Enter ordinate and abscissa points.

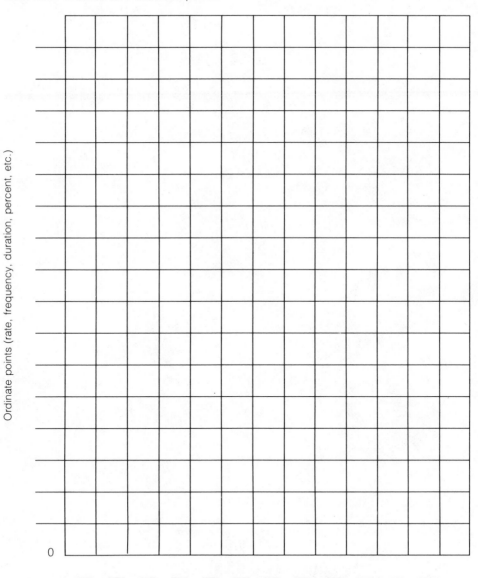

Ordinate points (rate, frequency, duration, percent, etc.)

0

Abscissa points (hours, days, sessions, treatment, etc.)

Behavior Chart

Child _____

Observer _____ Date _____

Target behavior _____

DIRECTIONS: Indicate rate, frequency, etc., for vertical axis; hours, days, etc., for horizontal axis. Enter ordinate and abscissa points.

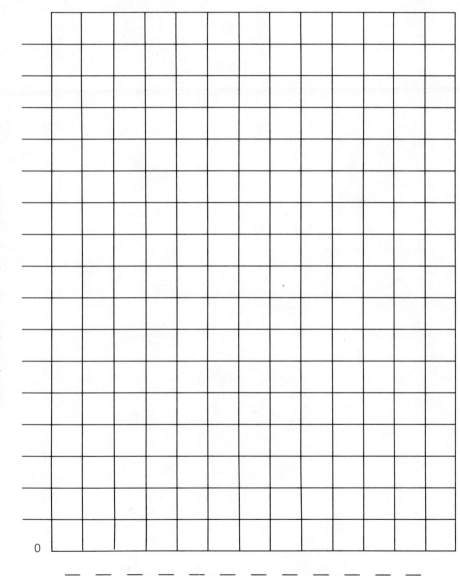

Ordinate points (rate, frequency, duration, percent, etc.)

0

Abscissa points (hours, days, sessions, treatment, etc.)

Behavior Chart

Child _____

Observer _____ Date _____

Target behavior _____

DIRECTIONS: Indicate rate, frequency, etc., for vertical axis; hours, days, etc., for horizontal axis. Enter ordinate and abscissa points.

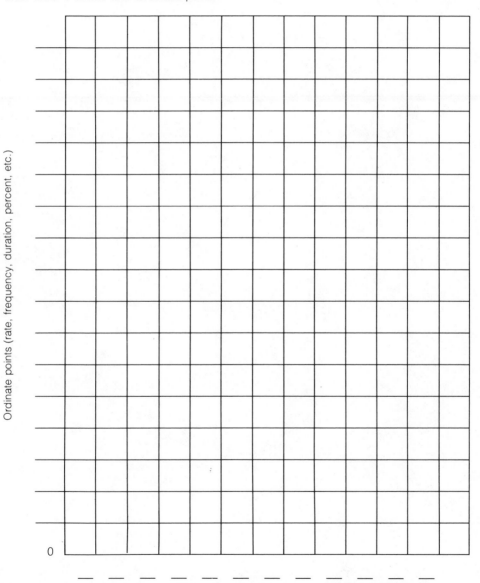

Ordinate points (rate, frequency, duration, percent, etc.)

0

Abscissa points (hours, days, sessions, treatment, etc.)

Contract Work Sheet

Child _____

Teacher _____ Date _____

(X)	Tasks	Comments
( )	1. Establish and maintain rapport.	
( )	2. Explain the purpose of the meeting.	
( )	3. Explain a contract.	
( )	4. Give an example of a contract.	
( )	5. Ask the child to give an example of a contract; if there is no response, give another example.	
( )	6. Discuss possible tasks.	
( )	7. Child-suggested tasks: _____ _____ _____ _____	
( )	8. Teacher-suggested tasks: _____ _____ _____ _____	
( )	9. Agree on the task.	
( )	10. Ask the child what activities he or she enjoys and what items he or she wishes to possess.	
( )	11. Record child-suggested reinforcers.	
( )	12. Negotiate the ratio of the task to the reinforcer.	

Continued.

Contract Work Sheet—cont'd

(X)	Tasks	Comments
( )	13. Identify the time allotted for the task.	
( )	14. Identify the criterion or achievement level.	
( )	15. Discuss methods of evaluation.	
( )	16. Agree on the method of evaluation.	
( )	17. Restate and clarify the method of evaluation.	
( )	18. Negotiate the delivery of the reinforcer.	
( )	19. Set the date for renegotiation.	
( )	20. Write two copies of the contract.	
( )	21. Read the contract to the child.	
( )	22. Elicit the child's verbal affirmation and give your own affirmation.	
( )	23. Sign the contract and have the child sign it.	
( )	24. Congratulate the child (and yourself).	

Contract Work Sheet

Child _____

Teacher _____ Date _____

(X)	Tasks	Comments
( )	1. Establish and maintain rapport.	
( )	2. Explain the purpose of the meeting.	
( )	3. Explain a contract.	
( )	4. Give an example of a contract.	
( )	5. Ask the child to give an example of a contract; if there is no response, give another example.	
( )	6. Discuss possible tasks.	
( )	7. Child-suggested tasks: _____ _____ _____ _____	
( )	8. Teacher-suggested tasks: _____ _____ _____ _____	
( )	9. Agree on the task.	
( )	10. Ask the child what activities he or she enjoys and what items he or she wishes to possess.	
( )	11. Record child-suggested reinforcers.	
( )	12. Negotiate the ratio of the task to the reinforcer.	

Continued.

Contract Work Sheet—cont'd

(X)	Tasks	Comments
( )	13. Identify the time allotted for the task.	
( )	14. Identify the criterion or achievement level.	
( )	15. Discuss methods of evaluation.	
( )	16. Agree on the method of evaluation.	
( )	17. Restate and clarify the method of evaluation.	
( )	18. Negotiate the delivery of the reinforcer.	
( )	19. Set the date for renegotiation.	
( )	20. Write two copies of the contract.	
( )	21. Read the contract to the child.	
( )	22. Elicit the child's verbal affirmation and give your own affirmation.	
( )	23. Sign the contract and have the child sign it.	
( )	24. Congratulate the child (and yourself).	

Contract Work Sheet

Child _____

Teacher _____ Date _____

(X)	Tasks	Comments
( )	1. Establish and maintain rapport.	
( )	2. Explain the purpose of the meeting.	
( )	3. Explain a contract.	
( )	4. Give an example of a contract.	
( )	5. Ask the child to give an example of a contract; if there is no response, give another example.	
( )	6. Discuss possible tasks.	
( )	7. Child-suggested tasks: _____ _____ _____ _____	
( )	8. Teacher-suggested tasks: _____ _____ _____ _____	
( )	9. Agree on the task.	
( )	10. Ask the child what activities he or she enjoys and what items he or she wishes to possess.	
( )	11. Record child-suggested reinforcers.	
( )	12. Negotiate the ratio of the task to the reinforcer.	

Continued.

Contract Work Sheet—cont'd

(X)	Tasks	Comments
( )	13. Identify the time allotted for the task.	
( )	14. Identify the criterion or achievement level.	
( )	15. Discuss methods of evaluation.	
( )	16. Agree on the method of evaluation.	
( )	17. Restate and clarify the method of evaluation.	
( )	18. Negotiate the delivery of the reinforcer.	
( )	19. Set the date for renegotiation.	
( )	20. Write two copies of the contract.	
( )	21. Read the contract to the child.	
( )	22. Elicit the child's verbal affirmation and give your own affirmation.	
( )	23. Sign the contract and have the child sign it.	
( )	24. Congratulate the child (and yourself).	

Contract Work Sheet

Child _____

Teacher _____ Date _____

(X)	Tasks	Comments
( )	1. Establish and maintain rapport.	
( )	2. Explain the purpose of the meeting.	
( )	3. Explain a contract.	
( )	4. Give an example of a contract.	
( )	5. Ask the child to give an example of a contract; if there is no response, give another example.	
( )	6. Discuss possible tasks.	
( )	7. Child-suggested tasks: _____ _____ _____ _____	
( )	8. Teacher-suggested tasks: _____ _____ _____ _____	
( )	9. Agree on the task.	
( )	10. Ask the child what activities he or she enjoys and what items he or she wishes to possess.	
( )	11. Record child-suggested reinforcers.	
( )	12. Negotiate the ratio of the task to the reinforcer.	

Continued.

Contract Work Sheet—cont'd

(X)	Tasks	Comments
( )	13. Identify the time allotted for the task.	
( )	14. Identify the criterion or achievement level.	
( )	15. Discuss methods of evaluation.	
( )	16. Agree on the method of evaluation.	
( )	17. Restate and clarify the method of evaluation.	
( )	18. Negotiate the delivery of the reinforcer.	
( )	19. Set the date for renegotiation.	
( )	20. Write two copies of the contract.	
( )	21. Read the contract to the child.	
( )	22. Elicit the child's verbal affirmation and give your own affirmation.	
( )	23. Sign the contract and have the child sign it.	
( )	24. Congratulate the child (and yourself).	

Contract Work Sheet

Child _____

Teacher _____ Date _____

(X)	Tasks	Comments
( )	1. Establish and maintain rapport.	
( )	2. Explain the purpose of the meeting.	
( )	3. Explain a contract.	
( )	4. Give an example of a contract.	
( )	5. Ask the child to give an example of a contract; if there is no response, give another example.	
( )	6. Discuss possible tasks.	
( )	7. Child-suggested tasks: _____ _____ _____ _____	
( )	8. Teacher-suggested tasks: _____ _____ _____ _____	
( )	9. Agree on the task.	
( )	10. Ask the child what activities he or she enjoys and what items he or she wishes to possess.	
( )	11. Record child-suggested reinforcers.	
( )	12. Negotiate the ratio of the task to the reinforcer.	

Continued.

Contract Work Sheet—cont'd

(X)	Tasks	Comments
( )	13. Identify the time allotted for the task.	
( )	14. Identify the criterion or achievement level.	
( )	15. Discuss methods of evaluation.	
( )	16. Agree on the method of evaluation.	
( )	17. Restate and clarify the method of evaluation.	
( )	18. Negotiate the delivery of the reinforcer.	
( )	19. Set the date for renegotiation.	
( )	20. Write two copies of the contract.	
( )	21. Read the contract to the child.	
( )	22. Elicit the child's verbal affirmation and give your own affirmation.	
( )	23. Sign the contract and have the child sign it.	
( )	24. Congratulate the child (and yourself).	

Date _____

Contract

This is an agreement between _____
Child's name

and _____. The contract begins on
Teacher's name

_____ and ends on _____. It will be re-
Date   Date

viewed on _____ .
Date

   The terms of the agreement are:

Child will _____

_____

_____

_____

Teacher will _____

_____

_____

_____

   If the child fulfills his or her part of the contract, the child will receive the agreed-on re-ward from the teacher. However, if the child fails to fulfill his or her part of the contract, the rewards will be withheld.

Child's signature _____

Teacher's signature _____

Date _____

Contract

This is an agreement between _____
Child's name

and _____. The contract begins on
Teacher's name

_____ and ends on _____. It will be re-
Date   Date

viewed on _____ .
Date

The terms of the agreement are:

Child will _____

_____

_____

_____

Teacher will _____

_____

_____

_____

If the child fulfills his or her part of the contract, the child will receive the agreed-on reward from the teacher. However, if the child fails to fulfill his or her part of the contract, the
rewards will be withheld.

Child's signature _____

Teacher's signature _____

Date _____

Contract

This is an agreement between _____
Child's name

and _____. The contract begins on
Teacher's name

_____ and ends on _____. It will be re-
Date   Date

viewed on _____ .
Date

The terms of the agreement are:

Child will _____

_____

_____

_____

Teacher will _____

_____

_____

_____

If the child fulfills his or her part of the contract, the child will receive the agreed-on reward from the teacher. However, if the child fails to fulfill his or her part of the contract, the
rewards will be withheld.

Child's signature _____

Teacher's signature _____

Date _____

Contract

This is an agreement between _____
                                              Child's name

and _____. The contract begins on
              Teacher's name

_____ and ends on _____. It will be re-
              Date   Date

viewed on _____ .
                          Date

The terms of the agreement are:

Child will _____

_____

_____

_____

Teacher will _____

_____

_____

_____

If the child fulfills his or her part of the contract, the child will receive the agreed-on reward from the teacher. However, if the child fails to fulfill his or her part of the contract, the
rewards will be withheld.

Child's signature _____

Teacher's signature _____

Date _____

Contract

This is an agreement between _____
Child's name

and _____. The contract begins on
Teacher's name

_____ and ends on _____. It will be re-
Date Date

viewed on _____ .
Date

The terms of the agreement are:

Child will _____

_____

_____

_____

Teacher will _____

_____

_____

_____

If the child fulfills his or her part of the contract, the child will receive the agreed-on reward from the teacher. However, if the child fails to fulfill his or her part of the contract, the
rewards will be withheld.

Child's signature _____

Teacher's signature _____

Point Card*

Child's name _____ Date _____

1	2	3	4	5	6	7	8	9	10
11	12	13	14	15	16	17	18	19	20
21	22	23	24	25	26	27	28	29	30
31	32	33	34	35	36	37	38	39	40
41	42	43	44	45	46	47	48	49	50
51	52	53	54	55	56	57	58	59	60
61	62	63	64	65	66	67	68	69	70
71	72	73	74	75	76	77	78	79	80
81	82	83	84	85	86	87	88	89	90
91	92	93	94	95	96	97	98	99	100

*Teacher circles the cumulative total.

Point Card*

Child's name _____ Date _____

1	2	3	4	5	6	7	8	9	10
11	12	13	14	15	16	17	18	19	20
21	22	23	24	25	26	27	28	29	30
31	32	33	34	35	36	37	38	39	40
41	42	43	44	45	46	47	48	49	50
51	52	53	54	55	56	57	58	59	60
61	62	63	64	65	66	67	68	69	70
71	72	73	74	75	76	77	78	79	80
81	82	83	84	85	86	87	88	89	90
91	92	93	94	95	96	97	98	99	100

*Teacher circles the cumulative total.

Point Card*

Child's name _____ Date _____

1	2	3	4	5	6	7	8	9	10
11	12	13	14	15	16	17	18	19	20
21	22	23	24	25	26	27	28	29	30
31	32	33	34	35	36	37	38	39	40
41	42	43	44	45	46	47	48	49	50
51	52	53	54	55	56	57	58	59	60
61	62	63	64	65	66	67	68	69	70
71	72	73	74	75	76	77	78	79	80
81	82	83	84	85	86	87	88	89	90
91	92	93	94	95	96	97	98	99	100

*Teacher circles the cumulative total.

Point Card*

Child's name _____ Date _____

1	2	3	4	5	6	7	8	9	10
11	12	13	14	15	16	17	18	19	20
21	22	23	24	25	26	27	28	29	30
31	32	33	34	35	36	37	38	39	40
41	42	43	44	45	46	47	48	49	50
51	52	53	54	55	56	57	58	59	60
61	62	63	64	65	66	67	68	69	70
71	72	73	74	75	76	77	78	79	80
81	82	83	84	85	86	87	88	89	90
91	92	93	94	95	96	97	98	99	100

*Teacher circles the cumulative total.

Point Card*

Child's name _____ Date _____

1	2	3	4	5	6	7	8	9	10
11	12	13	14	15	16	17	18	19	20
21	22	23	24	25	26	27	28	29	30
31	32	33	34	35	36	37	38	39	40
41	42	43	44	45	46	47	48	49	50
51	52	53	54	55	56	57	58	59	60
61	62	63	64	65	66	67	68	69	70
71	72	73	74	75	76	77	78	79	80
81	82	83	84	85	86	87	88	89	90
91	92	93	94	95	96	97	98	99	100

*Teacher circles the cumulative total.

Point Tally Form

Child _____ Date _____

Monday													
Tuesday													
Wednesday													
Thursday													
Friday													

TOTAL

Monday	
Tuesday	
Wednesday	
Thursday	
Friday	
Week	

Point Tally Form

Child _____ Date _____

Monday

Tuesday

Wednesday

Thursday

Friday

TOTAL

Monday	
Tuesday	
Wednesday	
Thursday	
Friday	
Week	

Point Tally Form

Child _____ Date _____

Monday

Tuesday

Wednesday

Thursday

Friday

TOTAL

Monday

Tuesday

Wednesday

Thursday

Friday

Week

Point Tally Form

Child _____ Date _____

Monday												
Tuesday												
Wednesday												
Thursday												
Friday												

TOTAL

Monday	
Tuesday	
Wednesday	
Thursday	
Friday	
Week	

Point Tally Form

Child _____ Date _____

Monday												
Tuesday												
Wednesday												
Thursday												
Friday												

TOTAL

Monday	
Tuesday	
Wednesday	
Thursday	
Friday	
Week	

Point Card for Multipurpose Token Economy

Child _____ Day _____ Date _____

Work period	Readiness	Social behavior	Work effort	Work success	Teacher comments
9:00-9:15			*	*	
9:15-10:00					
10:00-10:30					
10:30-10:45			*	*	
10:45-11:30					
11:30-12:00					
12:00-1:00			*	*	
1:00-1:30					
1:30-2:45					
2:45-3:00			*	*	

*Points for work effort and work success are not available during these periods due to the nature of the activity: opening exercises, recess, lunch, and closing exercises.

Point Card for Multipurpose Token Economy

Child _____ Day _____ Date _____

Work period	Readiness	Social behavior	Work effort	Work success	Teacher comments
9:00-9:15			*	*	
9:15-10:00					
10:00-10:30					
10:30-10:45			*	*	
10:45-11:30					
11:30-12:00					
12:00-1:00			*	*	
1:00-1:30					
1:30-2:45					
2:45-3:00			*	*	

*Points for work effort and work success are not available during these periods due to the nature of the activity: opening exercises, recess, lunch, and closing exercises.

Point Card for Multipurpose Token Economy

Child _____ Day _____ Date _____

Work period	Readiness	Social behavior	Work effort	Work success	Teacher comments
9:00-9:15			*	*	
9:15-10:00					
10:00-10:30					
10:30-10:45			*	*	
10:45-11:30					
11:30-12:00					
12:00-1:00			*	*	
1:00-1:30					
1:30-2:45					
2:45-3:00			*	*	

*Points for work effort and work success are not available during these periods due to the nature of the activity: opening exercises, recess, lunch, and closing exercises.

Point Card for Multipurpose Token Economy

Child _____ Day _____ Date _____

Work period	Readiness	Social behavior	Work effort	Work success	Teacher comments
9:00-9:15			*	*	
9:15-10:00					
10:00-10:30					
10:30-10:45			*	*	
10:45-11:30					
11:30-12:00					
12:00-1:00			*	*	
1:00-1:30					
1:30-2:45					
2:45-3:00			*	*	

*Points for work effort and work success are not available during these periods due to the nature of the activity: opening exercises, recess, lunch, and closing exercises.

Point Card for Multipurpose Token Economy

Child _____ Day _____ Date _____

Work period	Readiness	Social behavior	Work effort	Work success	Teacher comments
9:00-9:15			*	*	
9:15-10:00					
10:00-10:30					
10:30-10:45			*	*	
10:45-11:30					
11:30-12:00					
12:00-1:00			*	*	
1:00-1:30					
1:30-2:45					
2:45-3:00			*	*	

*Points for work effort and work success are not available during these periods due to the nature of the activity: opening exercises, recess, lunch, and closing exercises.

Time-out Log

Child _____

Supervisor _____

Date _____

Time		Behavior before time-out	Behavior during time-out	Behavior after time-out
Enters	Leaves			

Time-out Log

Child _____

Supervisor _____

Date _____

Time		Behavior before time-out	Behavior during time-out	Behavior after time-out
Enters	Leaves			

Time-out Log

Child _____

Supervisor _____

Date _____

Time		Behavior before time-out	Behavior during time-out	Behavior after time-out
Enters	Leaves			

Time-out Log

Child _____

Supervisor _____

Date _____

Time		Behavior before time-out	Behavior during time-out	Behavior after time-out
Enters	Leaves			

Time-out Log

Child _____

Supervisor _____

Date _____

Time		Behavior before time-out	Behavior during time-out	Behavior after time-out
Enters	Leaves			

Behavior Log Form

Target behavior _____

Child _____

Observer _____

Date	Time		Antecedents	Consequences	Applied interventions	Comments
	Begins	Ends				

Behavior Log Form

Target behavior _____

Child _____

Observer _____

Date	Time		Antecedents	Consequences	Applied interventions	Comments
	Begins	Ends				

Behavior Log Form

Target behavior _____

Child _____

Observer _____

Date	Time		Antecedents	Consequences	Applied interventions	Comments
	Begins	Ends				

Behavior Log Form

Target behavior _____

Child _____

Observer _____

Date	Time		Antecedents	Consequences	Applied interventions	Comments
	Begins	Ends				

Behavior Log Form

Target behavior _____

Child _____

Observer _____

| Date | Time | | Antecedents | Consequences | Applied interventions | Comments |
	Begins	Ends